THE PARADISE OF TRAVELLERS

By the same author

Les Sources françaises de Goldsmith
Paris, 1924 (Prix Bordin of the French Academy)

The Early Life of J.-J. Rousseau
Cambridge, 1929

Earth of the Tarentines: a novel
London, 1940

The Italian Influence in English Poetry
London (George Allen & Unwin) and Bloomington, 1955

Animal Poetry in French and English Literature and the Greek Tradition
Bloomington, 1955; London, 1956

The *Memoirs of James II* (critical edition)
London and Bloomington, 1962

In preparation

The Italians in Stuart England

Poetry and the Fine Arts in Seventeenth-Century Britain: the Italian inspiration

1. *Solfatara near Naples*

See pp. 178, 196

The Paradise of Travellers

THE ITALIAN INFLUENCE ON ENGLISHMEN IN THE SEVENTEENTH CENTURY

BY

A. LYTTON SELLS

How beautiful is sunset, when the glow
Of Heaven descends upon a land like
thee,
Thou Paradise of exiles, Italy!

Julian and Maddalo

London
GEORGE ALLEN & UNWIN LTD
RUSKIN HOUSE MUSEUM STREET

FIRST PUBLISHED IN 1964

PRINTED IN GREAT BRITAIN
in 10 point Juliana type
BY EAST MIDLAND PRINTING CO. LTD
BURY ST. EDMUNDS

To Ripley and Lilian Cutler

INTRODUCTION

THE present work is designed as the first part of a sequel to the writer's earlier essay on *The Italian Influence in English Poetry: from Chaucer to Southwell.*[1] The original intention had been to study the effects on English poetry, painting, architecture and the natural sciences, of Italian work in these fields and to use the personal and political contacts between the two peoples as a background. But the story of the diplomatists and expatriates, and especially of students and travellers, has proved so extensive that I have been obliged to defer the other enquiry to a complementary volume. The scope of this one is entirely historical, and in large part biographical.

Of the hundreds of figures involved, a number are well-known, and on the life and work of a few there exist good editions or monographs. These I have not hesitated to use. As regards other persons, equally interesting or significant, the available information is scattered or less abundant. I have tried to draw it together and where possible supplement it. Thus, while I have been indebted to critical biographies and articles for parts of the work, the chapters on the travel-books, which form the main substance of what I have to offer, are drawn from primary sources.

The travellers studied here are limited for the most part to those who were not regular *literati*, poets, artists or art-collectors. Thus the experiences of Inigo Jones, of Nicholas Ferrar, of Milton and Crashaw, of the Earl of Arundel and the men who collected paintings for Charles I—these are reserved for a companion volume in which the influence Italy exercised on them and through them can be properly examined.

While the present volume was taking shape, I realized that the story of the travellers could scarcely be seen in focus without some indication of the social, economic and even financial structure of the age; and that whereas readers would be familiar enough with the political and military history of Britain in that era,[2] they might not be so well acquainted with what was happening in Italy or with social conditions in that country. Hence a few 'background' chapters which are inserted where they seem to be most useful.

[1] London and Bloomington, 1955.

[2] For *general* histories of seventeenth-century Europe, see G. N. Clark, *The Seventeenth Century*, Oxford (2nd edition) 1947; Henri Hauser, *La Prépondérance espagnole*, Paris, 1948; E. Préclin et V. Tapié, *Le XVIIe Siècle*, Paris, 1949.

The relations between Stuart Britain and the Italy of the Seicento were less conspicuous for any direct literary influence of the latter on the former, except as regards the Jacobean stage, than they had been in Tudor times; but more conspicuous in the natural sciences and in the diplomatic sphere. Great Britain, Protestant on the one side, and the independent states of the Italian peninsula, Catholic on the other, were then drawn more closely together by common interests and perhaps too by a temperamental affinity, a something between 'Spanish gravity and French levity', as a Venetian ambassador put it. Another link, which of course affected France and the Netherlands as well, was a common enthusiasm for the pursuit of the natural sciences. Anglo-Italian relations after the Restoration and prior to the age of Gray were mainly scientific, at a time when English literature had come under the spell of French.

The seventeenth century was a troubled era. The doctrines and policies that had issued from the Council of Trent were only then exerting their full influence, and the results were so complex that it is not easy to disentangle them. It seems a paradox that the greatest Italian prose-work of the century was—if we make an exception for the writings of Galileo—an indictment of the Council of Trent. Another and later paradox was the spectacle of an intelligent Pope reproaching Louis XIV for his persecution of the Huguenots. But if attitudes were changing in Italy, they were changing more drastically in Britain. The continued growth of a well-to-do middle class together with the predominance of a powerful squirearchy involved fearful political readjustments. And the impact of Cartesian metaphysics and psychology,[3] accompanied by the revelations of physical science, imposed a revision of traditional beliefs which was potentially more poignant. In short, the social and political crises were followed by a crisis of conscience.

Medieval monism, for one thing, had been replaced by Cartesian dualism. Again, medieval man had not conceived of humanity as progressing. Some such notion had arisen among the Greeks, but it was born anew in seventeenth-century France and brilliantly formulated by Descartes and Pascal. Hence the optimism of later thought and particularly of the 'Enlightenment'. 'The world is old today and we have more experience,' wrote Descartes. Knowledge was accumulating. And so the idea of progress, strengthened by a belief in the power of reason in mankind and at the same time by a gradual abandonment of the doctrine of original sin, was to take hold of the educated public; and it is only in the present century that this too facile optimism has been seriously undermined. Original sin, or what-

[3] Basil Willey, *The Seventeenth-Century Background*, London, 1934, new edition 1946.

ever you like to call it, is incomprehensible; but it is a fact of experience. The Voltairean belief in a 'reasonable' mankind is in ruins. But—contrary to what many people seem to fear—there is hope in applied science. It is on this that a belief in progress may perhaps be founded. Descartes, Pascal, and their disciples had had an inkling of it, and we are their spiritual heirs.

We are the heirs of the Seicento, because we are trying to work out—we are beginning to work out—what the philosophers and scientists of that time had a glimpse of, and were making possible. By the end of the century educated men were *thinking* differently, and feeling *differently*, from the way their grandparents had thought and felt. The world on which Shakespeare's contemporaries looked out was not, it is true, that of the high Middle Ages, a single world in which everything fitted into an intellectually satisfying pattern. But it was probably nearer to that world than to the universe as it appeared to the contemporaries of Newton.

The face of England was changing; but the way of looking at it had been transformed. Of an Elizabethan it could not have been said that

> A primrose by the river's brim
> A yellow primrose was to him,
> And it was nothing more . . .

It had a moral and spiritual meaning behind its surface appearance; and the same held true of everything, in the mind of everyone. Of this attitude to life and the world, the widespread vogue of emblems was perhaps the clearest manifestation; but the whole attitude of people's minds was 'emblematical' and remained so until the 1660's.[4] Shakespeare had been ready enough to think of the planets as 'quiring with the young-eyed cherubins'. Kepler and Galileo knew better than that, and Restoration England had digested their lessons. Small wonder if Dryden and his friends thought Shakespeare needed revision and that, if his fantasies were remarkable, his 'judgment' was not.

If today we could go back and converse with the subjects of James I and Charles I, it would not be their dress, their queer table-manners and their brutish amusements that would most astonish us, but habits of thought and feeling radically different from ours. In Restoration England, on the contrary, we should feel far less *dépaysés*. Rarely have a father and son been more different intellectually than Charles I and Charles II. Charles I was a medieval-minded man; Charles II was a modern man. We should have understood him; he would understand us.

[4] cf. Rosemary Freeman, *English Emblem Books*. London, 1948, especially pp. 48-51, 91-98.

Nevertheless, the real significance of the scientific revolution of the seventeenth century was not apparent to most of those who were carrying it through, and this for two reasons.

Immense as were the advances in mathematics and physical science, their ultimate consequences could not be foreseen. Although many of the philosophers, following Francis Bacon, believed that the application of science to industry, agriculture and medicine would transform human life for the better, no one could foresee the incredible changes in thought and in the conditions of life that have taken place in the past sixty years. The fact is that the mathematicians and physicists of the Seicento were simply preparing the way for the decisive discoveries of the twentieth century. When Lord Rutherford not so very long ago exclaimed: 'This is the heroic age of science! This is the Elizabethan age,' he, as Sir Charles Snow has pointed out, 'was absolutely right'.[5] But, now, applied science has caught up; and the consequence has been the appearance, as it were overnight, of an 'industrial society of electronics, atomic energy, automation', which (if I may again cite Snow) 'is in cardinal respects different in kind from anything that has gone before, and will change the world much more'.[6] Nothing analogous to this took place even in the eighteenth century.

There was, however, a second reason why the great thinkers of the Seicento did not realize the significance (and the dangers) of what they were doing. Scientists were then men of letters, literary men took a keen interest in the scientific movement. Most educated people read, or discussed, the works of that 'grand Secretary of Nature, the miraculous Descartes', just as many of them understood the *Dialogues* of Galileo. Descartes himself was metaphysician and psychologist as well as mathematician and physicist. If there were already two cultures, a scientific and a literary, no one seems to have been aware of it, because the greatest minds were at home in both. Pascal is the outstanding example. Gassendi had revived the atomic theory along with epicurean philosophy and reconciled them both with revealed religion. Robert Boyle, the great English exponent of the 'mechanical philosophy', was a zealous Christian. Not that all the scientists saw eye to eye. Hobbes was the boldest and most revolutionary thinker, and his irreligious attitude was abhorrent to the scientists. He proposed in the *De Corpore* to apply the findings of the new science to society and human life as a whole.[7] This alarmed

[5] *The two Cultures and the Scientific Revolution*. Cambridge, 1959, p. 5.

[6] *Ibid.*, 31.

[7] See, among other works, M. H. Carré, *Phases of Thought*, Oxford, 1949, pp. 224-79, and in particular A. Rupert Hall, *The Scientific Revolution* (2nd edition, London and New York, 1962) and Marie Boas (Mrs A. R. Hall) *The Scientific Revolution, 1450-1630* (New York, 1962).

people when they read the *Leviathan*. But the kind of thing he suggested is now, willy-nilly, taking shape.

The main point, however is this: what was healthy about the seventeenth-century situation and what differentiates it sharply from our own, is that no real gulf existed between men of science and men of letters: they could and did communicate, at least until the latter part of our period. It was with Newton's *Principia* (1687) that communication first began to break down, when Locke admitted that he could not follow the mathematics. Today there is a gulf, and the problem of education is to bring the two cultures together.

Not that everything in the later seventeenth century was new. Long before that time, scepticism had been formulated by Pomponazzi, and the maxims of modern statecraft by Machiavelli. Modern capitalism had established itself long before the arrival of democracy, its natural concomitant. Even in minor respects, as I shall try to show, the world we now live in was revealing a few of its peculiarly unpleasant features. The significance of some of these changes was apparent to contemporaries but, as I have said, the implications of the metaphysical and scientific revolutions were not. None of our travellers, except perhaps Thomas Hobbes, seems to have been aware that European man had crossed the watershed and was headed for an unknown extremely uncertain, though not devoid of hope.

While it has appeared fitting to outline the intellectual importance of the age, the present work has no pretensions to be other than a contribution to diplomatic history and especially to social history and the 'daily-life' genre: a record of private lives the sum of which goes to make up a national life; and hence a background to the study of arts, letters and science.

* * * *

It would have been impossible to write this book but for the facilities generously afforded by the Graduate School of Indiana University. In the course of a visit to Florence I was assisted by Professor Carlo Pellegrini and Professor Piero Rebora. The latter put me on the track of material I might otherwise have missed and gave me a number of offprints of articles relating to my subject. In Padua the keeper of the University archives, the Librarian of the Cathedral Library and the Director of the Museo Civico placed their resources at my disposal. I am indebted to Professor and Mrs A. R. Hall for helping me to understand the nature of the Scientific Revolution. To these and many others I tender grateful thanks.

A.L.S.

Indiana University,
September, 1963.

CONTENTS

ILLUSTRATIONS

B

PART I

Italy in the Seventeenth Century

CHAPTER I

History of the Seicento: Politics and War

IT is not simply an exaggeration to speak—as historians have been prone to speak—of seventeenth-century Italy as decadent, it is an error. The recession in industry and commerce, the decrease in population, the political and military weakness of the country were not primarily due to Italy's being divided into a number of principalities and republics; because medieval Italy, although divided, had comprised wealthy and powerful states. Doubtless, had Machiavelli's dream of a federated Italy been realized, the country would have played an important part in European affairs, and the balance of power in the seventeenth century might have been re-established and maintained with less cost of life than in fact it was. A certain economic and political decline seems to have been inevitable. The advance of Ottoman power in the eastern Mediterranean, the rise of great monarchies in Spain, France and England, were bound to throw the Italian republics into the shade. The opening up of a new sea way to Asia and the discovery of America—in which Italians played a leading part—were to prove most profitable to the Portuguese, the English and Hollanders. But the evil days on which Italy had fallen in the sixteenth century and which continued until the early eighteenth can be ascribed mainly to the dead weight of Spanish domination.

The Peace of Cateau-Cambrésis (1559) had registered the hegemony of Spain in Europe and America. It had excluded the French from Italy and fixed the Spanish yoke on Lombardy,[1] Naples, Sicily and Sardinia.[2] The Genoese Republic was little more than a vassal

[1] But Spanish Lombardy was not then as large as modern Lombardia. It did not include the territories of Bergamo and Brescia (which belonged to Venice) or Mantua.

[2] cf. Henri Hauser, *La Prépondérance espagnole* (1559-1660), Paris, 1948, pp. 1, 13, 14. See also H. Hauser et A. Renaudet, *Les Débuts de l'âge moderne*, Paris, (1929), 1956, passim, especially pp. 40, 361 et seq., for the importance of banking and finance in the struggle between the House of France and the House of Austria. Also R. de Roover, *L'Evolution de la lettre de change*, Paris, 1953, p. 67. Charles V had been financed by the Fuggers and the

of the Spanish monarchy, but a very valuable one. No Italian rulers other than the Dukes of Savoy and the Venetian Republic dared for a time to assert their independence.[3] The activities of the Society of Jesus and the work, generally, of the Council of Trent fortified in the intellectual field what Spain had conquered and consolidated in the military. And it looked as though she would become the mistress of Europe, the more so as France was distracted with civil war and it had not at once been certain whether the young Elizabeth would carry England into the Protestant camp.

Resistance developed however in the course of time. Emmanuel-Philibert of Savoy was so far from intending to become a vassal of his former ally that he was planning territorial expansion on his own account.[4] The United Provinces seceded from the Spanish Empire. An attempt to invade England met with resounding disaster; and the attempt to prevent Henri IV from becoming master of France also ended in failure. But the core of Spanish power remained intact. Spain with her great colonial empire, her possession of much of Charles the Bold's dominions, including what is now Belgium and Franche-Comté; with the support of Genoese finance and naval ability; with also the prestige of a brilliant literature, inspired a fearful mixture of dread and admiration. And the admiration was not to be discounted. It befuddled the policy of James I and was partly responsible for the reversal and weaknesses of French policy after the death of Henri IV and prior to the rise of Richelieu. A circumstance that further strengthened the Spanish position was the alliance with the House of Austria and for a time with the Papacy. Since the time of Paul IV none of the Popes had dared to talk of 'liberating Italy' from the foreigners. If there were weaknesses in the colossus—and there were—these were not very apparent. Philip III (1598-1621) and Philip IV (1621-1665) were men without character or capacity; but this handicap was offset by the ability of the minister Olivarès, by Spain's tireless and brilliant diplomatists, and by the capable and aggressive viceroys in Milan and Naples. The Spanish and Walloon soldiery were very hard to beat as long as they were led by Italian or Walloon generals—by an Alessandro Farnese, an Ambrogio Spinola, or a Tilly[5]—; less effective when, in the campaigns in north-eastern France in the 1650's, they were commanded

Genoese bankers, and his successors were able to maintain their hold on Italy and wage war from the Netherlands until 1659, thanks to the quantities of gold and silver which they imported from America and which enabled them to continue paying their troops.

[3] La Prépondérance espagnole, 15, 16.

[4] *Ibid.*, 16.

[5] *Ibid.*, 264. The fact that Spain produced no general of the first rank is one of the most curious features of the age.

by Spaniards like Caracena and Don Juan who, however brave, always liked to take their after-lunch siesta, even when the enemy was at hand.[6]

What ultimately decided the outcome of the struggle was not simply the military genius of Turenne, but the economic and financial basis on which military predominance must in the end be founded.[7]

I

But the decline of Spanish power had been hardly perceptible for many years and there were few visible signs of it prior to the middle of the century. In Italy the Spaniards stifled the industrial and commercial prosperity of the Milanese and ruthlessly exploited the kingdom of Naples and Sicily. In the early sixteenth century there had been 200,000 people in Milan; in the early seventeenth there were only 100,000.[8] The populace of southern Italy rose several times in rebellion, aided and encouraged on occasion by France and Savoy. The insurrection of 1637 took some time to quell. That of 1647, led by Tommaso Aniello, was a more serious affair. A republic was proclaimed, Henri de Lorraine, Duc de Guise, was appointed its 'duke', and Mazarin sent a fleet to support the rebellion. But the rebel forces were at cross-purposes, the French fleet was severely damaged by a storm, and it was only because Guise's friends deserted him that Don Juan was able to recapture Naples and instal a new vice-

[6] See the present writer's edition of the *Military Memoirs of James II* (London, 1962, 231-35). The young Duke of York served for some time, rather unwillingly, with the Spaniards in the later 1650's and was constantly amazed by the slowness of the senior generals, their adherence to text-book routine and especially their siestas.

[7] If France in the 1650's was weakened and impoverished by war, although potentially rich in agriculture and industry, the industrial and agricultural resources of Spain herself were meagre. Moreover the gold and silver she drew from the New World did not operate quite as much to her advantage as one might suppose, because by the 1570's, if not earlier, the European exchange-rates had been regularly adverse to Spain, so that in the end she lost the advantage of all the bullion she was importing from America and exporting in Europe. To transfer credit *from* Spain to another European market cost 8%; to transfer credit to Spain cost only 5%. Prices in Spain were relatively high and therefore encouraged imports, but discouraged the export trade (R. de Roover, *L'Evolution de la lettre de change*, 81-2). What on the other hand assisted the French was not simply the diplomatic stamina of Richelieu and Mazarin nor even the military brains of Turenne, though without these assets France could not have won; but the alliance with England, a wealthy modern state with a rising industry, a prosperous agriculture and one of the best armies in Europe.

[8] Edmond Préclin et Victor Tapié, *Le XVIIe siècle* (1610-1715). Paris, 1949. 25.

roy.[9] It was because they were so firmly established in Lombardy and southern Italy that the Spaniards were able to overawe the peninsula and hold the independent states in check.

II

Of the independent and the vassal states there were a large number. In the north-west, the Duchy of Savoy, with a territory comprising Piedmont and the present-day French departments of Savoie and Haute-Savoie, was already a notable power. The capital had been moved from Chambéry to Turin, and the Dukes were meditating expansion eastward and southward. Already to Charles-Emmanuel I had come the dream of a powerful Alpine kingdom, stretching from the Lake of Geneva to the Ligurian Sea and from the Lac du Bourget to the line of the Adda.[10] In furtherance of this policy the Dukes usually allied themselves with France, but on two occasions (1613 and 1628) with Spain: a dangerous game to play and very costly between 1628 and 1630 when the French crossed the Alps and fought it out with the Spaniards in Piedmont. The outcome was to bring Savoy back into the French alliance. Louis XIII retained the fortress of Pinerolo, with its Alpine approach, and that of Casale in Montferrat.[11] On the whole, however, the Savoyard *politica del carciofo* (one leaf of the artichoke at a time) was to prove brilliantly successful. Piedmont was a prosperous country, agriculture was encouraged; and, apart from the senseless persecution of the Waldensians and a short period of civil war during the childhood of Victor-Amadeus II, the Savoyard state was well governed. The Marquisate of Montferrat, lying to the south-east of Turin, had belonged to the Gonzagas of Mantua, but part of it was assigned to Savoy by one of the treaties of Cherasco (1631) when Richelieu consolidated the ground he had recovered or gained in north-west Italy.

South of Piedmont and occupying the seaward-facing slopes of the Maritime and Ligurian Alps, the Republic of Genoa subsisted in a state of magnificence so curious as to call for explanation. In the twelfth and thirteenth centuries, after a series of wars with the rival maritime republic of Pisa, the Genoese had secured naval predominance in the Mediterranean. They were at this time a great commercial power, in possession of Corsica, islands in the Levant and trading-posts as far afield as Syria. But in the later fourteenth century the Venetians replaced them as masters of the Mediterranean. The political régimes in Genoa itself were unstable, and

[9] *Ibid.*, 25-6; H. Hauser, *op. cit.*, 381-2.
[10] H. Hauser, 307.
[11] *Ibid.*, 308-9.

party strife led to the intervention of foreign princes who were from time to time recognized as lords of the State. In the struggle between France and the Emperor Genoa sided with the former, and the city was taken and sacked by the Imperialists (1522); but in this juncture Andrea Doria, a member of one of the old families who had become Doges of Genoa, went over to the side of Charles V, secured the liberation of his country and contrived to prevent its becoming an actual Spanish possession. It was not possible to do more. The Republic was henceforth and until the later seventeenth century reduced to the condition of a vassal of Spain, to whom she supplied military commanders and technical experts.[12]

During all these vicissitudes the Banco di San Giorgio,[13] perhaps the oldest in Europe, remained virtually untouched. As the power of the old aristocracy declined, that of the financial aristocracy went from strength to strength. They had branches in Castile and at Besançon in Franche-Comté (A Spanish possession) and became bankers for the King of Spain. Spanish bullion from the New World passed into Europe through Genoa, at least until the 1630's when the flow appears to have dried up and, as a consequence, the importance of Besançon declined.[14]

In the early Seicento Genoese territory included the county of Nice and stretched as far as the borders of Tuscany. The Republic had recovered possession of Corsica, but Charles Emmanuel I was entertaining designs against it. During the war of the Valtellina he tried (1628) to promote a revolution in his favour, which however did not succeed; and a similar plot by Charles Emmanuel II in 1672 also came to nothing.

The city of Genoa presented no outward sign of decadence. The later sixteenth and early seventeenth centuries witnessed the rise on the hillside above the harbour of the most superb palaces that any Italian city could boast: skyscrapers of a uniform grandeur whose apartments were to be adorned with paintings by Rubens and Van Dyck for the delectation of the great financiers.[15] John Evelyn, in

[12] E.g. Ambrogio Spinola (1569-1630), who was responsible for the cutting of the famous canal from Ghent to Bruges, which struck John Evelyn in 1661 as 'a wonderful piece of labour' (*Diary*, ed. de Beer, Oxford, 1955, II, 74). Spinola commanded the Spanish army in Piedmont in 1628-9.

[13] St George is the patron of Genoa and many churches in the region are dedicated to him. It is said (I do not know with how much truth) that once when Richard I was returning by sea from Palestine, he ran into a storm off the mountainous promontory of Portofino and swore that if he got safely ashore, the patron of the nearest church should become the patron of England. He did of course make a safe landing, and that is how we got our patron saint.

[14] R. de Roover, *op. cit.*, 78 and passim.

[15] H. Hauser, *op. sit.*, 496, 500, 501.

October, 1644, was particularly impressed by the Strada Nova;[16] 'It is for statlinesse of the buildings, paving and evenesse of the Streete, certainly far superior to any in Europ for the number of houses.'[17] The Genoese did not suffer immediately from the decline of Spanish power. The city was to be very roughly handled by the French in 1684; but the 'capitalists of St George' maintained their primacy in banking until the early years of the eighteenth century.[18]

The Grand Duchy of Tuscany[19] was a state of some importance. It is true that the textile industries which had once made Florence so prosperous and the Medici Bank the wealthiest in Europe, had fallen into decay. Under authoritarian rule party strife had vanished and public morale declined; while private morals had improved. After the demoralizing reign of Cosimo I, Ferdinand I had pulled the country together, undertaken important public works and left the reputation of an enlightened prince, tolerant in matters of religion and independent of the Papacy. His successors, Cosimo II (1609-1621) and Ferdinand II (1621-1670) were less incompetent than has been averred. As the Spaniards had the right to maintain garrisons in Tuscany, the Medici princes were not in a position to annoy the Spanish viceroys. But they were decidedly Anglophile; with the technical assistance of the exiled Earl of Warwick they had built up an effective little navy, which enabled Cosimo II to make war on the Turks. Their free port of Livorno was the principal Mediterranean depot of the Levant Company. Scientific research was encouraged at the State University in Pisa, and Tuscany at this time produced some of the greatest scientists in Europe.

South and east of Tuscany lay the Papal States, stretching from the Tyrrhenian Sea to the Adriatic and including, in the north, the territories of Bologna and Ferrara. In the eastern Apennines the Duchy of Urbino, which had belonged to the Della Rovere family, was annexed by the Pope in 1531. Papal policy[20] varied with the character of the reigning pontiff and according as he was Francophile or had been elected by the Spanish faction. But, as compared with their sixteenth-century predecessors and with Clement VIII who died in 1605, the Popes tended to be increasingly mild and to preserve at least an outward show of neutrality as between Spain and

[16] The present-day Via Garibaldi.

[17] *Diary*, ed. de Beer, II, 176.

[18] R. de Roover, *op. cit.*

[19] Medieval Florence had subjugated most of the surrounding cities and finally absorbed Pisa and Siena. The tiny republic of Lucca alone had avoided being swallowed up and was at this time fiercely jealous of its independence.

[20] There is an excellent chapter on 'Papal Policy, 1590-1648' by Moritz Brosch, in the *Cambridge Modern History*, 1906, IV, 666 et seq., to which I am indebted in the following account.

France. Paul V (1605-1621) began by asserting the rights of the Church and wresting concessions even from Spain. He next joined the Spanish viceroys in an attempt to assert his power over Venetia; but here he met his match and had to climb down. It is most improbable that he connived at the Spanish plot to destroy Venice from within (1618)[21]; he refused to have any part in the massacre of the Protestants of Sondrio and Tirano (1620) or to approve it; and indeed his latter days revealed Rome as less Catholic than Madrid and Vienna. On the other hand both Paul V and Gregory XV (1621-1623) were of course anxious to further the cause of the Counter Reformation. Protestantism was almost everywhere in retreat and was to suffer further reverses in Germany, in the Valtellina and in France in the years to come.

Meanwhile, as we shall see, the subjugation of the Grisons by Austrian and Spanish troops had excited consternation in Venice and Turin, and some alarm in Paris. There, in the Rhaetian Alps and the Valtellina, was the most valuable square on the international chess-board. The French negotiated with Madrid and it was decided that, as an interim measure, the Pope should be asked to place his own troops in the Valtellina strongholds. His brother therefore led a Papal army into the Alps and the Spanish garrisons withdrew. It was like a United Nations arrangement and was to prove about as effective.

This was the situation that Cardinal Maffeo Barberini inherited on his election as Pope in 1623. The sympathies of Urban VIII, as he styled himself, inclined rather more to the French and Venetian side than to the Spanish; but in any event he would have been pleased to add the Valtellina to the Papal States. He had difficulty however in paying his soldiers there, the Spaniards began to return and replace them, and then a formidable new player began to take a hand in the game. In 1624 Richelieu, who had just joined Louis XIII's council, came to an agreement with Savoy and Venice; he sent an army to the Grisons and assisted by the Venetians frightened the Spanish and Papal garrisons into withdrawal; after which the valley was declared a French protectorate. But Richelieu's policy was undermined at this time by the 'parti des dévots', and in the negotiations that led to the Treaty of Monzon (1626), Urban intrigued successfully against him. It was agreed—to the disgust of Venice, Savoy and the Grisons[22]—that Spanish as well as French troops should have the right of passage. The Spaniards had gained all they needed.

In Germany the Catholic reaction was triumphing; in France

[21] See below, chapter III, p. 70.

[22] Moritz Brosch, in *Cambridge Modern History*, IV, 675.

Richelieu was setting himself to destroy the Huguenot party as a political force. But once this object was achieved, once England had been frustrated in the project of assisting La Rochelle, the Cardinal would probably need English support against Spain. And although Urban had connived for so long at the Spanish hegemony in Italy, the war of the Mantuan succession caused him to change his mind. If the Spaniards contrived to seize Mantua and the marquisate of Montferrat, the whole of Italy, including the Pope, would be at their mercy. It was for this reason that Urban now moved over to Richelieu's side. He asked Louis XIII to intervene in Piedmont, where the Duke had unwisely allied himself with Spain. It is true that when the French crossed the Alps and brought the Duke to terms, Urban thought twice about sending them the help he had promised. He was not sure that they would stay. Richelieu was in fact obliged to move his troops back to France; whereupon the Spaniards under Spinola once again took the offensive, while an Imperialist army came down the Valtellina, defeated the Venetians and Mantuans at Vallegio and after a long siege took and sacked Mantua. This was a notable horror, which must have made the Pope regret having meddled at Monzon. He now threw his influence wholly on to the French and Venetian side. His emissary at Ratisbon co-operated with Father Joseph (Richelieu's 'Eminence grise') in detaching Maximilian of Bavaria from the Emperor Ferdinand II, and in leading the latter to dismiss his ablest general, Wallenstein. Richelieu next promoted a truce between Poland and Sweden, so as to enable Gustavus Adolphus to intervene in Germany, and he himself brought an army back into Piedmont and seized Pinerolo. He then arranged that France and Venice should subsidize the Swedish king, and in 1631 formal alliances were concluded between France and Sweden, and France and Bavaria. The Emperor and the King of Spain were naturally appalled by this diplomatic defeat as much as by what must have seemed to them an act of apostasy on the part of the Cardinal. Philip IV sent a protest to Rome; but the Romans, rallying round the Holy Father, declared that Heaven had brought the King of Sweden into Germany in order to save Rome from the designs of Spain and Austria![23]

Urban VIII himself did not say as much: he moved prudently behind the scenes, rejoicing in secret over Gustavus's victories, promising money-grants to the Emperor and refraining, in the event, from giving him more than a very little. The death of Gustavus at Lützen (1632) and the Protestant disaster at Nordlingen (1634) filled him with grief. These setbacks led him to step more warily, though he remained in close touch with Richelieu. He expended large sums

[23] *Ibid.*, 680.

in building up an army, but its morale was poor, and when put to the test, in the war with Parma, the sword of the Pope was not the sword of Gideon. His domestic policy was neither kind to his subjects, who were heavily taxed, nor happily conceived. It has been suggested[24] that he was hoping perhaps that some resounding French victories would enable him, in a subsequent congress, to become ruler of Naples and the south. His diplomatic support of France and the Protestant states did not imply sympathy for Protestantism. It seems likely that he thought it would gradually wilt and perish owing to its internal divisions and under the pressure of Catholic logic and proselytism. But what perhaps best explains his policy is that he was an Italian as well as a Churchman, that the cry of 'Libertà d'Italia' was going up, and that the only way of lightening the country's servitude was by bringing in a strong French element to counterbalance the Spanish.[25] Urban VIII was a forerunner of the Risorgimento and a sort of prophet of Napoleon III.

His policy, however, did not triumph. Richelieu died in 1642; in 1644 Urban himself died; and Innocent X who succeeded him had been elected by pro-Spanish votes and was opposed to Mazarin. It is of interest in this connexion to recall that Giulio Mazzarini, the future ruler of France, had served his apprenticeship in diplomacy under Urban VIII[26] and that Richelieu had singled him out for preferment as early as 1630.

The little principalities of north and north-east Italy, Parma, Modena, Mantua and Urbino, had something to fear from the Pope and a great deal from the Spaniards. We have seen what happened to Urbino. The others looked for support to France and Venice. The Venetians could not single-handedly cope with both Germans and Spaniards, and Richelieu's hand could hardly reach as far as Mantua, though his diplomacy could and did; but the city of the Gonzagas never recovered from the three days' pillage to which the Imperialists had subjected it. In 1642 Urban VIII tried to destroy the Duke of Parma, first by financial operations and then by excommunication and the threat of war. But the Duke, a Farnese, was not intimidated. Tuscany, Modena and Venice rallied to his support, while he himself took the offensive, hustled the Pope's soldiers and invaded the Papal States. This war ('the war of the Barberini') went on for upwards of two years, ending with a victory for Parma, considerable damage to the Pope's dominions and a return to the *status quo* (March, 1644).

[24] By Moritz Brosch, *op. cit.*, 682. [25] H. Hauser, *op. cit.*, 308.

[26] *Ibid.*, 309. He belonged to a family of Roman origin and had been born in the Abruzzi.

III

The Venetian Republic, oldest, most stable and most remarkable of polities, was the principal independent state in Italy. Its territory was considerable, stretching from the Dalmatian coast and the Carnic Alps in the east to Bergamo and Brescia in the west. It controlled all the eastern passes into Austria, its armies were not negligible and its fleets, manned by experienced sailors, were a force to be reckoned with. Venetian policy during the Seicento was a model of what could be done by a small power which combined caution with consistency and audacity. During the early years of the century, Venice successfully resisted the threats of the Pope and the Spanish viceroys.[27] When the Archduke Ferdinand incited the Uskok pirates against the Republic, the Republic made war on them both (1616-17) and then assisted the Protestant party in the Grisons in its struggle against Spain and Austria. Venice was constantly on the alert to support the enemies of Spain, and it was only after the Peace of the Pyrenees (1659) had marked the ascendancy of France that the Republic was prepared to assist the declining power of the Emperor against the Turks; and the great and indeed sensational triumphs of Venice were reserved for the end of the century.

IV

Of the Spanish possessions in Italy, the Milanese had the greatest strategic importance because only from there could the viceroy hold out a hand to his ally in Vienna. Milan commanded the approach to several of the great Alpine passes: the Simplon, the St Gothard, the Grisons passes and the Stelvio. But most of these led into Switzerland. To the east the Venetians controlled all the passes, including the Brenner and those at the head of the Val Camonica. Thus the Stelvio, which could be reached by the Lake of Como and the Valtellina, was the only sure means of communication between Milan, Innsbruck and Vienna. The Valtellina was therefore the bone of contention. To the Spaniards and Austrians, control of this highway —and if possible of the county of Chiavenna, which commanded the approaches to the Splügen and the Maloja—appeared a strategic necessity. To the Grisons, the Venetians, the Savoyards and the French, it appeared equally desirable to prevent such control.

The Valtellina, which is the upper valley of the Adda, runs east and north-east from the head of the Lake of Como to Bormio and the Stelvio Pass; bounded on the north by the Bernina massif, the strong-

[27] For the details of this contest and the part played in it by James I and especially by his ambassador Sir Henry Wotton, see Chapter III below.

hold of one of the Protestant leagues,[28] and on the south by the Alpi Orobie much of which belonged to Venice; so that by the Gavia and Aprica passes the Venetians could send help to their Grison allies.

In 1386 one of the Visconti had ceded his rights over Chiavenna and the Valtellina to the Bishop of Chur. In 1530 the Grey Leagues took over from the Bishop. Apart from their flocks, herds and timber, these mountaineers had little natural wealth, and the Valtellina, which was good farming and wine-growing country, was a most valuable acquisition. Moreover they now controlled all the passes from the Splügen to the Stelvio, and as by the early seventeenth century the Grisons were in a majority Protestant, they were not likely to favour the Austro-Spanish coalition. Hence the struggle for mastery over the Valtellina. It led to civil war in 1618 and 1619, then to open intervention on the part of Spain and Austria and finally to an international conflict.[29]

The men of the Valtellina, nobles and peasants, hated their Grison overlords; and the fact that the latter were themselves divided in religion became a source of weakness which the Spaniards were quick to exploit. In 1601 the French, in 1603 the Venetians secured treaties with the Grisons, thanks to a liberal distribution of money; but the new situation so impressed Count Fuentes, the viceroy in Milan, that he began to build a fort at the head of the Lake of Como, which enabled him both to threaten the Grisons and to strangle or even to cut off their trade with the Milanese. It was a brilliant move: without striking a blow, he created dissension among the Grey Leagues. In 1607 the Catholic and pro-Spanish party in the Grisons met at Chur and cancelled the treaties with France and Venice; whereupon the Protestants caught and beheaded the leaders of that faction. In 1610 the assassination of Henri IV led to a change in French policy which now ceased for a time to be anti-Spanish. Venice, however, still supported the Protestant party, so did Bern and Zürich; and the internal struggle for power in the Grisons became more and more exacerbated. In 1618 a party of Protestant firebrands kidnapped the old arch-priest of Sondrio and tortured him,

[28] The lower Engadine and the Prätigau (Davos and Klosters) were Protestant; the 'Gotteshaus', with Chur as its centre, mainly Catholic; the Grey League proper, with Ilanz and Disentis in the valley of the Vorderrhein, partly Protestant and partly Catholic.

[29] There is an excellent, detailed account of the affairs of the Valtellina by Horatio Brown in the *Cambridge Modern History*, 1906, Vol. IV, Ch. II, pp. 35-63, to which I am indebted. For a mise-au-point in the light of subsequent research, see H. Hauser, *op. cit.*, 263 (period 1603-4), 288-9, and especially 297-302, 324, 326. The story of the Valtellina war is to be read in the light of the diplomatic struggle between Richelieu and Olivarès, as well as of the fortunes of war in France, Savoy and elsewhere.

so that he died. This atrocity provoked a general massacre of the Protestants in Tirano and Sondrio (1620); and the Duke of Feria, then viceroy in Milan, took the Valtellina under his protection. The Grisons had lost their wealthiest province.

Reinforced by troops from Switzerland and supplies from Venice, the Protestant party recaptured Bormio, but were not strong enough to hold it. The Catholic party, acting independently, came to an agreement with Feria (February, 1621) by which the Grisons were to have a merely nominal lordship over the Valtellina while the Spaniards exercised practical control. The result was a very horrible civil war in the Grisons, in the course of which the Catholic party was crushed.[30]

France and Venice, however, had already intervened on the diplomatic level. Marshal Bassompierre had gone to Madrid and induced Philip III's government to agree not only to restore the Valtellina to the Protestant Grisons but to permit the exercise of their religion there (Treaty of Madrid, April, 1621). Olivarès, however, had no intention of carrying out these terms,[31] and Feria ignored them. When Jürg Jenatsch, a sort of fighting parson, modelled on the more lively characters in the book of *Judges*, made another attempt on Bormio, the Viceroy in Milan and the Archduke Leopold in Tyrol decided on war. While Feria's troops took possession of Chiavenna and the Val Bregaglia, of Poschiavo, and also of Bormio, the Austrians invaded the lower Engadine, then subdued the Prätigau[32] and marched down on Chur. The Treaty of Madrid was a dead letter and the Grisons were at the mercy of the victors. By the treaty of Lindau (September, 1622) they lost Chiavenna, the Val Bregaglia, the Munstertal, the lower Engadine and the Valtellina. More than that, they undertook to allow free passage through their territory for Spanish troops, to refuse such passage to the enemies of Spain, and to submit to being a Spanish protectorate.[33]

But Gregory XV had been persuaded by the Venetian ambassador that the growth of Spanish power represented a menace to his own. And now the conquest of the Grisons aroused Venice and Savoy to the need for action. Both governments appealed to Paris[34] and when at last Richelieu came into power, action was taken. In 1624, to the great joy of the Protestant Leagues, a French expeditionary force under the Marquis de Coeuvres arrived in the Prätigau, crossed into the Engadine and descended on Tirano. Here they were joined by

30 Horatio Brown, *op. cit.*, IV, 51-2.

31 H. Hauser, *op. cit.*, 298.

32 This is the valley that goes up from Lanquart and includes Klosters and Davos.

33 Hauser, 298.

34 See above, p. 27.

reinforcements and siege-artillery which the Venetians had brought over the Aprica pass; and in face of these forces the Papal and Spanish troops retired from the Valtellina. The Archduke Leopold had been induced to withdraw from the lower Engadine, and the triumph of the Grisons and the Venetians appeared to be complete.

Unfortunately, as related above, Urban VIII, the new Pope, was annoyed at having lost any control in the Valtellina; the 'parti des dévots' was active in Paris, and in the negotiations that followed, the Spaniards won a brilliant diplomatic victory by the Treaty of Monzon (March, 1626).[35]

For now, in spite of the Franco-Venetian victory in the Grisons, the Valtellina was open for the passage of Spanish and Imperial troops. The Venetians, a cool-headed folk, contained their resentment. But the Grisons wondered whether they could in the future trust France to back them up consistently. The ultimate effects of Monzon became apparent only between 1637 and 1639; the immediate effects were felt almost at once. In 1627 the throne of Mantua became vacant. Charles de Gonzague, Duc de Nevers, the legal heir, was accepted by the people. He was a staunch Catholic, and the French candidate. But Ferdinand II declared that Mantua, a fief of the Empire, was at his disposal and in 1629, as will be remembered, he sent troops down the Valtellina to enforce his will.

Having taken La Rochelle in the autumn of 1628, Richelieu, a prelate in armour, led his troops across the Mont Genèvre in March, 1629, compelled the Duke of Savoy to abandon the Spanish alliance and reinforced the French garrison in Casale. But he had to cope with a Spanish offensive, and then to return to France where he wished to complete the subjugation of the Protestant party. Peace with England was signed in May, and the Huguenots submitted at the end of June. But now (October, 1629) the Imperialists laid siege to Mantua, and the prospects of relieving the place were small. In the winter of 1629-1630 the Cardinal brought another army into Piedmont and took possession of Pinerolo. Heavy fighting was renewed, the country was devastated, and Charles Emmanuel died at the moment when his fortunes were at their lowest ebb. His son and successor married a French princess and moved back into the French orbit. Casale held out against the Spaniards, but Mantua, too far away to be relieved, was taken by storm and suffered a dreadful fate.

A young Roman officer who had taken part in this war, had laid aside the sword for the cassock on entering the diplomatic service of

[35] Horatio Brown, 'The Valtelline', *op. cit.*, IV, 59; Moritz Brosch, 'Papal Policy', *ibid.*, 675; H. Hauser, *La Prépondérance espagnole*, 301-3. Hauser explains the great difficulties with which Richelieu had to contend in France before he could concentrate his efforts on war with Spain.

Urban VIII. Giulio Mazzarini possessed the political foresight and astuteness needed to impress the great Cardinal, and the handsome person and exquisite manners that were destined to win the heart of a Queen.

In these years all events and circumstances in western Europe were interlocked and interdependent. The Huguenot rebellion in France produced repercussions in Piedmont and the Valtellina; while a withdrawal of French influence from the Grisons had led Charles Emmanuel in disgust to desert the French alliance, and it had also spelt the doom of Mantua.

In spite of his success in Piedmont Richelieu was harassed and thwarted by his enemies at home: by the Queen-Mother, by Gaston d'Orléans and the ultra-Catholic party. The King's illness gave them an opportunity to seek the Cardinal's overthrow; and for a moment (10th November: 'La Journée des Dupes') it looked as though they had succeeded. Louis XIII, however, stood by his minister and the latter gradually recovered control. He had been ill served in the negotiations at Ratisbon, where the French envoys signed a general peace without his assent;[36] and in the following spring he took the question of the peace treaties personally in hand. In this matter he was aided by the Pope's envoy, Mazzarini, who had intervened so adroitly between the French and the Imperialists that while the French were ostensibly to abandon Casale, they actually remained in control of the citadel. By the treaties of Cherasco (1631) Victor Amadeus I, the young Duke of Savoy, returned to the French alliance, promised free passage for French troops and ceded Pinerolo; while the Duc de Nevers was restored to the throne of Mantua. The French now had free access to Italy, but this was the limit of their success for the moment. True, the great Cardinal was now secure in the royal favour. Archbishop Marillac, his ecclesiastical enemy, was disgraced, the Maréchal de Marillac, beheaded, while the Queen-Mother took refuge in the Spanish Netherlands. Richelieu himself was created a Duke.[37] But the Cardinal-Duke was not yet strong enough to give further assistance to the Grisons or to obtain for them any effective control of the Valtellina; and in 1632 he fell sick.

And now the loss of the Valtellina involved the allies of France in great misfortune. In 1633 and 1634 the Austro-Spanish coalition moved 21,000 men up from Italy into Germany, and these enabled the Emperor's general, Piccolomini, to overwhelm the Protestant

[36] Hauser, *op. cit.*, 310. It is not known whether he had failed to give le Père Joseph, his personal envoy, precise instructions, or whether Father Joseph's sympathies led him to favour the Catholic party.

[37] *Ibid.*, 310.

army at Nordlingen (September, 1634). The news, when it reached Rome, came as a bitter pill for Urban VIII. But where the Pope was dejected, the Cardinal-Duke was galvanized. He resembled that Hindu deity with arms extending in every direction as he gathered himself together for an assault on the Austro-Spanish hegemony. Vindictive or magnanimous as it suited his designs, he had treated the Huguenots with real toleration and even generosity. So far from humiliating their general, Duc Henri de Rohan, he had restored his estates and had simply exiled him to Venice where he would be among political friends but not among heretics. Rohan was now recalled home and entrusted with a task at once military and diplomatic: to re-establish the power and authority of the Grey Leagues.

Those who today visit the upper Engadine and go over Maloja and down the steep descent to the Val Bregaglia, or over the Bernina and down to Tirano, by well-engineered roads which are still sensational enough for the most exacting, may wonder how three centuries ago armies with their equipment moved rapidly up and down these and even more difficult passes; how also the Venetians hauled their cannon up the Val Camonica and over the Aprica pass. The Valtellina, once bitterly contested, has long since recovered its ancient peace. And only here and there, as by the ruins of Fort Fuentes, is one visibly reminded of the past.

Rohan reached Chur with a small army in March, 1635, and was joined by Jürg Jenatsch and the Grison forces. The strategy he planned was good, the execution of it brilliant. Jenatsch was sent to seize Bormio, while a French regiment occupied the Val Livigno to secure his rear. Rohan himself, with a larger force, descended the Val Bregaglia and occupied Chiavenna. To a less experienced commander the situation would have appeared hopeless. To the northeast, beyond the Stelvio, the Emperor's general Fernamond had an army of 10,000 Germans and Austrians; to the south a Spanish force under Serbelloni was moving up from Como. Only the swiftest and best calculated moves could prevent them from joining forces in the Valtellina, whether at Sondrio or Tirano. Though telephones had not been invented, 'intelligence' seems to have been good. Rohan heard that Fernamond's troops had driven Jenatsch out of Bormio and then moved up the Val Livigno against the French; who, heavily outnumbered, had withdrawn into the Engadine. The Imperialists, however, had been slow-witted enough to linger in Livigno. Rohan, seeing the danger to his rear, hastened back to the Engadine (anyone who knows the Val Bregaglia and the ascent to Maloja will guess what this involved), crossed the Casana pass[38] to the Val

[38] The approach to this pass, which is parallel with the Bernina, starts a few miles below Zuoz.

Livigno, surprised the Germans who were asleep and drove them back to Bormio. He then turned, crossed a little-frequented pass to the Bernina road and descended on Tirano. Fernamond was coming down from Bormio and Serbelloni might soon be advancing up the valley from the west. Rohan sent a column to hold up Fernamond. The latter repulsed it, thought he had finally beaten the French and let his men drink heavily and go to sleep. 'Veltliner' wine is potent and Rohan knew something about Germans and strong drink. In the early hours of the morning he was upon them. They were utterly routed and fled back to Tyrol.

Rohan now turned west to deal with Serbelloni, but that prudent commander did not wait to be attacked. In the autumn the French general moved up towards the Stelvio, was joined by Jenatsch and dealt Fernamond the final blow (13th October). He then marched down the valley. Serbelloni offered battle and was defeated. Rohan was now master of the Valtellina. But he was dependent on Paris for money to pay the Grisons, who were always in need of money; and the Grisons were growing suspicious of France and the Valtelliners were hostile to the Grisons. While awaiting a decision from Louis XIII, Rohan proposed that the Grey Leagues should have suzerainty over the Valtellina, except in matters of justice and religion. It was an equitable proposal, but it did not suit the Grisons, and now, after hunting with the hounds, they decided (September, 1636) to run with the hare. They sent envoys to Innsbruck where the Austrians were offering them what they thought better terms; and when at last the money arrived from Paris the mischief had been done. Rohan and his troops left Chur in May, 1637, overwhelmed with thanks for his services, which had indeed saved the Grey Leagues; and in the autumn of 1639 the latter signed peace at Milan. They were to be sovereigns of Chiavenna and the Valtellina, except in religion; but the Viceroy was to have the right of transit for troops between Milan and Innsbruck.

Exactly why France sacrificed the position Rohan had secured for her—a key-position in the open war now being waged against Spain and the Empire—may never be known; and more than one reason could be adduced. The whole situation, military and diplomatic, after 1635 was extraordinarily complex. In 1636 the Emperor had declared war on France, who was already at grips with Spain; and the French now suffered fearful reverses in Picardy and the eastern provinces, while in the Mediterranean the Spaniards seized the Iles Lérins, near Cannes. Richelieu was probably too deeply involved in these and other troubles to spare more men and money to hold the Valtellina.

The War of the Valtellina was nevertheless the most important of all those that were fought in or on the borders of Italy in the seventeenth century. The campaigns in Piedmont were in a sense part of it. And the final settlement marked by the diplomatic success of the Austro-Spanish coalition, assured the continuance of Spanish domination in Italy.

Though no major wars apart from these were fought in Italy until the so-called War of the League of Augsbourg in the 1690's, no part of the peninsula enjoyed unbroken peace except Tuscany. The revolt in Sicily in 1674 ended in the Spaniards' regaining control. But by this time Spanish power was declining. The Treaty of the Pyrenees (1659) had confirmed the ascendancy of France, and in the 1670's that ascendancy became a preponderance. A shift of alliances was soon to follow, hastened and largely occasioned by the religious policy of Louis XIV. The Dutch and finally the English moved into opposition. Savoy, for so long faithful to the French alliance, also turned against Louis XIV, and this led to Marshal Catinat's campaigns in Piedmont. In 1696 Victor-Amadeus II came to terms with Louis XIV; but in 1704, during the War of the Spanish Succession, he rejoined the allies and in the next few years northern Italy was the scene of warfare between greater armies and on a greater scale than anything in the seventeenth century.

The Dukes of Savoy had, as long before as the War of the Mantuan Succession, been pursuing the *politica del carciofo*, as Italian historians call it. This policy involved changes of alliance somewhat blatantly Machiavellian. In 1631 Savoy had obtained part of Montferrat; in 1707 she secured another part. In 1713 Sicily fell to the Duke's lot, in 1720, Sardinia, with the title of King.[39] As Piedmont-Savoy waxed more powerful, the Republic of St George declined. Genoa had been seriously disabled by the French in 1684 and 1685, and found it increasingly hard to retain control of Corsica.

V

The resurgence of Turkish power and aggressiveness in the 1640's posed an immediate threat to Venice and an ultimate threat to Austria and Poland. In 1645 the Turks had invaded Crete, a Venetian island, and in 1648 laid siege to Candia. The Venetians defended themselves bravely and stubbornly. Their navy, ably commanded by Francesco Morosini, frequently worsted the Turks at sea, and Candia held out until 1669, when most of the island fell into Turkish hands.[40] The Sultan's armies meanwhile had overrun

[39] But he lost Sicily.

[40] See Richard Lodge, 'Austria, Poland and Turkey', in *Cambridge Modern History*. Cambridge, 1908, V, 342-3, 348-9.

Hungary and advanced into Austria (1664). It was a peril that united Christian Europe, if only for a time. Louis XIV sent a French force to assist the Italian generalissimo Montecuculi, who commanded the Austrian army and its German auxiliaries; and in the battle of St Gothard (August, 1664) Montecuculi routed the invaders. The ensuing treaty left the Turks in possession of Hungary, but Austria had been saved—for the moment[41]—and the northern flank of Venetian territory remained covered.

In face of the Turkish peril, Vienna, now supported by Venice, remained the rallying-point for volunteers in the crusade against Moslem aggression. It was apparent in 1682 that the worst was to be feared. In 1683 a Turkish army of 250,000 men invaded Austria and laid siege to Vienna. Montecuculi, the Emperor's ablest general, had died in 1681 and the Imperial army was now under the command of Charles de Lorraine, with whom Eugene of Savoy was serving as a young officer. Greatly outnumbered by the enemy, Charles had withdrawn to harass Turkish communications and wait for the Emperor's appeal to bring up reinforcements and allies. Two of the German Electors responded to the cry for help, but more effective aid came from John Sobieski of Poland. In the early morning of September 12th Sobieski, Lorraine and the German princes attacked the Turkish army that was besieging Vienna, put it to flight and pursued it into Hungary. In 1684, after a Holy League had been signed by Poland, Austria and Venice, the Venetians undertook the reconquest of Dalmatia from the Turks and dispatched Morosini, assisted by German auxiliaries under Count Königsmark, to invade the Peloponnese, or Morea, as it was then called. In 1685 most of this part of Greece had been taken, and in 1687 the Venetians laid siege to Athens. The Turks at last surrendered the city, but it was not possible to hold it for more than a few months. Morosini was now seventy—an advanced age for a field commander. After returning home for a time, he came back to Greece to direct operations, but died there in 1694. The whole of the Peloponnese had, however, now been conquered by Venice,[42] and the southern flank of the Turkish Empire rather materially undermined. The Russians meanwhile were advancing towards the Black Sea, but in spite of this favourable diversion, the Imperialists (who had been holding a line of defence in Hungary) suffered bad reverses in 1695 and 1696.[43] In 1697, however, Prince Eugene, whose kinsman the Duke of Savoy had just come to terms with France, took command of the Imperial army and almost annihilated the Turks at Zenta. By the peace of Carlovitsi (January, 1699) the Emperor recovered

[41] *Ibid.*, 347-8.
[42] *Ibid.*, V, 365.
[43] *Ibid.*, V, 369.

Hungary, while the Venetians retained Dalmatia and southern Greece.[44]

By the end of the century the balance of power in Europe had been radically changed and the shadow of Spanish domination had passed away. For a time, after 1701, it looked as though the French would become masters of Lombardy, but they were obliged to withdraw in 1707,[45] and it was Austria, or, strictly speaking, the Emperor who, by one of the treaties of Utrecht (1713), entered into possession of the Milanese; while by another of the same group of treaties France restored to the Duke of Savoy the county of Nice and the Duchy of Savoy which had been taken from him.

None of the wars of the Seicento prevented or seriously affected travel in Italy, but they determined the routes it should follow or at least those which it would not. Travellers would not go to Italy by way of the Grisons (a favourite route) between 1618 and 1627 or again between 1635 and 1639; nor would they think of crossing the Mont Cenis between 1629 and 1631. There were times also when Naples was in the throes of rebellion or revolution. But other parts of Italy would remain open, Tuscany and Venetia in particular, and the Thirty Years' War, part of which was fought on Italian soil, did not disrupt commerce and travel to the same extent that an international war today would do.

VI

While the Papacy during the Seicento had lost much of its old power in Europe and was unable to destroy Protestantism or free thought, it exercised a valuable and growing influence in America and Asia. The personal character of the Popes had greatly improved. Their temporal power in Italy had been limited, as we have seen, by the exorbitant power of Spain; and as Spanish predominance passed away, they found themselves challenged by the growth of Gallicanism in France and by the dictatorial Church politics of Louis XIV. The rise of Jansenism and later of Quietism, not to speak of the excesses of casuistry, demanded for their solution the utmost care and wisdom. It was a question of holding the Church together and steering a middle course—the sort of problem that sooner or later faces any organization in which sincere and intelligent men are involved.

Relations with Great Britain were intermittent and informal, except during the pontificates of Innocent X and Innocent XI. To have added Ireland to the Papal States would have been very satisfactory to the Pope; but if the English were ousted from Ireland—an im-

[44] *Ibid.*, V, 370-1.

[45] Convention of Milan, March, 1707. *Ibid.*, V, 415.

probable contingency—the French or the Spaniards might well step in to replace them.

Urban VIII, whose political activities have already been noted, was one of the most gifted and intelligent pontiffs of the age. He appears to have believed in the Copernican system and he certainly encouraged Galileo, who was a personal friend, to write the now famous *Dialogue on the two principal systems of the world* (1632).[46] But its publication and the flutter that ensued caused him apparently to change his mind, or at least his attitude; whether because the Jesuits had put pressure on him, or because he believed himself to have been caricatured in the person of Simplicio.[47] Not only did Urban VIII promote the interests of the Church everywhere he could, including Canada and China, but he was himself a very cultured prince and a competent writer of verse in Greek, Latin and Italian.[48]

Innocent X who succeeded him (1644-1655) was too old and lacking in character, too 'cautious' and 'dilatory' in policy (in the words of an Italian historian) to make an effective Pope. He felt sympathy for Queen Henrietta-Maria in exile, and was induced by her representative, Sir Kenelm Digby, to send her 20,000 scudi to procure arms for Charles I; but declined to give any more money to an obstinately Protestant king who was fighting a losing war against even more deplorably Protestant subjects.[49] This was perfectly natural. It was his subservience to his sister-in-law, the imperious Olimpia Maldacchini, that lowered the prestige of the Holy See.

Alexander VII (1655-1667) pursued a much more vigorous policy. He induced the Serenissima to readmit the Jesuits to Venetian territory, and in matters theological he decidedly favoured the Society of Jesus. It was he who condemned the famous five propositions, declaring at the same time that they *were* in Jansen's *Augustinus*, a point to which the Jansenists demurred. He, no more than his predecessor, felt any liking for Mazarin.[50]

Clement IX (1667-1669) on the other hand, a gentle and conciliatory soul, kept on good terms with both France and Spain. He was deeply interested in the war against the Turks, and the fall of Candia, after its long and heroic resistance, seems to have been his death blow. He had been essentially a peacemaker, and Clement X (1670-1676) who inherited his policy would have been a peacemaker too. The contentions in which he became involved with Louis XIV, mainly as regards ecclesiastical administration and finance, were not of his making. It was some consolation to this unaggressive pontiff

[46] E. Préclin *XVIIe siècle*, 539, 603.
[47] H. Hauser, *op. cit.*, 484.
[48] Préclin, 603.
[49] See below, Chapter IV.
[50] Préclin, 604-5.

that he was able to improve the organization of Catholic missions in Canada and China.

But by far the greatest of the Popes since the Middle Ages was Innocent XI (1676-1689). The excesses of Jesuit casuistry, which had excited such scandal and had exposed the Society to the devastating sarcasm of Pascal, met with short shrift from this learned and scrupulous theologian; but he also discouraged the more extreme forms of Jansenism and Quietism. In home affairs he attacked every form of nepotism, simplified the Papal administration and established the budget on a sound basis.[51] In foreign affairs he vigorously opposed Louis XIV, and disapproved of the Revocation of the Edit de Nantes, knowing well that souls are not won over by cruelty and oppression. Through his nuncio in London he warned James II of the unwisdom of his behaviour, and if James had listened to him he might have retained his throne—and probably would.

The reigns of Alexander VIII (1689-1691) and Innocent XII (1691-1700) were marked by an improvement in relations with France and a final settlement of the points in dispute. It was only with Clement XI (1700-1721) that the chair of St Peter was occupied by a statesman comparable in some respects to Innocent XI.

If political weakness and a certain degree of economic stagnation are infallible signs of decadence, then seventeenth-century Italy was decadent. But civilization and moral progress depend on other factors, besides, as I shall try to indicate in another chapter. It was, one may recall in this connexion, at a time when Palestine was under foreign rule that she gave birth to the greatest agency for progress that the world has seen.

[51] *Ibid.*, 606.

CHAPTER II

Envoys and Diplomatists

DURING the reign of James I diplomatic relations with northern and central Italy acquired, owing to the need of re-establishing a balance of power, exceptional importance. Spain was now solidly entrenched in Lombardy and Naples: and her very presence in northern Italy constituted a threat to Venice, to Savoy, to Tuscany and to the Grisons. For a time, therefore, the embassy at Venice and the residency at Turin became focal points of British Foreign Policy. James desired to check the advance of Hapsburg and Papal power: and it was through Venice, as much as through Paris and the Hague, that it seemed possible to promote that end. There were other, non-political reasons why Englishmen of all classes were interested in the Venetian Republic as well as in Tuscany, a wealthy and independent little state, and why Venetia in particular loomed larger in English eyes than she had in the days of Elizabeth. These interests were, however, furthered by the new diplomatic and the older commercial relations between England and Italy.

The political and spiritual structure of medieval Europe had not required the existence of a diplomatic corps. When some problem arose, a special envoy was sent out to deal with it. But the formation of national states created the need for a balance of power and solicited a more formal machinery. Henry VII instituted the system of resident ambassadors at foreign courts.[1] He was a close-fisted man and selected persons of humble origin who would be inexpensive to maintain. Henry VIII, who vied with François Ier in a taste for splendour and display, appointed men of birth and standing; and this example was generally followed by his successors. But few positions in the state were closed to men of talent and character.[2]

Elizabeth I encouraged young men to go abroad to learn languages and acquire a knowledge of Continental politics; she sometimes subsidized them: and in this way she formed the *cadre* of a gifted and competent foreign service,[3] consisting of men who had learned in

[1] L. Pearsall Smith, *The Life and Letters of Sir Henry Wotton*. Oxford, 1907, I, 46.

[2] The rise of the Cecil family is one of many instances.

[3] Pearsall Smith, I, 8-9.

the school of experience. A number of them, perhaps a majority, acted for Sir Francis Walsingham who maintained one of the best secret services of the time—or of most times. Essex had his own service. The Queen herself maintained ambassadors at the principal courts of the Continent; and on the other hand France, Spain and other powers had ambassadors or residents in London.

Henry VII and Elizabeth had been careful and practical statesmen, averse to an excess of display, or at any rate of expenditure. The Stuarts liked magnificance; and with the accession of James I diplomacy became more splendid and also more active. The King's earlier life had been passed in an atmosphere of peril and conspiracy, which had taught him to play the fox rather than the lion. Accession to the throne of England opened a wider field of action but authorized no radical change in policy. The desire was to maintain the balance of power without recourse to war. James both feared and admired Spain, and he moved warily in a Europe in which he could hope to exert strong influence only in association with states that were opposed to the Hapsburg coalition. France, the United Provinces and the German Protestants were potential allies; but it might be possible also to engage Venice or one of the Italian principalities on his side.

Not that his preoccupations were solely political and military. England was a trading nation, with an expanding economy. The outlets through Antwerp and into the Baltic, even in Muscovy, where English merchants had established depots at Moscow and Vologda[4] were insufficient for her needs. She was now putting out feelers across the Atlantic and also, round the Cape of Good Hope, to the East Indies.[5] But the Mediterranean trade was still the richest, and most of the exports from India and the Spice Islands still passed through Aleppo or other ports in the Levant. The Venetians handled a large part of this merchandise; but the Turks could control the passage of goods through Syria. English ships carried woollen textiles to Turkey, and also tin, an essential commodity in war, as it was needed for the manufacture of cannon;[6] they brought back currants and cotton. In 1593 Ferdinand I, Grand-Duke of Tuscany, had opened Livorno (Leghorn) as a free port. The harbour facilities were before long to be greatly improved by an English engineer, an expatriate son of the Earl of Leicester:[7] and Livorno was now the greatest depot for the Mediterranean trade as a whole.[8]

[4] G. D. Ramsay, *English Overseas Trade*. London, 1957, p. 27.

[5] James Lancaster's first venture was in 1591. He was more successful in 1601-3, when he brought back cargoes from Sumatra and Java (Ramsay, pp. 67-8).

[6] Cannon were made of bronze. See also Ramsey, 42.

[7] See below, pp. 97-100.

[8] Ramsey, 50-51.

It is not surprising if, in these circumstances, James sent out splendid embassies, not only to Constantinople and even to the court of the Great Mogul, but especially to Venice. An English ambassador, on his way to a foreign court, was likened to a comet, blazing in gold and crimson and followed by a sparkling 'tail' of splendidly attired gentlemen and servants.[9] London might—and did—appear to Italian visitors a rather mean-looking place, with its low Gothic mansions and half-timbered shops and dwellings—a town not comparable for beauty with Genoa or Venice or a dozen other Italian cities. But an ambassadorial train showed that this was but the modest exterior of a rich and powerful nation, which Venice—and other states—would do well to cultivate as an ally.

Venice was still a considerable power, and a wealthy one. Her alliance was therefore of value to the Protestant states, and especially to England. The same might be said of Tuscany and Savoy, both of which were well disposed and anxious to marry their children into the English royal family. Fear of the Hapsburgs and of the Papacy drew them together. To seek allies in the midst of hostile territory was, in the eyes of London, an obviously desirable policy: while the Venetians, being on bad terms with the Court of Rome, were glad to obtain what help they could from England, as Savoy was from France.

There were other, and more particular reasons, as Pearsall Smith indicates in his *Life of Wotton*, why the English ambassador should receive from the Doge and Senate a welcome as magnificent as that which had been accorded to the representatives of France and Spain.[10] The loss of Cyprus had been a severe blow to the military and naval power as well as to the commerce of the Republic.[11] Add to this that the opening of a passage to India round the Cape of Good Hope had injured the eastern trade which the Venetians had formerly handled by way of the Levant. It is true that the Republic was far from being impoverished. What had been lost in trade was largely made up for in banking; and the erection and decoration of new and splendid palaces, both on the island and along the Brenta canal,[12] were not, as might appear, the wasting of a once splendid patrimony. But trade remained essential. In this matter the English frequently assisted; but they also competed. There had been disputes; and the absence of an English representative in Venice had not facilitated their settlement. These disputes had arisen out of the practices of the Levant Company, which had on occasion ignored Venetian monopolies and interests, but above all from the fact that many

[9] Pearsall Smith, *op. cit.*, I, 48. [10] *Ibid.*, 50-1.
[11] *Ibid.*
[12] This continued right on into the eighteenth century.

English ships were engaged in piracy.[13] The Venetians retaliated when they could, but they naturally preferred to remove the nuisance by negotiation,[14] the more so as the horizon was black with menace.

Hence a period, after 1601 and even more after 1604, of intense diplomatic activity, and the peculiar importance of the Venetian embassy in London, and of the English embassy in Venice and the residency in Turin. So keen did the contention grow between Venice and the Papacy that a movement for ecclesiastical separation arose, led by Fra Paolo Sarpi and the Protestant-minded element in the nobility, and it appeared not impossible that Venice might turn Protestant and that a form of Anglicanism might be established there.[15]

Englishmen were quick to seize the many opportunities for advancement which the foreign service afforded. On going abroad, an ambassador or a 'resident' took with him a considerable 'household'.[16] He had a chaplain, one or two secretaries of whom the senior would represent him in his absence, a secretary who was a native of the state in question or at least an expert in the language, and a number of gentlemen whom he selected privately as his servants. Thus Wotton took his nephew Albertus Morton as first secretary, and Nathaniel Fletcher as chaplain. In 1608 Fletcher was succeeded by William Bedell, who assisted the ambassador in attempting to convert Venice to Anglicanism. He translated the English Prayer-Book into Italian and later translated into English parts of Sarpi's *History of the Council of Trent*. He kept in touch with England by corresponding with the Masters of Emmanuel and Sidney Sussex Colleges as well as with prominent courtiers: and finally he became Bishop of Lismore. Isaac Bargrave, who was chaplain in Venice from 1616 to 1618, ended up as Dean of Canterbury. A period of service in Venice, Florence or Turin was equally valuable to the layman.[17] Thus Albertus Morton, after serving in Venice, was appointed resident in Turin; and later, after his return to England, Secretary of State (1625). Sir Dudley Carleton who, in 1610, succeeded Wotton as ambassador to Venice, was transferred to the Hague in 1616 and became Secretary of State in 1628. The experiences of Sir John Finch, later in the century, are even more instructive.

It was useful, on any score, to be attached to the embassy in Venice. A man so placed could not only hope for other and better

[13] G. D. Ramsay, *op. cit.*, 41-43. [14] Cf. Pearsall Smith, I, 72-73.
[15] See below, Ch. III.
[16] J. W. Stoye, *English Travellers Abroad* (1604-1667). London, 1952, 148-9.
[17] Mr Stoye traces the successive stages in political advancement (p. 129).

appointments; he could spend three or four months of the year studying Medicine, Anatomy, Languages or Law at Padua; he could acquire beautiful manners that would enable him to shine in Whitehall; he could purchase paintings and specimens of the exquisite glass-ware of Murano, which might be shipped home and presented to some *grande dame* or powerful lord in gratitude for benefits to come.[18]

Sir Henry Wotton, whose knowledge of Italy was unique among Englishmen at that time, represented King James in Venice from 1604 to 1610 and again from 1616 to 1623. Meanwhile, as we have seen, James had appointed Albertus Morton as his agent in Turin. In 1616 Morton was succeeded by Isaac Wake (1582?-1632), who had been Carleton's secretary at Venice from 1610 to 1615, and who remained at the court of Charles-Emmanuel until he was appointed to succeed Wotton at Venice in 1624. On this occasion he entered Venice in great style, 'as well in liveries, flaunting feathers, and the like, as in number of followers . . .'[19] But he was often short of money, and had the greatest difficulty in obtaining from London the remittances that were due to him.[20] After his departure, Thomas Rowlandson, whose family appears to have had its home in Venice, acted as *chargé d'affaires* until the arrival of Sir Basil Feilding, Charles I's ambassador; but there was also a British Consul who looked after the commercial and maritime interests of his countrymen.

The outbreak of the Civil War, and still more the execution of Charles I, dislocated the foreign service and at times interrupted regular intercourse with Venice; but the *Calendar of State Papers: Venetian* enables one to trace something of what was happening in both capitals.

Feilding's departure left a vacancy which was ultimately to be filled, though not for long, by Thomas Killigrew, the future dramatist and theatre-manager.

Killigrew[21] belonged to a prominent Cornish family and was a great friend of the poet Thomas Carew, in whose company his portrait was painted. He had visited Italy in 1636 with the Honourable Walter Montague. The latter, who had gone over to the Catholic Church, joined the Order of the Oratory in Rome;[22] he was later to become one of the most prominent of the English Royalists

[18] One may recall in this connexion the names of George Rooke and Michael Branthwaite (Pearsall Smith, II, 478 & 464).

[19] *The Court and Times of James I.* London, 1848, II, 454.

[20] *State Papers: Savoy.*

[21] See Alfred Herbage, *Thomas Willigrew, Cavalier Dramatist* (1612-1683). Philadelphia, 1930.

[22] *Ibid.*, 59.

in Paris, and, as the abbé Montaigue, to be head of the monastery of Saint-Martin de Pontoise.[23] Killigrew had no such bent. He was interested in the theatre, as can be judged from the tragi-comedies of *Claricella* and *The Princess* which were written about this time and appear to owe something to his knowledge of Italy. During the ten years that followed his first visit, he remained mostly in England; but towards 1647 we find him in the service of Prince Charles who had taken refuge in France and who now sent him to Italy to raise money—the raising of money being a matter of the greatest urgency, not only then but during the whole period of the Royal Family's exile on the Continent. We know that Killigrew was at Padua in July, 1647, and he probably called on English merchants in Venice, Florence, Livorno and possibly even Naples in order to borrow money. That he borrowed a good deal is certain.[24]

In 1649 the Prince, who had now been proclaimed King as Charles II, appointed Killigrew as envoy extraordinary to Turin, Florence and Venice, and as Resident in Venice. But his tenure of this once coveted position was uncomfortable and short. He presented his credentials to the Doge and the Collegio in April, 1650.[25] As, however, the Commonwealth government was not long in intimating its displeasure, the Venetians bethought themselves to accuse Killigrew of irregular practices, and even to arrest his gondolier. Finally, when Lorenzo Paulucci, their representative in London, reported that Sir Oliver Fleming was complaining of Killigrew's presence in Venice, they contrived to get rid of him.[26] The Republic appeared to be firmly established in England, London was soon offering naval assistance in the defence of Crete, and the Venetians were as practical as Mazarin in their diplomacy.

From this moment and for many years to come there was no English Resident in Venice, and Charles II on his restoration did not at first trouble to appoint one. The Venetians, who were maintaining Piero Mocenigo as ambassador in London, regarded this as a slight,[27] and Charles at last decided to fill the vacancy. A number of prominent men were anxious to go. Henry Howard, the Catholic Earl of Arundel, was one; but his devotion to Venice, and the expenses he defrayed in the negotiations with Muley Roshid, king of Taffilet, 'do not suffice', Mocenigo reported to the Senate, 'to recom-

[23] J. W. Stoye, *op. cit.*, 432-4.

[24] *Historical MSS Commission* (Report on the Pepys MSS in the Library of Magdalene College). London, 1911, 263.

[25] *Calendar of State Papers: Venetian*, Vol. XXVIII (1647-1652). London, 1927, 136, 140, 141, 143-5.

[26] *Ibid.*, 250, 256.

[27] *Calendar of State Papers: Venetian*, Vol. XXXVI (1669-1670). Edited by A. B. Hinds. London, 1937, Preface, p. li.

mend him for an honour he so greatly desires'.[28] Sir William Temple also wanted the post, and Sir John Finch, who was then Resident in Florence, had strong support. But the position had been virtually promised to Sir Thomas Belasize, Viscount Falcombridge; and although at one moment it looked as though Finch would be chosen, Falcombridge intervened and, with the support of the Duke of York, was appointed.[29]

It is a curious fact that our knowledge of all this, and of his mission to Italy in general, is derived from the dispatches of Venetian diplomats and other secret papers in the Archives of Venice—documents that were not published until 1937. One gathers that he had sought the office partly on account of his wife, Mary Cromwell, whose position at Court the Royalist ladies had made uncomfortable. It was her money that was to pay most of the expenses, and one can imagine her feelings when the king prevented her from accompanying her husband. Although ambassador to Venice, Falcombridge had other duties to perform in connexion with Savoy, Genoa and Tuscany. The Duke of Savoy, who wished to promote an active commerce with England through the ports of Villefranche and Nice, had sent a generous present of wine to Charles II, and the latter then instructed Sir John Finch to cultivate good relations with the Savoyards.[30] Falcombridge's first task therefore was to discuss practical arrangements. On arrival in Turin, he found that the Genoese were raising objections, but as it soon appeared that these were invalid he promised that a British Consul should be sent out to facilitate the commerce in question. He himself was very courteously received and taken to see a ballet at Valentino which was attended by 'a swarm of ladies.'[31] He next proceeded to Genoa and thence to Livorno, where there was a large English colony. From this port Tuscany had been shipping some 24,000 barrels yearly of salt fish to England. Venice, which had only exported 4,000 barrels in 1669, wanted a share of the trade; and the English on their side desired to import more currants from the Ionian Islands (which belonged to Venice), and also to export cloth to Bosnia, which was in the Venetian sphere. As, in all this, three independent Italian states were involved, a certain amount of bargaining must have been involved.

Falcombridge's next stage was at Florence where he was lodged in the Palazzo Pitti, the residence of the Grand Duke. And at the beginning of July (1670) he reached Venice, his arrival being an-

[28] *Ibid.*, 69.

[29] Dispatch from Mocenigo, No. 106. C. S. P.: *Venetian* XXXVI, 93-4.

[30] Dispatch from Mocenigo, 6th April, 1669. C. S. P.: *Venetian*, XXXVI, 42.

[31] Dispatch from Francesco Michieli, Venetian ambassador in Turin (No. 201), 8th May, 1670. *Ibid.*

nounced to the Secretary to the Senate, Angelo Zon, by George Hailes, the British Consul. The Cavaliere Michiele Morosini was commissioned to introduce him, and on 7th July, in the Monastery of the San Spirito, he was formally received by the Doge and Collegio and read an address in English.[32]

His mission appears to have been successful; the Venetians were pleased with the standing and manner of the ambassador.[33] It seems doubtful, however, whether they derived much benefit from all this.

The Commonwealth had shown more practical sympathy with Venice in her periodical wars with Turkey. Thus on 14th August, 1651, Angelo Ciera had announced to Killigrew the news of a naval victory off the isle of Paros, in which the Venetians had burned five Turkish ships and captured ten: whereupon Killigrew, says Ciera, 'rejoiced at the news I gave him and that the flags of his country were fighting under the happy auspices of General Mocenigo.'[34] One finds no record of any such assistance from Charles II: on the contrary the Venetian ambassador in London, Piero Mocenigo, could obtain no help for the defence of Crete and Charles even prevented Louis XIV from sending the Scottish guards under Lord George Douglas and Sir George Hamilton to the relief of the Venetian fortress which the Turks were beleaguering. It was this disappointment, more than anything else, that led Mocenigo to press for his recall home.[35]

Venice did not apparently profit, either, from the commercial point of view. The English trade seems to have declined; whereas, paradoxical as it might appear, the English were now increasing their hold on the seaborne trade of southern Italy, which was a Spanish possession. They dominated the shipping to and from Naples. In 1675 the British Consul there reported that there were on an average sixty ships loading for England every year and sixty for other destinations.[36] The volume of trade through Livorno was of course greater; and here, as in Naples, English textiles had acquired a grip on the Italian market, where the native textile industries were in decay.[37]

32 Nos. 241, 245. C. S. P. Venetian, XXXVI, 221, 222, 223.

33 They wrote to Charles II on 9th July to this effect (No. 247).

34 *C. S. P.: Ven.* XXVIII (1647-1652). London, 1927, 194. This was Tomaso Mocenigo who was killed in the battle.

35 *Ibid.*, XXXVI (1669-1670), Nos. 23, 30, 31, 38.

36 Koenigsberger, 'English merchants in Naples and Sicily in the seventeenth century.' *English Historical Review*, LXII, 317, cited by G. D. Ramsay, *op. cit.*, 49.

37 C. D. Ramsay, p. 51 (citing C.-M. Cipolla, 'The Decline of Italy' in *Economic History Review*, Series II, Vol. V, 178-87). There has of course been a brilliant resurgence of Italian industry in recent times, particularly in engineering, electrical equipment and a variety of wonderful textiles.

Savoy and Tuscany were more anxious to maintain Residents in London than London was to reciprocate the arrangements. James I had, as already mentioned, been represented in Turin; but the subsequent neglect of Savoy was an error, because a British Resident might have mitigated or even prevented the persecution of the Waldensians. Tuscany maintained a permanent Resident in London, but British representation in Florence was neglected.[38] It was not until 1665 that Sir John Finch, who held the Chair of Anatomy at Pisa and was in high favour with the Grand Duke, was appointed as Resident. Prior to that time the interests of Englishmen and Scotsmen in Tuscany seem to have been left in the hands of the Livorno merchants or, more often, to the good nature of the Florentines themselves. Milton was apparently entertained in the Palazzo Gaddi, which in those days had a wonderful garden, the 'Paradiso dei Gaddi', stretching along the Via del Melarancio. Noblemen, however, were usually lodged in the Palazzo Pitti itself.[39]

The English Consuls were usually selected from among the merchants resident in the big ports, or in Florence. One of the first commercial agents in the Tuscan capital was a certain Humphrey Dethick. He had reached Italy about 1589; in 1602 he went to Scotland with the supposed intention of assassinating King James; was overcome with remorse and confessed; and was finally treated as a simple madman.[40] As early as 1608 several English merchants were established in Florence, and the names of Aldrich, Tracy and Stock have been preserved.[41] James Howell, who visited Naples in 1620, reported the presence there of a number of representatives of English firms and said that they 'live in better Equipage and in a more splendid manner . . . than their Masters and Principals in London'. But the largest commercial colonies were those in Venice and Livorno. A number of these merchants were very well-to-do. In Venice, Henry Parvis was known to be a rich man; and it is unlikely that Thomas Guther, who was Consul there in 1620, and John Hobson, who was appointed to represent the Trinity Company towards 1650,[42] were anything but men of substance. The colony at Livorno was even more conspicuous, this port being the principal English emporium for the Mediterranean. From the narratives of travellers we learn that the Englishmen here were hospitable as

38 Sir Stephen Le Sieur had been sent as a special envoy in 1608.

39 As when James Hamilton and Mr Savile arrived in August, 1670, to offer condolences to Cosmo III on the death of his father Ferdinand. (Dispatch from Ottavian Valier, Venetian Secretary in Florence, No. 273. C. S. P.: *Ven.* XXXVI, 245).

40 *State Papers: Scotland*, Vol. LXVIII, 43 *et seq.*

41 J. W. Stoye, 114.

42 C. S. P.: *Venetian*, XXVIII (1647-52), p. 62.

well as wealthy; it was probably usual for them to entertain their compatriots. Sir Kenelm Digby may have stayed with the Consul at Livorno[43] after leaving Rome early in 1648; he had, at all events, as we shall see, been negotiating with him for the loan of several vessels to assist the Duc de Guise. Some of these men acted as bankers, and travellers in Italy were accustomed to replenish their funds by means of a bill of exchange on Livorno or Venice.[44] They also received trunks or other luggage which travellers had sent by sea from London; and they attended to the dispatch by sea of such articles as books and works of art which Englishmen had collected.[45]

[43] This may have been Santhill, who, however, resided mostly in Florence.
[44] Mr Stoye cites one of these bills in full, from Harleian MS. 943, folio 119 (*op. cit.*, 193).
[45] Milton records having had his books shipped home in this way from Venice. See also Stoye, 186.

CHAPTER III

Sir Henry Wotton and the Venetian Embassy

AMONG the men who represented England in seventeenth-century Italy, three deserve special attention, not because they were the greatest or most successful of our ambassadors abroad (the embassies in Paris and Madrid were more important) but because, for a knowledge of Anglo-Italian relations, cultural, artistic or scientific as well as political, their careers are exceptionally informative. These were Henry Wotton, Kenelm Digby and John Finch.

I

Thanks to Wotton's voluminous correspondence which has been edited by the late Pearsall Smith,[1] to the *Calendar of State Papers: Venetian*, which became available in the nineteenth century and have been translated and edited, thanks also to many other documents, we are better informed about the life and doings of Wotton than of most of the other envoys to Italy; and indeed they afford the key to much that would otherwise be obscure in our foreign policy. Unlike Digby (born in 1603) and Finch (born in 1626), Henry Wotton was a child of Elizabethan England; one of the most remarkable linguists in an age of linguists, one who could and did pass as a German for months among Germans; an eloquent, humorous and successful orator in Italian; a kind of oracle for the younger generation—as witness the testimony of Milton and Izaak Walton; a good poet, and probably the most Italianate of all Englishmen then living. With his unrivalled knowledge of Italy and its people, he figures as the great herald of the new Italian period in English literature.

Henry Wotton came of a Kentish family long distinguished for

[1] Logan Pearsall Smith, *The Life and Letters of Sir Henry Wotton*. Oxford, 1907, 2 vols. The following pages are based largely on this standard work, a model of its kind; partly on other sources.

its public spirit. He had been born in 1568 and educated at Winchester and Oxford. Here he made friends with John Donne, and here too, in 1586, he wrote and produced a play, *Tancredo*, based on the *Gerusalemme Liberata*. Of this we should have known nothing but for the record in Izaak Walton's *Life of Sir Henry Wotton*:[2] but the knowledge of Italian to which it points may have brought him into touch with the jurist, Alberico Gentili, who became Professor of Civil Law at Oxford in 1587. In any event, a Latin treatise which Wotton composed about this time so greatly impressed Gentili that he conceived the warmest admiration for Wotton and moreover, as Walton says,

> . . . there was in Sir Henry such a propensity and con-naturalness to the Italian language, and these studies [Law and Mathematics] whereof Gentili was a great master, that this friendship between them did daily increase, and proved daily advantageous to Sir Henry, for the improvement of him in several sciences, during his stay in the University.[3]

Henry's elder brother, Sir Edward, was at this time ambassador in Paris, and it was almost certainly in preparation for a diplomatic career that Henry now decided to travel on the Continent with a view to acquiring a knowledge of languages and a familiarity with affairs—and with secret service procedure. His first object was apparently to learn German, next to study Law under the French jurist, François Hotman, who was professor at Bâle, and then to proceed to Italy. He set out in 1589 and, after spending the winter at Heidelberg, found himself in the spring of 1590 at Frankfort where he may have met Giordano Bruno. Next, because he had learned of Hotman's death, he made a sojourn at Altdorf, the University associated with Nuremberg, and finally reached Vienna where he made friends with the librarian to the Emperor, the Dutchman Hugo Blotz. By the autumn of 1591 he was ready for the exciting and perilous adventure that lay ahead.

The moment was a critical one in the affairs of the nation. The Armada had been defeated, but England was still at war with Spain, and Spain was the greatest power in Europe. She was firmly established in what is now Belgium as well as other parts of the former empire of Charles the Bold; in the Milanese; and in southern Italy. And her alliance with the Court of Rome which was rigorously prosecuting the Counter-Reformation created a very formidable *bloc*,

[2] *The Life of Sir Henry Wotton* (in *The Lives of Donne, Wotton, Hooker, Herbert and Sanderson*), ed. S. B. Carter, London, 1951, p.71.

[3] *Ibid.*, p. 77.

animated by the kind of thing that Burke afterwards described as an 'armed doctrine'. The only power capable of serious opposition was France, but that country was still torn with civil strife. Henri de Navarre, now its rightful king, was besieging Paris; but a Spanish army was intervening against him. In these circumstances, to visit Spain itself would be an enterprise of the greatest peril. Italy, however, lay more open, as Tuscany and the Venetian Republic were not unfriendly to England. Approaching by way of their territories, one might reach Rome in disguise and learn something of the enemy's dispositions.

That the young Wotton had received a special assignment before leaving England is not unlikely. Some experience in the secret service was a recognized part of an apprenticeship in diplomacy, and Wotton was now well equipped for work of this kind. He let it be known in Germany that he was leaving for Constantinople, and then quietly descended into Venetia in the guise of a German Catholic. The charm of the Italian character was the first thing to impress him. Years afterwards, in June, 1616, on the occasion of his second embassy to Venice, he spoke to the Doge and the *Collegio* of '*una inclinatione quasi naturale alla natione Italiana, amata et estimata da me . . . con affetto particulare, ch'io le presi fin dalla prima volta che passai le Alpi.*'[4] He reached Venice on November 4th but after four days proceeded to Padua where he had a letter of introduction to Gian Vincenzo Pinelli, a famous patron of men of letters. Much as Wotton liked the average Italian he decided that in this country one had to be guileful, or, as he put it in a letter: '*Qui vult esse in Italia semper incolumis, non debet semper esse bonus*'.[5] He spent the winter in Padua with Lord Zouche,[6] an influential peer who befriended him; and they were probably in touch with Lord Darcy[7] who was in Venice at this time and who, a little later, wrote to the Lord Treasurer on their behalf. Whether these lords were travelling incognito it is difficult to say; they were certainly proceeding with circumspection. In March, 1592, in the company of a German baron who took him for a German and was not undeceived, Wotton crossed the Apennines to Rome, and here he went about conspicuously, wearing 'a mighty blue feather in a

[4] *Esposizioni Principi, Archivio di Stato*. Venezia. June 27, 1616. Cited by Pearsall Smith, I, 147, note 2.

[5] In a letter to Blotz.

[6] Edward la Zouche, 11th Baron Zouche (1556-1625). He was subsequently employed as a special envoy to Scotland and Denmark, and in 1602 appointed Lord President of Wales.

[7] Thomas Darcy (1565-1640), 3rd Lord Darcy; created Viscount Colchester in 1621, and Earl of Rivers in 1626.

black cap',[8] drinking copiously with German priests and learning all he could about the Papal Court, the Jesuits and the English Catholics. This continued without a hitch for five weeks or so, after which he paid a visit to Naples. His biographer suggests that he may have met the Marchese di Villa and his guest Tasso at this time;[9] had he done so, he would surely have referred to it in his letters. After a week in Naples, Wotton returned to Rome; but an encounter with a compatriot whom he suspected of being a Catholic spy, sent him flying for safety to Florence.

He reached sanctuary just in time. The Papal authorities were on the look-out for him and also for Lord Zouche, who had been one of the judges of Queen Mary Stuart; and as both were now out of reach, letters were written to them from Rome purporting to come from English outlaws with whom they had been in touch—letters which were then intercepted with a view to incriminating them both with the government in London. Fortunately these missives fell into the hands of Lord Darcy, who then wrote to Lord Burghley to clear his friends of suspicion. Wotton's trip to Rome had been costly —'146 crowns, with the best frugality I could use,' as he mentioned pathetically in writing to Zouche.[10] It might have proved more costly.

In Florence he lodged in the Via Larga, now the Via Cavour, in the house of a certain Baccio Buoni,[11] who was good only in name but from whom he must have learned much worldly wisdom. Buoni charged him ten crowns[12] a month: 'the times are dear in extremity,' Wotton sighed. He regarded the city as 'a paradise inhabited by devils' but this did not prevent his staying there through the summer and early autumn or sending at intervals to Zouche the political and social news he was gathering. There is much curious matter in these letters, about the Court of Rome, the movements of Church dignitaries, and any sensations or horrors that came to his notice. On August 14th he reports that Antonio Perez, secretary to Philip II, 'having been with the King of France . . . is gone to Her Majesty'. The defection of this influential personage, who had been Philip's right-hand man, was one of the sensations of the age.[13] On August 29th Wotton announces the marriage of Leonora, the Grand-Duke's niece, to the Conte di Santo Fiore.[14]

[8] Letter to Lord Zouche. Florence, May 8, 1592. *Letters*, I, 271-2.
[9] Pearsall Smith, *op. cit.*, I, 20.
[10] Florence, August 14, 1592. *Letters*, I, 284.
[11] To Zouche, May 29, 1592. *Letters*, I, 278.
[12] About £7 sterling, i.e. over £60 in present-day value.
[13] See Gregorio Marañon, *Antonio Perez*. Translated by C. D. Ley. London, 1954.
[14] *Letters*, I, 285.

All the Florentines were not devils. There was Lorenzo Guicciardini, a man of high repute both at home and in London. He sent news-letters to Secretary Walsingham and also acted informally as English Consul in Florence, where he took care of visitors like Wotton. Roberto Titi, the lawyer poet, proved a very good friend to the young Englishman. And the Grand Duke Ferdinand I inspired such confidence that Wotton was subsequently to envisage the prospect of entering his service. At the moment, however, it seems to have been Titi's influence, and not the wickedness of Florence, or rather the high cost of living, that decided him to move, in October, to Siena.[15]

His sojourn in the old hill-town, most refined of Italian cities for its landscape, its atmosphere and the language of its natives (the very children have been said to answer a casual question in verse) was the happiest period in his wanderings. He lodged with a certain Scipione Alberti. Many years before, this upright man had been steward to that Duke of Palliano who had murdered his wife and been subsequently executed. This was one of the grim Italian tragedies which, recorded in brief 'chronicles', were to furnish material for the Websters, Fords, Shelleys and Stendhals. Alberti had survived the vengeance that fell on his employer, but he had learned that in this world he who would sleep securely should preserve *i pensieri stretti ed il viso sciolto*, and he impressed the truth of this maxim so effectively on Wotton's mind that the latter only once departed from it (though that 'once' probably lost him the appointment to the office of Secretary of State); and that years later, when the young Milton called on him at Eton, he passed on the maxim as the best passport for foreign travel. For the rest, Wotton seems to have devoted himself to the study of Italian literature under the guidance of a Sienese named Orazio Lombardelli, to whom Titi had given him an introduction. These lessons were as much in language as in letters. It was not unusual in the following century for Englishmen to linger at Siena precisely for this purpose. John Raymond in his *Mercurio Italico*,[16] says that for three months he did nothing but study Italian there. On the present occasion Lombardelli became so much interested in his pupil that he composed and dedicated to Wotton a book on the principal writers of Tuscany, a book published in Florence in 1598 and in which he speaks of Wotton's '*innata bontà, cortese piacevolezza, . . . bellissimo ingenio, finissimo giudizio*' and excellence in languages and science.[17] Aside from this, he met at Siena a certain Girolamo Emo, to whom he refers obliquely as 'the nephew of the Cardinal of Verona, one of my very intrin-

[15] *Letters*, I, 287-289.

[16] See below, Part II, ch. XIV, p. 213.

[17] Pearsall Smith, 'Life of Wotton,' in *Letters*, I, 22.

sical acquaintance and that hath some light of the truth'.[18] Emo belonged to the noble Venetian family which still possesses an old palace in Padua, and he, in fact, had Protestant leanings.

If Wotton considered his duties to consist in visiting the strongholds of Catholicism and Protestantism, then he took them very seriously. He even, at the beginning of 1593, went back to Rome for a few weeks. Returning thence by way of Florence, he made his way to Geneva, not by the Simplon which would have been the nearest route, but by one of the Grison passes, probably the Septimer. This had involved a halt at Chiavenna which still belonged to the Grisons and had for long been the only Protestant city of refuge on that side of the Alps. It seems likely that he had crossed the mountains from Brescia, which then belonged to Venice, and reached Chiavenna by the Valtellina. In this ancient and austere little town Wotton lodged with Scipione Lentulo, a Neapolitan who had once been a Cardinal's secretary and was now a Protestant pastor.[19] Lentulo put him in touch with his son Paolo, who was living in Berne and who later supplied Wotton with information regarding Henri IV's relations with the Swiss.[20]

What Wotton thought of the Alps, whether he crossed by the Splügen or the Septimer, we do not know. His letters are full of international politics. But he tells Zouche of his 'very great contentment' in lodging with Isaac Casaubon, the French scholar who was then Professor of Greek in Calvin's Academy, and it is clear that he stayed there mainly to improve his French and because of his admiration for Casaubon. Geneva itself seemed to him 'marvellous unpleasant'. There is a certain nostalgia in this letter for wicked and 'discreet' Italy. He remarks amusingly that 'we are here [in Geneva] rather scholars than politicians, and sooner good than wise'.[21]

Back in England by the end of 1594, he spent the next five or six years in the service of Lord Essex, whom he followed in the expedition to Cadiz, when Donne was his companion; and in the expeditions to the Azores and to Ireland. But the Earl's fall from favour threatened to ruin Wotton's career and he judged he would now be safer abroad. He chose Tuscany, in spite of its wickedness, as his place of refuge and set out in December, 1600, in company with his nephew Pickering Wotton and a certain Alessandro Antelminelli, a refugee from Lucca, who was being pursued by the assassins of that jealous little Republic.

The move was more astute than it might appear. By going to

[18] Letter to Zouche. Geneva, August 22, 1593. *Letters*, I, 299.
[19] Letter to the Earl of Essex (winter of 1594-5). *Letters*, I, 300.
[20] Letter to Essex. Plymouth, October 30, 1597. Ed. *cit.*, I, 304.
[21] To Zouche. August 22, 1593. *Letters*, I, 295-6.

Florence, Wotton would in no way offend the Queen or Sir Robert Cecil—on the contrary. There was no city in Europe where Elizabeth would have been more pleased for one of her subjects to reside. She had for many years been on excellent terms with Grand Duke Ferdinand who was opposing the extension of Spanish power and who, since the death of Sixtus V in 1590, had also been on unfriendly terms with Rome. At the present moment she had even more cogent reasons for cultivating good relations. Clement VIII had played her a scurvy trick in mediating the Treaty of Vervins between France and Spain. She was angry with Henri IV for making peace with her enemy—and also for not paying his debts; and it was necessary in this juncture to look round warily for more active allies. Hence a readiness to welcome any advances that might come from Boris Godunov in Moscow or Ferdinand I in Florence. She knew Tuscan well and spoke it beautifully. It pleased her to be called 'the Florentine'. Ferdinand was moreover one of the wealthiest princes in Europe, his cipher-name in the secret service being in fact 'Riches'. And he, for his part, greatly admired the spirit and naval prowess of England. He maintained an agent in London, Filippo Corsini, a well-to-do merchant, and he was beginning to attract Englishmen and English ships into his service. Early in 1600 when William Cecil, son of Lord Exeter and nephew of Sir Robert Cecil who was now Secretary of State, visited Florence, he was lodged in the Palazzo Pitti and hospitably entertained by Don Virginio Orsino, Duke of Bracciano, Ferdinand's nephew. It was only a few weeks after Wotton's departure from England that Don Virginio arrived incognito in London, was received almost as a royal personage and, on January 6th, (being Twelfth Night) entertained in the Palace of Whitehall to the *première* of a comedy in which the noblest personage was, by a seemingly delightful coincidence, a Duke Orsino like himself.[22]

Travelling by way of Lyon and Pisa, Wotton reached Florence on March 4, 1601, and here he fell in with a kinsman, Sir Anthony Sherley who had been in Persia and Russia and was now bent on creating, in concert with those powers, a coalition against the Turks. Sherley introduced him to the Grand Duke, and Wotton then accompanied Sherley and the Persian ambassador to Rome where they were received with immense honour by the Pope. In May, however, he was sent back by Sherley to Florence with letters for Ferdinand. By some means or other he was at once in great favour with the Grand Duke,[23] and it may have been at this time that he met Belisario Vinta the Secretary of State. In a little over a week

[22] Leslie Hotson, *The First Night of 'Twelfth Night'*. London, 1954, passim.

[23] As Thomas Wilson, one of Sir Robert Cecil's agents, wrote to London (Pearsall Smith, I, 39-40).

after his return to Florence, on June 9th to be precise, he left the city quietly, it being understood that he was travelling by way of Venice as an envoy to some of the German princes.[24]

Really he was on his way to Scotland with a message of warning to James VI. It was feared that Elizabeth's end was near, and everyone knew that the succession was in doubt. The best claimant on the Protestant side was James; on the Catholic side, the Infanta Isabella of Spain. If James could be removed, it seemed not impossible that a Catholic might be seated on the English throne, and in that event the Spanish coalition would triumph on the Continent, France would be overawed and immobilized, and the independent Italian States, Venice, Savoy and Tuscany would probably share the fate of Milan. Ferdinand, good Catholic as he was, had no fancy for being swallowed up by the Spaniards or the Pope. Now he had just discovered a plot to poison the Scottish king, possibly the plan which Humphrey Dethick made a half-hearted attempt to carry out. He therefore chose Wotton as his secret envoy, entrusted him with an important dispatch regarding the English succession and also a '*vasetto d'antidoto contraveleno*'[25] which James could have recourse to in the event of his actually being poisoned—Ferdinand enjoying the reputation of knowing more about antidotes to poison than any other prince of his time. Finally, Wotton carried a letter of greeting from the young Prince of Tuscany to Prince Henry.

He travelled in the guise of a 'Signor Ottavio Baldi', and reached Scotland by way of Denmark. The king, who was at Dunfermline, was naturally surprised at learning of the arrival of an Italian envoy: but when Ottavio Baldi had been 'requested to lay aside his long rapier', Walton tells us, he was admitted to the presence and the King

> bade him be bold, and deliver his message: for he would undertake for the secrecy of all that were present. Then did Octavio Baldi deliver his letters and his message to the King in Italian; which when the King had graciously received, after a little pause, Octavio Baldi steps to the table, and whispers to the King in his own language, that he was an English man, beseeching him for a more private conference with His Majesty, and that he might be concealed during his stay in that nation; which was promised, and really performed by the King . . .

[24] *State Papers: Tuscany*, Sept. and Oct., 1601.
[25] *Archiveo Mediceo* 3004, Oct. 7, 1617. Cited by Pearsall Smith, I, 40, note 3.

Walton adds that Ottavio Baldi left Scotland 'as true an Italian as he came thither'.[26]

Both James and he enjoyed this experience: James on account of its atmosphere of melodrama and also because he was now forearmed against poisoners; Wotton, because he had made a powerful friend in Scotland and at the same time consolidated his position in Tuscany. It seems more likely that he expected to make his career in Italy than that he foresaw the day when he would be in the foreign service of his native land; but when, in later years, he was so employed, he often signed his letters to the King with the name of Ottavio Baldi—a joke which they both appreciated.

II

Wotton returned to Florence in the late Spring of 1602, but the year 1603 and the accession of James to the throne of England brought a change in his fortunes. Not only was the King predisposed in his favour, but Sir Robert Cecil had begun to think well of him, and his prospects suddenly became as brilliant as they had formerly been uncertain. From Venice in the spring of 1603 he wrote to Sir Robert expressing the hope that he might be given a Crown appointment and, the answer being presumably favourable, he reappeared in London early in 1604. Walton's statement that the King offered Wotton the choice of the embassies in Paris, Madrid or Venice can scarcely be credited. It is clear that James meant to appoint him to Venice, Sir Robert having so informed Nicolò Molin, the Venetian ambassador, in the previous winter.[27] Early in July James knighted the ambassador designate and later in the same month Sir Henry set out with his train.

The story of his first period as ambassador (1604-1610) was not without influence even on the history of literature, because the part he played in Venice raised the already great prestige of the Republic in English eyes, and also because the English colony at Padua was in close touch with the embassy in Venice. It is significant that *Othello* was first produced in the winter of 1604.[28]

Wotton appears to have crossed the Alps by one of the Grison passes to Chiavenna and to have reached Venice on September 23rd.[29] The Republic welcomed him, as we have seen, partly because it had grievances in regard to the Levant Company and serious complaints in respect of piracy and it hoped that these annoyances might be mitigated; but especially because of the perils that were now threat-

[26] Izaak Walton, *Lives, ed. cit.*, pp. 82-3.
[27] Pearsall Smith, I, 45.
[28] Cf. *Ibid.*
[29] *Ibid.*, I, 49.

ening, perils directed from Madrid and supported in Rome and Vienna. Spain was now in possession of Sicily, the whole of southern Italy and also the once powerful Milanese. From Milan she was threatening to link up with Austria by way of the Valtellina; while the Pope gave support from central Italy. The Republic was thus hemmed in, except on the side of Tuscany and the Grisons, by hostile states, and her only hope of salvation lay in obtaining support from England and France. It was equally to the interest of these states to support her, and they did so, Henri IV by following the astute policy of which he was a master, James I with more of hesitation.

Wotton rested for a few days at the embassy, which was at Canareggio, near where the Grand Canal enters the Lagoon. Then came the official reception, which was magnificent. On September 30th, in a fleet of gondolas occupied by the English residents in Venice and the students at Padua, he proceeded to the Isola dello Spirito Santo, where he was received by sixty notables and escorted back to the embassy. On October 1st he proceeded down the Grand Canal, landed at the Piazzetta and was received in the Palazzo Ducale by the Doge Marino Grimani and the 'Collegio', that is, the Council of twenty-five senators who directed the principal affairs of state.[30] After this, he quickly took the tone of the place. He made himself charming to his opposite numbers from Paris and Madrid, was correct in his dealings with the Papal Nuncio and on easy terms with the residents of Tuscany and Savoy. Tuscany, of course, met him more than half way. Count Asdrubale di Montauto received regular consignments of table delicacies from Florence, which he was used to distributing throughout the Diplomatic Corps, so much so that, whenever a new consignment arrived, everyone turned up at the Tuscan embassy as by a miracle of timing to have his share in the largess.[31]

Wotton's charm of manner and readiness of wit captivated the Venetians. He set about rendering services to his colleagues, doing good turns to any Italians who might later befriend him and keeping a paternal eye on English travellers. In an address to the Doge and the Collegio in January, 1605, he eulogized in magnificent language the institutions of a Republic which had subsisted intact for twelve hundred years and was governed with a wisdom and a justice so profound.[32] Having thus ingratiated himself in an appropriate manner, he seized the first opportunity of promoting the policy he had at heart. It was not exactly James's policy, nor Sir

[30] *Ibid.*, I, 51-52. The account is in the *Calendar of State Papers: Venetian*, X, 183.

[31] Pearsall Smith, I, 61-62.

[32] C.S.P. *Venetian*, X, 121-13 (cited by Pearsall Smith, I, 54).

Robert Cecil's; but in general they approved of it. An opening was afforded by the sensation of the Gunpowder Plot. The Jesuits denied that they had been concerned in this; whereupon Wotton, in an address to the Doge, poured ridicule on them.

In the meanwhile he made himself comfortable by renting a villa at Noventa on the Brenta canal for the summer months. Here and at the Canareggio he entertained young men from Oxford and Cambridge; at Noventa, some of the English students from Padua. In the autumn he would visit the Lake of Garda.[33] In 1607 William Bedell came out as his chaplain and this energetic Anglican soon made the acquaintance of Fra Paolo Sarpi, theological counsellor to the Republic, and brought him into touch with Wotton at a moment when this exactly suited the latter's plans.

These were to alienate Venice and the northern Italian principalities from the Papacy, to persuade Venice to ally herself with England and the United Provinces, and by the same means to create a Protestant movement in Venice. Now it so happened that the policy of Paul V, who had succeeded Clement VIII in 1605, and also the inclinations of a powerful group in Venice, played into Wotton's hands. An influential party among the nobility was disposed to take an independent line in religion. The brain behind this party was Paolo Sarpi, but it had gained new strength from the election of one of its members, Leonardo Donato, as Doge in 1605, and he now became its leader.[34] Sarpi proceeded cautiously (all the Venetians were prudent and sphinx-like); but the time was not distant when he would be ready to organize a National Church in Venice which would have borne some resemblance to the Church of England.

Before this moment arrived, however, Paul V picked a quarrel with the Republic. He revived some of the old Papal claims and, in particular, demanded that the Venetians should hand over two priests whom they had arrested as malefactors. This they refused. The Pope then issued a bull of interdict and excommunication against the Republic. A similar thing had happened some five hundred years before, and Venice had not been greatly moved. She considered St Mark as great an apostle as St Peter. So, now, the Republic declared the bull null and void and retaliated by expelling the Jesuits from its territory. This precipitated an international crisis.

The Pope was furious and prepared for war; Spain decided to support him; and the courts and embassies were in a flutter. The Catholic powers sent envoys with (as one of them put it) buckets of water to extinguish the flames; while Wotton, in the words of the

[33] Pearsall Smith, I, 57-58. [34] Pearsall Smith, I, 77.

French ambassador, threw wood on the fire to keep it going.[35] He revealed to the Doge and the Collegio the existence of a Spanish plot to seize a town in Venetian territory and suggested to the Venetians that they should enter into a secret alliance with England, France and the Protestant Cantons of Switzerland. This was exceeding his instructions, as the Venetians must have known. Proceeding cautiously, they instructed Giustinian, their ambassador in London, to sound James himself on the matter. The King promised to help them 'with all my heart in all that depends on me', and Sir Robert, now Lord Salisbury, wrote to Wotton to convey this promise, though he added a more definite and sensible proviso. The King, however, had been drinking, he was in a martial mood—for the moment—and he made Salisbury instruct the ambassador to encourage Venice to resist.

It was a most hazardous move, as Salisbury feared; but Wotton desired nothing better. He sought an audience of the Collegio and in a resounding declaration offered the assistance of King James 'with all his counsels, friends and forces, both terrestrial and maritime . . .'[36] The Venetians, tremendously impressed, thanked James for his 'heroic resolution' and referred to the proposal of a league as though it had been the King's and not Wotton's. But Lord Salisbury had no desire to see England involved in open war with Spain while France stood aloof, and he wrote to Wotton advising him to be more wary and telling him that the proposal of a league was 'very improper'.

But his rash promises had their effect. Everyone now knew that James I was backing the Venetians; and though the latter suspected that, if the worst came to the worst, his government would not let him do as much as he had promised, they had nevertheless been emboldened by his coming out on their side. The truth seems to be that no one desired war; and Henri IV, who was perfectly aware of this, now moved with his usual dexterity. He sent the Cardinal de Joyeuse to Rome and hinted to the Pope that a triumphant Spain might prove extremely embarrassing to him, and that, on the other hand, if he pushed Venice to desperation she would secede from the Roman communion. His Holiness was now thoroughly scared. He agreed to remove the Interdict and Excommunication. The Venetians, on their part, handed over the two priests to the French ambassador, explaining, however, that they were doing this simply out of respect for the King of France. They also accepted absolution, very privately, from the French cardinal. But they maintained their

[35] *Ibid.*, I, 79 and 374, note 1.

[36] Pearsall Smith, I, 82. The words are translated from the *Esposizioni Principi, Archivio di Stato, Venice,* Sept. 5, 1606.

laws, they did not readmit the Jesuits,[37] and at the same time they extricated themselves from a situation of extreme peril. They had, to speak the language of chess, 'won on the exchange'.

The English Lion, or rather Sir Henry Wotton, had roared; and while everyone was wondering what would happen next, the intervention of France had brought triumph for Venice, a setback for the Pope, and relief for Lord Salisbury. The Venetians recognized how much James I had assisted them in what we should now call a war of nerves: they were grateful to Wotton and more disposed to coquet, albeit secretly, with his desire to introduce Anglican doctrines into the Republic.

Circumstances at this moment seemed to favour the policy. On the one hand, William Bedell was a man of learning and energy; on the other, Paolo Sarpi was not only the greatest scholar and historian of his time, but was at heart, as Bossuet perceived well enough, a Protestant. He and his associate, Fra Fulgenzio, conferred secretly with Bedell every week, and Wotton also met them in secret. But Sarpi was not willing to proceed hastily or to take a line independent of his native country. Whether he was deeply attached to the cult of Our Lady and the Saints, or to the ritual of the Roman Church, one may doubt. But he probably saw no harm in them. On the other hand he had the backing of a majority of the aristocracy in very bitter opposition to the Holy See, and for this reason was ready to make some advance in the Protestant direction. For the rest, it is impossible to know and idle to guess how many real Protestants there were in Venice. Wotton told Donne in a letter that there were 14,000. One doubts it.

In October, 1607, two men who must have been partisans of the Papacy tried to assassinate Sarpi. He recovered from the attack and remarked wittily of the dagger they had left behind that he 'recognized the *style* of the Holy See', punning on the two senses of 'stilo' in Italian.[38] Shortly after this he and Fulgenzio suggested to Wotton that he should invite Giovanni Diodati, the Genevese theologian, to Venice—a very daring *démarche*. Now Diodati was translating the Bible into Italian, and one can guess what this would lead to. Some time in 1608, probably in July, Diodati, having taken advice from the French Protestant leader Du Plessis-Mornay and being accompanied by the latter's representative, De Ligues, made his way secretly to Venice, where he began to confer with Sarpi and Wotton. Meanwhile Bedell had translated the English liturgy with a view to its adoption by the Venetian Church that was being planned; and in Venice itself the movement was supported by Francesco Biondi,

[37] *Ibid.*, I, 85.
[38] These picturesque details are not mentioned by Pearsall Smith (I, 88).

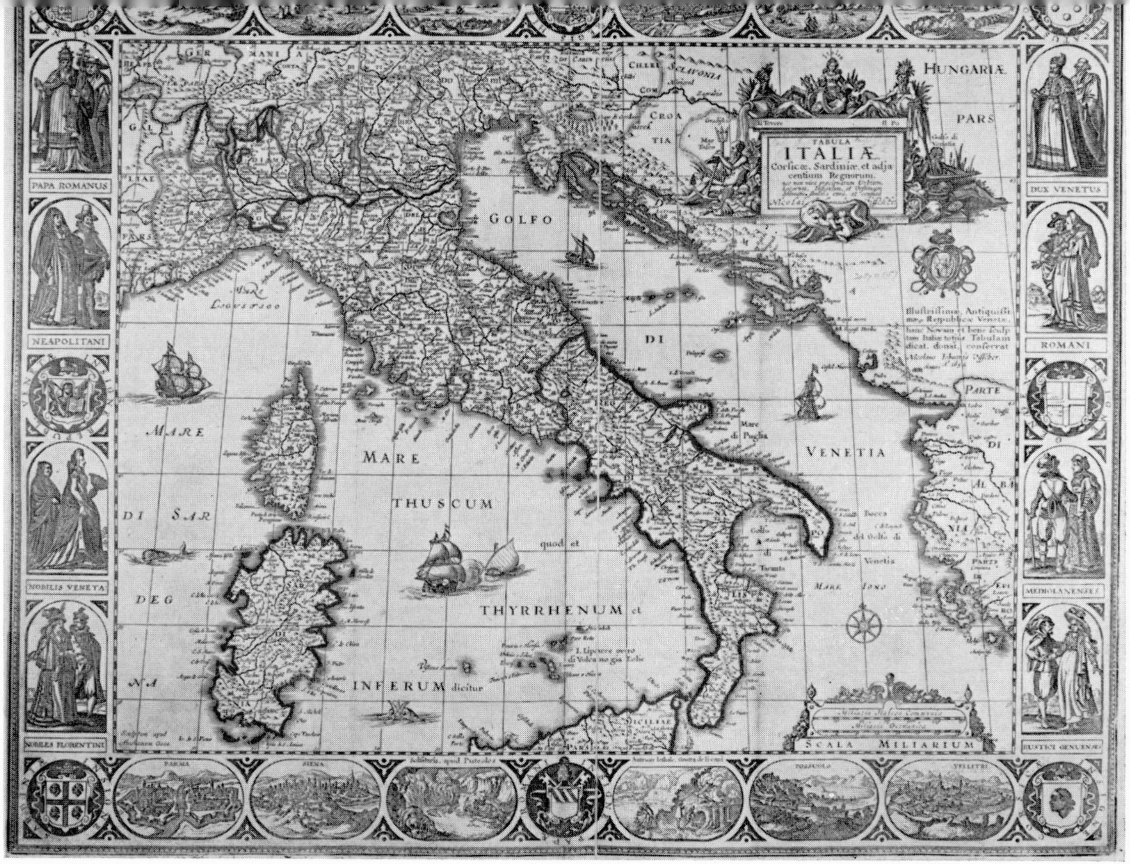

2. *Map of Italy in the seventeenth century*

(British Museum. Reproduced by permission of the Trustees.)

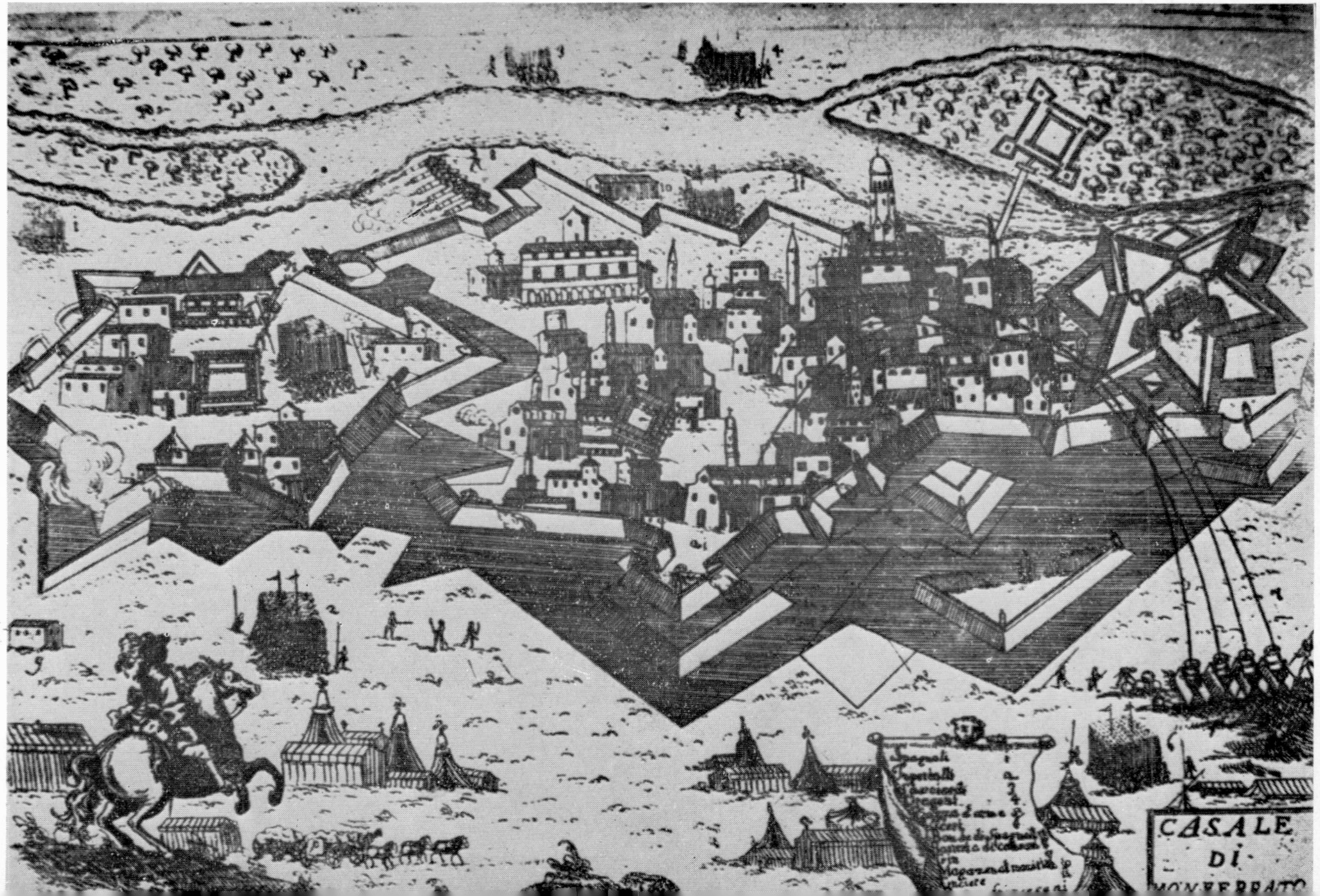

3. *Siege of Montferrat in 1630.*

See p. 24.

a convinced Protestant and by a Huguenot named Papillon. This Papillon had the entry of many noble houses, and he fancied that the task would be easier than it was:[39] but Diodati had some insight into the difficulties. He penetrated Sarpi's real attitude which was, that forms and observances are of no great importance as long as mind and soul are right with God[40]—a view as obnoxious to Geneva as it was to Rome. On the other hand Sarpi was certainly planning the formation of an independent Church by means of education and quiet propaganda; and it seems that Protestant pamphlets were now circulated and Bibles in Italian distributed in Venice. In 1609, through the intermediary of Biondi who was sent to England, Sarpi proposed to James I that he should head a league of Protestant powers, ostensibly political, but that in reality he should assist the introduction of 'la religione', that is Protestantism, into Italy. He suggested that Geneva might send three or four theologians, and finally James was advised to found a College for Italian refugees in England, and a College in the Valtellina to train Protestant missionaries for Italy.[41]

Already, as early as 1607, the Papal Nuncio had been very much disturbed by what was going on and bitter complaints were made to the Venetian ambassador in Rome. To these both ambassador and Senate replied by denying the rumours.[42] But in 1608 another dispute had arisen with the Papacy,[43] and, Venice being legally in the right, this may explain the audacious step which followed. In Lent, 1609, Fra Fulgenzio preached a series of sermons in which he advocated the study of the Scriptures and the offering of prayers in Italian, and defended such doctrines as that of justification by faith.[44]

The Reformation seemed to be making headway; and it might have continued to do so but for some incredible bungling on the part of James and his ambassador; and also, but for the assassination of Henri IV in 1610. *Le mauvais goût mène au crime*; or, if not always to crime, at least to blunders which may be worse. James had written a book of apologetics in which he not only expounded Protestant doctrine and controverted the arguments of Cardinal Bellarmine, but made jokes about Our Lady and identified the Pope with 'the Whore of Babylon that rideth upon the beast'. Worse still, he dedicated this *Premonition*, as he called it, to the Emperor and the various Kings and Princes with whom he had diplomatic relations. And worst of all he sent presentation copies to them, and even to the Spanish Viceroy in Milan. One can imagine the embarrassment of the ambassadors who were required to present these copies. None

[39] Pearsall Smith, I, 89-93.
[40] *Ibid.*, I, 88.
[41] *Ibid.*, I, 93-4.
[42] *Ibid.*, I, 95.
[43] *Ibid.*, I, 98.
[44] *Ibid.*

of them liked it, except apparently Wotton; and he, totally misreading the situation, presented the book to the Doge who politely accepted it. No sooner, however, had he withdrawn than the book was locked up in a secret place and the circulation of any copies in Venetia was forbidden. In this juncture Wotton behaved even more madly than James. He supposed that the Inquisitor had prohibited the book and rushed back to complain: and when the Senate replied that the prohibition was not due to the Inquisitor, but to a committee, and that they endorsed its decision, Wotton resigned his post and withdrew in dudgeon to Noventa.

The Venetians who were not temperamental and had not supposed the English were either, were astonished at this petulance. The Senate was indeed so much alarmed that it dispatched an envoy with a message to Marc Antonio Correr, their ambassador in London, explaining the position. And Correr immediately sought out the King and treated him to 'an hour's vehement oration' regarding Anglo-Venetian friendship, which ought to grow, he said, 'even finer with age'. James perfectly understood the Venetian position. He admitted that, had the boot been on the other leg, he would have acted as the Venetians had; and he wrote an amusing account of the interview to Lord Salisbury. The latter sized up the affair at once and expressed to Correr his hope that the Doge would not feel resentment against Sir Henry; while James wrote personally to assure the Venetians of his goodwill.[45] But this was not the first time that Wotton's zeal had outrun common sense, and it was fortunate for him that Salisbury was not a man to let annoyance sway his judgement. In Venice Wotton was amiably reproved by the Doge; while Francesco Contarini, arriving in London as ambassador extraordinary, was magnificently entertained; and so the affair was glossed over.

In fact in 1610 events still seemed likely to further Wotton's policy. Henri IV made an agreement with Charles Emmanuel, Duke of Savoy, to co-operate in driving the Spaniards from Milan;[46] in other words, to achieve very much what Napoleon III was to achieve some two hundred and fifty years later. The success of the 'Great Design' would have transformed the situation: and in that event there is little doubt but that a national church would have been set up in Venetia, very Catholic in doctrine and ritual but independent of the Papacy and probably in communion with the English Church. The assassination of Henri IV put an end both to the hope of liberating northern Italy and also to the realization of Sarpi's plans; and

[45] *Ibid.*, I, 100-106.
[46] Letter to Lord Salisbury, March 13, 1610 (I, 487).

at the end of the year Wotton was recalled to England and replaced by Sir Dudley Carleton.

III

The death of Henri IV had left Charles Emmanual in a desperate plight, exposed, without an ally, to the resentment of Spain. He therefore turned to England and proposed the marriage of his son to the Princess Elizabeth and of one of his daughters to the Prince of Wales.[47] This was not entirely a new plan but, in the circumstances, it was a sound one as Wotton saw. On the one hand it would help to check the advance of Hapsburg power; on the other, it might be a means, as both Wotton and Sarpi perceived, of strengthening Protestant influence in Italy. Wotton therefore returned home by way of Turin, where he conferred with the Duke;[48] and soon after this the latter sent an envoy to London to treat of the suggested marriages. James seems to have been incapable of pursuing a consistent policy. He thought it would be wonderful to marry Prince Henry into the Royal Family of Spain; and the Spanish ambassador, being perfectly aware of this, dangled the bait. James's attitude to Spain, whether it was to be deprecated or not, seems perfectly comprehensible. I think he admired in that gallant nation the qualities of steadiness and consistency which were lacking in his own character. Perhaps, too, in his unconscious (if this is not too Freudian), he respected that attachment to the past to which his mother had been a martyr. Much of James's vacillation may be traced to the misfortunes of his tragic childhood. Had he been a Catholic like his French and Italian friends, Spain might have fascinated him less. However that may be, he now proposed simply that Elizabeth should marry the Duke of Savoy's eldest son, the Prince of Piedmont. The Duke agreed to this, only to find to his chagrin that James had changed his mind and was going to marry her to the Elector Palatine. The Savoyards were naturally incensed by such treatment, but they were quickly avenged by James's discovery that the Spaniards had no intention of marrying their Infanta to the heretic Prince of Wales. He now therefore returned to the plan of an Italian marriage for Prince Henry and with this in view despatched Wotton as ambassador to Turin, bearing costly presents and accompanied by great noblemen.[49]

This pleased Charles Emmanuel. The English party was received with splendid honours which began at Chambéry and culminated in Turin; and Wotton did his best to promote the match between

[47] Pearsall Smith, I, 113-14.
[48] *Ibid.*, I, 114.
[49] *Ibid.*, I, 119-20.

Prince Henry and the Infanta Maria of Savoy. The Duke himself was so anxious for this marriage to take place that a portrait of the Infanta of Savoy was sent to London for Prince Henry to see. Wotton then returned to England, where he urged James to agree to the marriage in spite of the deference which James still showed for the wishes of the Spanish court. The Prince of Wales liked the portrait of his proposed consort and was attracted for other reasons by the plan:[50] and it only depended on James to complete the arrangements. But the dowry of 700,000 crowns which the Duke offered did not seem enough, and he was now actually negotiating for a French marriage. Lord Salisbury, the only person who might have influenced James for good, had died in May; and finally, in November, Prince Henry himself died, and all Wotton's efforts had some to nothing. Not only so, but he had lost a friend in the Prince and a wise patron in Salisbury; and to crown all, a scurrilous controversialist in Germany had discovered that, when at Augsburg in 1604, Wotton had written in a friend's album, in Latin, a description of an ambassador which when Englished read: 'an ambassador is an honest man sent to lie abroad for the good of the state.'[51] He now published this and embellished his pamphlet with observations so damaging to James that the latter was beside himself with indignation and called Wotton to account at a Court dinner. Sir Henry managed in the end to exculpate or at least excuse himself, but for some months he remained under a cloud and it was during this period that he wrote the lines 'On the Character of a Happy Life'—one of the most thoughtful and beautiful of the short poems of the age:

> How happy is he born and taught
> That serveth not another's will;
> Whose armour is his honest thought,
> And simple truth his utmost skill . . .

Prospects brightened in the spring of 1613 with the arrival from Turin of the Marchese di Villa, who proposed a marriage between one of the princesses of Savoy and Prince Charles.[52] Wotton again supported this, but without success; and, in view of what subsequently happened to James I's children, one wonders whether the King would not have done far better to marry them both to Savoyards. Elizabeth's marriage to the Elector Palatine involved her in the German hornets' nest and finally left the poor 'Winter Queen' an impoverished exile in Holland. Prince Charles's marriage to Henriette Marie was personally a suitable and happy one; but she was a more uncompromising Catholic than the Savoyard princesses,

[50] *Ibid.*, I, 121-24. [51] *Ibid.*, I, 49 and 126.
[52] *Ibid.*, I, 129-31.

and the Puritans disliked her. The Infanta Maria of Savoy was much more accommodating in the matter of religion. 'It is not perhaps too much to say,' writes Pearsall Smith, 'that this marriage, so earnestly promoted by Sir Henry Wotton, might have saved the House of Stuart.'[53]

In 1614 Wotton was sent as special ambassador to the United Provinces to take a hand in settling the Cleves-Juliers question; but, owing to the handicaps under which he laboured and also to the cleverness of the Spaniards, he was hardly successful and was glad to return home. In this juncture Sir Dudley Carleton, who was better capable of handling Dutch affairs, was transferred from Venice to the Hague (1616), and Wotton was once again sent to Venice. His particular mission was to promote an alliance between Venice, Savoy and the Elector Palatine, and if possible associate this league with other German Protestant states and with the Dutch. This was sound policy and, had James stuck to it, might have succeeded in establishing an equilibrium. Wotton began by spending six days at Heidelberg, where the Electress Elizabeth was finding life troublesome and difficult. He next proceeded to Turin. Here he found that the Duke, in spite of the humiliating rebuffs he had received from James, was fully in agreement with the present English policy.[54] Finally, leaving Isaac Wake as Resident in Turin (Morton having been transferred to Heidelberg), he moved on to Venice which he reached on June 9th. His reception lacked nothing in splendour, and the speech he delivered was judicious. He spoke of his admiration for 'questo stupendo e bel governo' (of the Republic), and also of the kindness he had formerly received from a people who had overlooked his faults.[55]

But the outlook in Italy was even more alarming than that in the Rhineland, and Venice was facing perils as great as those of 1606. She was engaged in a war with the Archduke Ferdinand of Styria and was being threatened by Osuna, the Spanish viceroy in Naples, who was planning naval operations in the Adriatic. At the same time, Don Pedro de Toledo, who was Viceroy in Milan, was threatening Savoy. For a time little of consequence happened and Wotton was at first less busied with military than with ecclesiastical affairs, of which the most sensational was the conversion of Antonio de Dominis, Archbishop of Spalato, to the Anglican Church. This had been on the way before Wotton's arrival, but it was only now that De Dominis left for London,[56] taking with him the manuscripts of his own *De Republica Ecclesiastica* and of Sarpi's famous *History of the Council of Trent*. Before long, however, the Spanish viceroys

[53] *Ibid.*, I, 116.
[54] *Ibid.*, I, 134-46.
[55] *Ibid.*, I, 147.
[56] He was made Dean of Windsor.

began to move. In September Don Pedro invaded Piedmont. The Duke appealed to London and the Venetians to Heidelberg; but it was the energy and courage of the Savoyards that thwarted Don Pedro, and it was a Venetian army that not only resisted the Archduke but seized part of his territory. The Spanish government did not, in point of fact, approve of its firebrands and a kind of peace was patched up by the Treaty of Madrid.

This, however, afforded little more than a breathing space, since Don Pedro paid small heed to it and Osuna, who was bent on the destruction of Venice, ignored it altogether. In 1617 he dispatched a large fleet into the Adriatic. The Venetians had already engaged a Dutch army, with an English contingent, to assist them, and they now applied to England for naval assistance. In 1618 a small fleet under Captain Bannister and Sir Henry Peyton joined the Dutch and Venetian fleets in the Adriatic, and this was enough to frustrate Osuna's attack. At the same time, however, a mysterious plot was formed, apparently by some agents in the pay of Osuna, to seize Venice from within, but this too was frustrated and 'Venice preserved'.[57]

It was natural that the north Italian states should be ready to welcome Protestant mercenaries. Protestants were indeed becoming increasingly numerous in Italy: the French as volunteers in the army of Savoy, the Dutch and English in the Venetian service. And so, while the Venetians had cooled off from their flirtation with the Anglican Church, Sir Henry Wotton still hoped that something might be done to further the interests of 'the religion'. He suggested to King James that a seminary should be founded at Sondrio in the Valtellina and that here missionaries should be trained for the Italian field. The plan, which was not new, appealed to James and by arrangement with the Grisons some buildings were taken for the purpose; but in 1620 the Spaniards occupied the Valtellina and the seminary disappeared.[58]

Meanwhile, however, a crisis had arisen in Prague through the Bohemians' defiance of the Archduke Ferdinand and their invasion of Austria. The cascade of misfortunes which followed is of no great relevance to Wotton's dealings in Italy. Although early in 1619 he was sent on a mission to the German princes, and on his return from England to Venice in the winter of 1620-1621 he was commissioned to assist the French in arranging an armistice, all his efforts were fruitless.[59] The Elector Palatine had not only accepted the crown of Bohemia but rejected the French and English proposal that he should make over his immediate claim to Ferdinand who

[57] See ch. I, p. 27.
[58] Pearsall Smith, I, 161-62.
[59] *Ibid.*, I, 170-75.

had now been elected Emperor. *Quem Deus vult perdere prius dementat.* On returning to Venice (March, 1621) Wotton met with a reception so perfunctory that he complained and had to be pacified. It was not hard to see that English prestige had sunk to a very low point, and Wotton would have been abnormal if he had not felt it. In the middle of April he withdrew to Padua for the rest of the year.[60] There seemed to be nothing he could do in Venice. The viceroy in Milan was attacking the Grisons and establishing garrisons in the Valtellina. France and the new Pope, Gregory XV, who was providentially anti-Spanish, were trying to support the Grisons, and they arranged with Madrid that the Valtellina should be handed back. But the viceroy ignored the orders of his own government and attacked the Grisons from the south while the Archduke Leopold invaded their territory from the north-east and seized Chur. The situation was so menacing that when Wotton reappeared before the Collegio in January, 1622, he was asked to urge King James to assist the Grisons.

James, however, was now trying to arrange a marriage between Prince Charles and the Spanish Infanta, and the Spaniards, as before, were deluding him with the impression that they might agree. The only material help—aside from the diplomatic support of France and Savoy—which the Grisons obtained in 1622 was from a Venetian army; and Wotton might now admit bitterly to himself that whatever James did or did not do made practically no difference to anyone on the Continent. He could certainly, however, notice that the French were rousing themselves from inertia and that a formidable figure was arising in the person of Armand du Plessis. In 1623 the latter became First Minister and a French army was dispatched to the help of the Grey Leagues. As for the Elector Palatine, nothing could be done to save him.

In Venice Wotton now found himself beset with problems and anxieties of a quite different kind. The trial and execution of Antonio Foscarini who had been ambassador in London, and whom Wotton had liked and supported, were a severe blow;[61] and this also, and as it might seem gratuitously, involved him in trouble with Lady Arundel. The wife of Thomas Howard, second Earl of Arundel and Surrey, was a person of difficult character. She had brought her sons to be educated in Italy and had taken the Palazzo Mocenigo in Venice as her winter residence and a villa at Dolo on the Brenta canal for the summer months. Now Foscarini had met her in England; and after his execution a story was circulated in Venice that he had been meeting foreign envoys at her house. Hearing this rumour, Wotton wrote to Dolo to advise the Countess to stay in the

[60] *Ibid.*, I, 176-78.

[61] I, 183-84.

country since, by coming to Venice, she might risk expulsion. But she took his advice amiss, protested her innocence, demanded an immediate audience of the Doge and insisted on Wotton's accompanying her. The Venetians managed to calm her, but she decided before long to return to England. Wotton may have acted injudiciously, though this is not apparent. In any event the part he had played in the *imbroglio* brought him into disrepute at home,[62] and his enemies rejoiced greatly against him. Finally, it was discovered in Venice, and publicly admitted by the Council of Ten, that Foscarini had been innocent. The false witnesses who had brought about his condemnation were executed and reparation was made to his family.

It was about this time that Paolo Sarpi died—a man whom Wotton revered above nearly all his acquaintances—and with Sarpi faded away any hopes that had once existed of creating a national church in Venice. Nevertheless Wotton had been happy, if not always in the island city, at least by the Brenta and in 'Padua the learned'; and when in 1623 he sought permission to come home on leave,[63] it is probable that he expected to return before long to Italy.

This was not to be. Wotton was now in bad health, and moreover he was poor. For every lucrative post that was vacant, there were many candidates. But the King was not insensitive to his merit, and in face of strong competition he was, in 1624, appointed Provost of Eton.[64] The years that followed may not have been as happy as Walton suggests, but they were relatively quiet. He took a keen personal interest in the boys, did a little literary work from time to time and, on summer evenings, fished in the Thames with the young Izaak Walton. It was on such occasions no doubt that he related the anecdotes which Walton afterwards retold in his *Life* of Wotton. In the spring of 1638 Sir Henry received a visit from Milton, and a little later, in response to the gift of a copy of *Comus*, he wrote that famous letter of advice for the journey to Italy in which he recalled the counsel he himself had received many years before from Scipione Alberti, that 'pensieri stretti' and 'viso sciolto' will take you safely through the whole world.[65] He died in 1639 at the age of 71, the same age as that of Sarpi.

IV

Though Wotton wrote little verse, what he wrote was exquisite. 'The Character of a Happy Life' is a breviary of Christian resignation. Happy the man

[62] 185-89. [63] 191-92.
[64] 199-201. [65] 220-21.

Who God doth late and early pray
More of his grace than gifts to lend;
And entertains the harmless day
With a religious book or friend!

This man is freed from servile bands
Of hope to rise, or fear to fall;—
Lord of himself, though not of lands,
And having nothing, yet hath all.

And no princess has ever received a lovelier tribute than the verses he dedicated in 1620 to 'his mistress the Queen of Bohemia', at a moment when catastrophe was impending.[66] Perhaps, as Pearsall Smith suggests, he was recalling images used by Petrarch in Sonnetto 182 in Vita:

Col suo bel viso suol dell'altre fare
Quel che fa'l dì delle minore stelle;

and in Sonnetto 211 in Vita:

I'la riveggio starsi umilmente
Tra belle donne, a guisa d'una rosa
Tra minor fior . . .

for these images are virtually identical with those Wotton uses in the first and third stanzas of his poem; but how perfectly they are renewed, even enhanced, and woven into a larger pattern which is Wotton's alone:

You meaner beauties of the Night,
  That poorly satisfy our eyes,
More by your number than your light,
  You common people of the skies;
  What are you when the Moon shall rise?

* * * *

You violets that first appear,
  By your pure purple mantles known,
Like the proud virgins of the year,
  As if the Spring were all your own;
  What are you when the Rose is blown?

So when my Mistress shall be seen
  In form and beauty of her mind,
By Virtue first, then choice a Queen,
  Tell me if she were not design'd
  Th' eclipse and glory of her kind?[67]

[66] For this noble and high-spirited Princess, who was to die in February, 1662, after surviving so many misfortunes, see Dr C. V. Wedgwood's recent article in *The Times* (February 13, 1962): 'Queen of Bohemia and Hearts'.

[67] *Ibid.*, I, 170-71.

Aside from his vast correspondence and his treatise on architecture, Wotton wrote very little. Yet his indirect influence on the literary life of his times was, I think, considerable. If the artistic climate of the age of James I and Charles I was as deeply Italianate as that of Elizabeth's reign, this was largely due to Wotton's activities. He knew Venetia as few Englishmen, before or since, have known that golden land. It was through him that certain distinguished Italians visited or settled in England: of these, Gasparo Despotini[68] who came to practice as a doctor at Bury St. Edmunds, and Sir John Biondi[69] who served for a time in the diplomatic corps and like Despotini married an Englishwoman, were the most notable. More important than this, Wotton had taken with him to Venice and to his house on the Brenta canal a number of young Englishmen, and he also entertained others, whether travellers like Coryate and James Howell, who visited him during his first term as ambassador and whose subsequent writings made Venice better known in England; or students at Padua who enjoyed his hospitality and remembered him afterwards. Whether Suckling who was in Italy in 1621 called on him, we do not know. Thomas Carew was at the Venetian embassy with Sir Dudley Carleton between 1610 and 1614, but he came into touch with Wotton soon after the latter's appointment to Eton.

While in Venetia, Wotton had begun collecting pictures for Sir Robert Cecil and, later, others for Buckingham. He even commissioned an artist, Daniel Nys, to travel round Italy in quest of suitable purchases;[70] and thus initiated a vogue that was continued by Charles I even before he came to the throne; and it may be that this greatest of art collectors owed his first enthusiasm to Wotton. We know that Daniel Nys, whom Wotton mentions twice in his letters,[71] subsequently purchased the Mantua collection for England.[72]

Finally, Wotton's sojourns by the Brenta canal, the banks of which are lined with country mansions designed by Palladio and others, explain how he had come to study the problem of designing country houses and gardens, and this was in part the subject of his principal piece of writing, *The Elements of Architecture*, which appeared in 1624.

[68] Wotton brought him over in 1611. See Pearsall Smith, I, 114 and II, 467-8.

[69] *Ibid.*, II, 463-4.

[70] Pearsall Smith, I, 59-60.

[71] Ed. Pearsall Smith, II, 210, 258.

[72] The great painting by Odoardo Fialetti of Wotton's reception in the Ducal Palace in 1604 is now at Hampton Court; and in 1636 Wotton presented to Eton College another picture by Fialetti, a kind of bird's eye view of Venice, which hangs in the Provost's Dining Room.

The work of Andrea Palladio is of special interest to the history of English architecture. Between about 1540 and 1580 he had designed a number of villas for the Venetian aristocracy in various parts of the territory. Some, like the villa at Maser, had had their walls or ceilings adorned by Veronese. The best known of his villas are the Rotonda on the hillside south-east of Vicenza and the Villa Foscari alla Malcontenta by the Brenta canal. Others are hidden away by country roads or on hill slopes like similar houses in England. In the book referred to above, Wotton commends the more recent Italian taste in architecture which was increasingly pure and severe. He tries to discover the laws of this art and to dive 'into the mysteries of proportion'. He instances the great Basilica of Santa Giustina near the Prato della Valle in Padua, which had been rebuilt between 1518 and 1570. This church, he says, ravishes the 'beholder . . . by a secret harmony in the proportions'.[73] But his main purpose is to show how a gentleman's country house should be designed, and there is no doubt that he wished to see in England a number of houses like those he had admired in Venetia. It is the art of Palladio, Vignola and Ammanati that he praises. He recommends Palladio's *I Quatri Libri dell'Architettura* as a book to be studied; and it may be recalled that at an earlier date, in 1612, he had brought back to England a number of Palladio's drawings. A special correspondent of *The Times*,[74] to whom I owe this information, thinks that Wotton may have shown these plans to Inigo Jones, who was familiar with them before he visited Vicenza, which was towards 1614. In this matter Wotton's taste was certainly in harmony with that of Inigo Jones and reinforced the influence the latter was exercising during the second quarter of the century: an influence that was to bear its full fruit only after the Restoration and in the eighteenth century. When on a hillside in the home counties or even further afield you see a mansion in classical style, with perhaps a beech-wood behind and a lake in front, you may be sure that its inspiration had come originally from Venetia.

These varied activities of Wotton were not of course designed to influence literature, but I think they did more than is realized to create the climate of taste and feeling in which the newer poetry was to flourish—not the 'metaphysical' genre and still less the florid poetry of Crashaw which, when they looked abroad, looked rather to Marino and to Jesuit art, but the plainer and classical manner of Waller and his successors. Between Venetia and the Jesuits, the gulf was much more than political. But long before the

[73] I, 194-97.

[74] 'Palladio's Villas for the Lords of Venice.' *The Times*, February 24, 1954. p. 9.

time of the Restoration Wotton's diplomatic activity had made Venetia and Venetian taste much better and more widely known than they had been before. There is, after 1604, a marked increase in the number of plays which have an Italian setting or are inspired by Italian models. It is true that Italy had figured rather prominently in the Elizabethan novel: but as regards the theatre, whereas prior to 1603 only those dramatists who, like Shakespeare and Marston, felt a special interest in Italy, had situated their plays in that country: after about 1603 almost every dramatist devoted at least one of his plays to the Italian scene, while some showed a preference for it. It may be that Henrietta Maria's interest in things Italian encouraged Ford to give four of his plays an Italian setting: we know that they were produced by 'The Queen Majesty's Servants'; but the reason for the Mediterranean colouring of Jacobean and Caroline drama must lie in the general trend of public taste, the taste not only of the cultured theatre-goer but of those Londoners who were not ardent Puritans.

More important, however, was the long-term influence which I ventured to ascribe to Wotton. If his taste in architecture was for the simple and even severe, his taste in literature was similar. His own verses are marked by firmness in design, by clarity, and even a certain plainness in diction. They reveal the influence of Palladio and not of Marino. And we know from his letter to Milton that this was what he admired in poetry. Speaking of *Comus* he wrote: 'I should much commend the tragical part, if the lyrical did not ravish me with a certain Dorique delicacy in your songs and odes.'[75]

Behind the movement that was carrying literature towards the pole of simplicity, 'reason' and 'nature', in England as in France, may thus be seen the influence of Italian critical theory.

[75] Letter to Milton, April 13, 1638. *Letters*, II, 381.

CHAPTER IV

The Queen's Chancellor

LONDON maintained no diplomatic agent at the Court of Rome. It had been unwise for many years for an English Protestant to live or even stay there. With the accession of Charles I, however, and his marriage to a Catholic princess, relations improved. The Pope was more kindly disposed, and Cardinal Francesco Barberini, Secretary of State to Urban VIII, came to be known as Protector of the English. Thus Protestants like Milton were entertained by this cultured and generous prince of the Church and even, on occasion, at the English College—much as the clergy of the latter had at one time been dreaded.

The misfortunes of Charles I, and the loyal manner in which the Catholic gentry supported him, raised hopes that England might be won back to the fold; and towards 1639 the trend of events offered the Pope a means of putting pressure upon the King. It was a few years later that that 'accomplished cavalier', Sir Kenelm Digby,[1] appeared on the diplomatic scene.

He had already had some experience of diplomacy, having accompanied his uncle, Sir John Digby, on a mission to Madrid in 1617.[2] In April, 1620, he had set out on the Grand Tour. He reached Florence in the autumn and for two and a half years that city was to be his headquarters in Italy.[3] In March, 1623, he rejoined his uncle the ambassador in Madrid, where negotiations had been reopened for a marriage between Prince Charles and the Infanta. The Spaniards had no intention of being drawn into such an alliance; but Digby's manners, like those of Prince Charles, won general esteem. Female hearts grieved over his departure, and it seems that his excellent bearing on this mission was the reason for his being knighted by King James.[4] His next achievement was to marry

[1] See R. T. Petersson, *Sir Kenelm Digby: the Ornament of England* (1603-1665), Harvard University Press, 1956; and Vittorio Gabrieli, *Sir Kenelm Digby*, Rome, 1957. Of Digby's relations with the Italian scientists and the part he played in the scientific movement of the age, I will speak in the companion volume.

[2] Petersson, 30-32.

[3] Gabrieli, 22 et seq. He visited Siena and other cities.

[4] It is true that the ceremony was one of the most grotesque on record.

Venetia Stanley, *bellissima donna*, in the same year (1625) in which Prince Charles married Henrietta Maria. The royal alliance did not however improve Anglo-French relations. Buckingham's attempt to relieve La Rochelle annoyed the French; and his inglorious failure humiliated the English. The two countries were now very much at odds, and on each side privateers plundered their enemy's shipping. It was in these circumstances that on January 6, 1628, Digby took three vessels to the Mediterranean, 'legally in the King's behalf', with the object of disrupting French trade with the Levant. Approaching Alexandretta (or 'Scanderoon' as the English called it) he heard that there were four French vessels laden with bullion, but escorted by four powerful Venetian warships. He boldly engaged the latter, without much success; then seized three of the French ships, but not before the gold had been removed.[5]

On his return home he was received as a conquering hero; but his victory, if such it could be called, was scarcely a diplomatic one. Venice demanded reparations; while the Vice-Consul and merchants of the Levant Company at Alexandretta, having been imprisoned and heavily fined in retaliation for Digby's exploit, raised a bitter outcry. However, once the scandal had subsided, he was appointed Commissioner for the Navy and rewarded with certain profitable monopolies.[6]

It is curious to reflect that his very undiplomatic behaviour was to lead indirectly to a great diplomatic appointment. He had begun to identify himself closely with the King's interests and with one of his dearest hopes. Charles desired earnestly to come to an understanding with the Papacy. A sincere Protestant, but without fanaticism, he regarded himself as King of all his people, Catholics, Anglicans and Presbyterians alike. He wished all Christians to be spiritually, if not formally, united. Discussing the matter with George Con, the Papal resident in London, he urged the latter 'to induce the Pope to meet me half way'. Now Digby, as everyone knows, was a Catholic—he was the son of that Sir Everard Digby who had been put to death for his association with a Catholic plot. To be a Catholic was regarded in England as unpatriotic. The Anglican Church, on the other hand, though rent with dissensions, counted in its ranks a vast number of learned and saintly men. It seems certain that Charles's attitude influenced Sir Kenelm because he now, late in 1630, met the King half way by becoming an Anglican.

His motives were probably not simply political.[7] Beneath—or above—all sectarian differences, deep currents of thought and feeling were affecting believers of every complexion. There was the

[5] Petersson, 76-81. [6] *Ibid.*, 82-3.

[7] They are excellently analysed and discussed by Petersson, pp. 93-5.

appeal of 'reason', especially strong among the Cambridge Platonists; and there was the movement towards a religion of individual prayer and personal devotion, and away from institutional worship. Strange as it may now seem, the taste for attending church and hearing sermons was markedly less keen in the 1630's than it was to be after the Restoration. To a cultured man these trends might appear favourable for some form of reunion. What neither Charles I nor Digby really grasped was that an effective majority in the nation was unwilling to tolerate Catholicism on any terms whatsoever.

Digby himself must soon have grown disillusioned, for in 1635 he returned to the Roman communion and settled for the time being in Paris. But in Great Britain the political situation soon began to deteriorate. The Scots, who were in no mind to tolerate the Anglican Prayer-Book, threatened war. They had sympathisers in England; and Charles, who was trying to govern without Parliament, naturally found himself in great financial difficulties. If Parliament were recalled, the outlook for the English Catholics, weak and unorganized as they were, would be of the grimmest. Hence it came about that when Digby returned home, in the winter of 1638-39, he was asked by the Queen—presumably on account of his influence with his co-religionists—whether he could assist in raising money for King Charles.

Not that the Catholics had anything to gain: the risk was that they might soon lose what little protection the King had been able to afford them. It was hard to know what to do. Cardinal Barberini was consulted, and on his approving of the scheme, it was decided[8] to address a circular letter to all the Catholics in England, followed by a personal letter from the Queen. The response was handsome. £10,000 was subscribed immediately, and a like sum was promised in three months' time.[9] This was helpful; but only for a season. In 1640 the Queen asked Urban VIII to provide £125,000 which would enable her to win over a certain number of M.P.s. The project was natural enough at that time. In the following century Sir Robert Walpole governed systematically on such lines; and had the money been forthcoming, it might have met with some success. It appears from a letter of March 2, 1640, addressed by Count Carlo Rossetti, Urban's personal envoy to London, to Cardinal Barberini, that Digby was proposing that he should himself go to Rome to negotiate.[10] This suggestion does not appear to have been welcomed, and His Holiness countered the Queen's appeal by suggesting that she should

[8] At a meeting held in George Con's house in London.

[9] Petersson, 152.

[10] *Roman Transcripts*, I, f. 143, in the Public Records Office. Cited by Gabrieli, 167.

convert her husband. Charles, however, was unalterably loyal to the English Church. Some notice of all these proceedings may, however, have leaked out, because in May, 1640, a Puritan mob broke into Digby's London house, rough-handled the master and damaged his property.[11] And Charles was in dire need of money. He was now compelled to recall Parliament, and this meant that the Catholics could expect the worst.

It was quick in coming. Some dozen priests were caught and put to death; and in the summer of 1641 Digby himself took refuge in Paris. He returned in November, but was arrested in August, 1642; then released and arrested again. Finally on July 30, 1643, in response to a letter from Anne of Austria, he was set at liberty on the understanding that he would leave the country and do nothing prejudicial to the safety of Parliament.[12] As though Parliament were the government! But a struggle for power was in progress and legality had gone to the wall.

Once more in exile, Digby composed, or completed, his *Two Treatises* (Paris, 1644), the first a compendious and most intelligent survey of the scientific and philosophical work of the age; the second, a metaphysical treatise on the soul. He now threw in his lot wholly with the Queen. She took refuge in Paris in July, 1644, and appointed him her Chancellor, or diplomatic representative, at a time when he had apparently been itching[13] to take active steps to assist the royal armies in England. They were in need of assistance. Parliament had found in Cromwell a commander of genius: and any slip or error on the part of the Royalists was likely to cost them dear. It happened at Marston Moor in July. The position now looked desperate; even Lord Newcastle gave up hope; and in January, 1645, Henrietta Maria decided to send Digby as her envoy plenipotentiary and resident in Rome, in succession to Sir William Hamilton.[14]

Accompanied by two of his sons, he left Paris in February, stopped at Turin to pay his respects to 'Madama Reale'—Christina, the Queen's sister—and probably at Mantua,[15] and reached Rome early in May. But the omens were scarcely favourable. Urban VIII, a Barberini, had died the previous year, and been succeeded by Innocent X, a Panfili. The Barberini family had been pro-French and well disposed to England: the new Pope's sympathies were rather with Spain; and Cardinal Francesco was not only no longer Secretary

[11] *Ibid.*, ff. 215 et seq. Gabrieli, 168.

[12] Petersson, 155, 158, 162-3; Gabrieli, 180.

[13] As early as February, 1644. The story of his missions to Rome has been studied in detail by Dr Gabrieli (pp. 188 et seq.), whose analysis I follow here.

[14] Gabrieli, 189-190.

[15] *C.S.P.: Venetian* (1643-47). Gabrieli, 191 note 2.

of State but was soon obliged himself to take refuge in Paris. Moreover the style of Papal diplomacy was, in Dr Gabrieli's words, 'dilatorio e sorvegliatissimo'—extremely cautious and watchful—and Sir Kenelm's hustling and flamboyant manner was unlikely to appeal to it.[16]

From a letter of June 26, 1645, which G.-G. Panciroli, the new Secretary of State, addressed to Cardinal G.-B. Rinuccini, the Papal Nuncio to Ireland, it appears that by that date Digby had been received several times by the Pope and by Panciroli, and had also presented a written statement.[17] We know that he submitted a further memorial on July 4th.[18] These interesting documents display more of eloquence and imagination than of diplomatic finesse. Sir Kenelm dilated on the (one time) scrupulous obedience of England to the Holy See. Even now, he intimated, despite the 'unfortunate withdrawal' (*l'infelice esito*) of Henry VIII, the country was still at heart devoted to the Supreme Pontiff. The Catholics of England had made the greatest sacrifices for the cause. Zealous laymen were every day devoting themselves to the conversion of Protestants.[19] The Queen above all, by 'her more than virile and truly heroic actions', though she had 'not in fact allayed the tempest of persecution', had at least mitigated it; so much so that the English Catholics might look to enjoying *un secolo d'oro*'. Even now, and even in London, 'thousands of persons heard Mass on Feast Days'. But, should Parliament gain the upper hand, all the Queen's good work would be undone; the flames of heresy would spread to Catholic countries, and the Papacy itself would be in danger of extermination. A victory for Charles I would, on the other hand, assure the conversion of England. It had to be remembered that the structure, organization and even revenues of the Church, although at present usurped by heretics, had remained virtually intact. The change-over would therefore be facilitated; and the conversion of England would constrain the Dutch and the French Huguenots to conform. All that was needed to promote these glorious ends was a suitable money-grant to furnish *i nervi della guerra*. Sir Kenelm went so far as to suggest that the breaking-up of silverware and the sale of Church ornaments would mark a return to the holy times of Ambrose and Paulinus.

The memorandum of July 4th contained specific requests. He

[16] Gabrieli, 190.

[17] G. Ajazzi, *Nunziatura in Irlanda di Mons. G.-B. Rinuccini negli anni 1645-49*. Florence, 1844, 444. Cited by Gabrieli, 195.

[18] *Codices Barberini Latini*, 8616, CVII, 3 ff. 115-22; Archivio Vaticano, Miscellanea, Vol. 16. Analysed by Gabrieli, 191-4.

[19] It was true that important conversions had been made.

wanted 100,000 scudi at once, and further subsidies to follow—namely, a credit for 500,000 scudi for seven years at 5%. The royal properties in Ireland would suffice to provide the interest to repay the capital.[20]

This sounded, and was, very nebulous. The Pope, moreover, being under the thumb of a grasping sister-in-law, was not anxious to return to the holy times of Ambrose and Paulinus. And apart from this, Digby was not popular in Rome. The Romans were not convinced of Charles I's good intentions regarding the English Catholics, while the inconsistencies and contradictions of his policy had given them a low opinion of his character.

Not that Innocent X himself was really ill-disposed. He promised a grant of 20,000 scudi for munitions 'as a mark of his very good will for the Queen'; but further than this he would not go. Had Digby been able to offer a substantial present to Donna Olimpia Maldacchini, the powerful sister-in-law, or again, had the Royalist armies won a notable victory, more might have been done. But the disaster at Naseby suggested that the end was near. Digby, however, persisted in his representations; and the Pope at last, in November, drew up the heads of a treaty under which, when it should be ratified by King Charles, he would make a grant of £72,000 at interest. Dublin and all the other Irish fortresses were to be handed over to the Catholics, and Ireland was to have a Parliament independent of England. In England all the penal laws against Catholics had to be removed, and the Catholics must have access to all public offices. An expeditionary force of 12,000 men was to be raised in Ireland, and this army, under the command of Catholic officers, would assist Charles—and, no doubt, it would see to it that he kept his promises.[21]

Such were the terms that Sir Kenelm took with him on a melancholy ride back to Paris. He had been consoling himself by corresponding with Cassiano dal Pozzo, a well-to-do Torinese and patron of the arts, of whom he was very fond; and with Cardinal Barberini in Paris; and now by calling on Dal Pozzo's friends in Milan. But of course none of them could help him; and despite his hopes, which Rinuccini thought purely chimerical, he must have been aware that Innocent's exigencies, though natural enough in themselves, would scarcely appeal to King Charles. And indeed, when he reached Paris in February, 1646, the Queen herself, though now in possession of the 20,000 scudi which the Pope had sent her, was sadly taken aback.

[20] Gabrieli, 192-4.

[21] *Clarendon State Papers*. Oxford, 1773, II, 298-9. See also S. R. Gardiner, *History of the Great Civil War* (1642-1649). London, 1901, III, 44, 49-50, 55. Cf. Petersson, 219 and Gabrieli, 195.

Perhaps, if Rome had granted a much larger subsidy a year or so earlier and exacted less rigorous terms, the Catholic cause in Ireland might have been advanced; but Charles's loyalty to the Anglican Church and, on the other hand, Rinuccini's too intransigent policy in Ireland, excluded the possibility of an accord. The Queen herself remained steadfast, but her constancy only stood out in contrast with the unpredictable movements of her husband. It is true that his position was growing desperate. Like a stag pursued by fierce hounds, every turn and twist he made involved him in worse perils. The project of bringing over an Irish army to assist him had been discovered; and in face of the tempest of indignation this let loose—for while it was perfectly right for English Protestants to send armies to hold down Ireland, it was perfectly wrong for Irish Catholics to bring an army to England—he disavowed his agent, Glamorgan. And of course the news of this disavowal reached Rome.[22]

In a letter of March 12, 1646, he authorized the Queen to promise that, in return for Papal subsidies, he would repeal the laws against the Catholics.[23] But in May he left Oxford in disguise and handed himself over to the Scottish army at Newark; but this was to place himself at the mercy of the Presbyterians, so that he would now have been incapable of giving effect to the treaty, even if he had wished to. If his first error had been to throw Lord Strafford to the wolves, this was another blunder.

As for Digby, while many people regarded him as a very unstable person, now sunk in melancholy, now bursting with enthusiasm, the truth is that he continued to serve the Queen with admirable constancy. In the autumn of 1646[24] he set out again for Italy, while scarcely hoping to obtain more than some personal aid for the Queen. But again the prospects were not bright, if we may judge from the letters written at this time by an English Benedictine in Rome to Cardinal Barberini, in particular a letter of October 22nd in which he speaks of the rumour that the Queen simply wanted money for her private expenses.[25] It is true that she was living in a state not far removed from penury.

Digby must have been conscious of the hostility with which so many influential Catholics regarded him; he knew that Rinuccini's uncompromising policy would also work against Henrietta Maria: and it seems evident that a few weeks in Rome brought his patience to an end. He asked for at least one grant of money for the Queen,

[22] Gardiner, *op. cit.*, III, 1893, 45.

[23] *Letters of King Charles I to Queen Henrietta Maria*. London, 1856, 24-5. Cited by Gabrieli, 200.

[24] Gabrieli, 199.

[25] *Codices Barberini Latini*, 8622, CVII, 9. Cited by Gabrieli, 200.

and then, taking the bit between his teeth, cast mildness, if not caution, to the winds. He defended Charles I's hesitations on the ground that Rome had encouraged plans for an invasion of England; he recalled the Irish rebellions and the 'barbarous and monstrous cruelty . . . exercised by the Irish Confederates against the unarmed English . . .'; and he told the Pope that many of Charles's supporters believed that Rome was really aiming at the maintenance in England of a party to assist those foreign powers who might be employed to unseat the legitimate sovereign.[26]

All this was probably true and must therefore have sounded very unpleasant. But Digby went further. He boldly asked, on the authority of the Queen, that Rome should appoint a more friendly nuncio to Ireland: and he attacked Rinuccini on the ground that the latter had used 'all his power to break the peace negotiations with the King, negotiations which had been practically brought to perfection' (*la trattatione di pace con il Re che era quasi ridotta a perfezione*). But what was far more likely to annoy the Pope was that the secular clergy in England wanted a greater measure of liberty[27] and that Digby not only warmly supported their desire, but was contemplating the propriety of some kind of agreement between the English Catholics and the 'Independents' in the Army, who now had the upper hand. Now the fact that Digby's headquarters were in Paris lent colour to the suspicion that Mazarin, who was promoting the aspirations to autonomy of the Gallican clergy, had encouraged Henrietta Maria's Chancellor to take this line.[28]

While awaiting a reply from His Holiness, Digby busied himself on behalf of various people who had been recommended to him by the Queen: one of them was Richard Crashaw—'*une personne de qui les Catholiques anglois ont conceu de grandes esperances et que j'estime beaucoup*', she wrote. He also embarked on literary studies and scientific research. He sent books to Barberini, in whose Roman palace he was now lodging, and corresponded with Dal Pozzo and with the scholar-poet Paganino Gaudenzi, a native of Poschiavo in the Grisons, and now Reader in Greek at Pisa.[29] But his principal correspondence was still diplomatic, he was still occupied on behalf of his co-religionists in England, and an extraordinary interest attaches to the letters exchanged at this time with Thomas White and those associated with him in what was known as 'Blacklo's Cabal': especially Henry Holden, an independent-minded theologian,

[26] Vatican Library, *Codices Chigiani*, 2879, III, 69, cc 176 et seq. Cited by Gabrieli, 201.

[27] Gabrieli (p. 202) points out that the regular clergy, and especially the Jesuits, would be dead against this.

[28] *Ibid.*, 203.

[29] *Ibid.*, 205-6.

and Peter Fitton, the dean of the Catholic clergy in England. The policy of this group, which included several men of distinction, was to establish in England a Catholic Church which should be national, and which would obey the Pope only with the consent of the State. The Inquisition, religious intolerance and the dogma of Papal Infallibility were to be rejected; and the first Bishop in the new organization was to be consecrated by a Frenchman, Gallican support being naturally indicated in this juncture.[30]

White himself (alias Albus, Le Blanc, Candidus and especially Blacklo) was perhaps more of a philosopher, mathematician and statesman than priest. He had been extremely successful in propagating his views at the English College in Douai[31] and was at present living in Digby's house in Paris; and Digby, who held him in great esteem, had now thrown himself heart and soul into the venture.[32] The longer he stayed in Rome, the more evident did it appear that the Papal Court was not merely corrupt but impious, and that Petrarch's three sonnets which castigated the corruption of the Courts of Rome and Avignon, fell somewhat short of the truth.[33] No spontaneous assistance could be expected from the present unworthy occupant of the chair of St Peter; only circumstances might force his hand.

It looked for a moment as if circumstances would. In the summer of 1647 Parliament, which was strongly Presbyterian, attempted to disband the Army, in which the 'Independents' were paramount. Once demobilized, officers and men would be at the mercy of a religious tyranny more fearful than that of Laud. 'New presbyter is but old priest writ large.' The generals, Cromwell, Ireton, Fairfax and others, refused to be tossed aside now that they had done the fighting, and as they had secured possession of the King's person, they drew up and offered him those famous 'Heads of the Proposals' which were designed to promote a final settlement. The King was once more to be Head of the State, but on a limited and constitutional basis; the Anglican Church was to be re-established, though without powers of coercion; and there was to be some form of religious liberty.

Any such proposal would be strenuously resisted by the Presbyterian M.P.'s; and it is probable that some of the generals, who were realists and more naturally disposed to tolerance than the Parlia-

[30] Petersson, 223-5.

[31] P. Guilday, *The English Catholic Refugees on the Continent*, 1558-1795. London, 1914, I, 250, 331. Cited by Petersson, 344.

[32] Gabrieli considers that the 'Blackloisti' were labouring under a 'growing delusion' (p. 208): Petersson regards their 'plan of schism' as 'fantastic' (p. 223).

[33] Letter to Francesco Barberini, April 28, 1647. Cited by Gabrieli, 206.

ment men, were looking for Catholic support against a body of opinion so powerful. That 'Blacklo's Cabal' saw in this situation a golden opportunity for the English Catholics is certain. Digby himself had acted with promptitude. On July 14th he had sought an audience with Innocent X, and pointed out that 'the royal part of the Independents' (as he called the army leaders) was contemplating the restoration of Charles and the revocation of 'all the penal laws in matters of religion', and that therefore the Pope might reasonably make some grant to the Queen.[34] On July 26th, after hearing that Fairfax had demanded of London that it should agree to the King's restoration, the dissolution of Parliament and religious liberty for 'tender consciences', he made further representations.[35] And finally, on August 3rd, he urged the Pope to declare that Rome did not regard England and Ireland as vassal states: the mere suspicion of which might wreck the possibility of toleration for the Catholics.[36]

Henry Holden, in the meantime, had been planning an agreement with the Independents under which an English Catholic Church would derive its authority from Parliament and not from the Papacy.[37] Were these schemes as illusory as Dr Petersson and Dr Gabrieli appear to suppose? They certainly depended for any possible success on Charles I's pursuing a consistent policy, quite as much as on Cromwell's good will. Cromwell was a hard though not unreasonable bargainer; but no one could foresee what the King would do next. And now, instead of accepting the Army's Proposals, which would, in all probability, have changed the course of history for the better, he played for time and in December came to terms with the English Presbyterians and the Scots—determined adversaries of religious toleration. The army leaders thought him impossible; also, he was cutting the ground from under Digby's feet. The Pope, on the other hand, was no more helpful than the King. Universal toleration did not appeal to him; he regarded the danger of a Catholic schism with contempt; and he continued to defer his reply to Digby.

Sir Kenelm, on his part, felt he could now hope for nothing from the Pope.[38] He may have been mistaken; a milder approach might

[34] See Gabrieli, 207.

[35] Vatican Archives, *Miscellanea*, Vol. 16 and P.R.O.: *Roman Transcripts*, IX, 994: analysed by Gabrieli, 207.

[36] Gabrieli, 208.

[37] Letters to Digby, 6th & 13th Sept., 1647. *Blacklo's Cabal*, 26-34. Gabrieli, 209.

[38] It is unlikely that he lent credence to the slanders then current in Italy regarding Innocent's relations with Donna Olympia (*Papa magis amat Olympiam quam Olympum*); but everyone knew that her influence was scandalous and exorbitant.

have had some effect; because the Sacred College had felt concerned, apparently in November, and while the Cardinals were decidedly opposed to the plea for an English Catholic Church dependent on the State, they did at last decide to offer some kind of help; but at that very moment a message arrived from the Pope to the effect that they were not, for the present, to do so. Digby was beside himself. 'He . . . hectored with His Holiness,' wrote Aubrey, 'and gave him the lie. The Pope said he was mad.'[39] He was not mad, but he was exasperated and suffering from a recurrence of the fever which had attacked him on his arrival. And when he left Rome, in February, 1648,[40] he had to be carried in a litter.

He had been engaged, during this second sojourn in Rome, in other activities which should be mentioned. Thus in 1646 he had offered to organize and lead a naval expedition against the Turks who were inflicting great damage on Venetian shipping. The English Consul at Livorno had just promised to assemble twenty-four ships for the purpose, and he himself hoped to bring the total number to forty armed vessels. The cost (for the Papacy) would be 80,000 ducats, and Digby was ready to offer the Crown jewels, which were at Amsterdam, as guarantee for repayment of the loan. He would ask Venice to lend him thirty or forty galleys, and with this force he proposed to attack the Turkish fleet. But when the Pope consulted the Venetian ambassador, Contarini disparaged Sir Kenelm as a man *pieno . . . di chimere*, and said that the Republic was not used to entrusting her fleets to other people.[41] Over a year later, in November, 1647, he was, however, able to assist the Duc de Guise in the latter's enterprising descent on Naples.[42] A revolution in the preceding July had overthrown the Spanish Viceroy, and the rebels had invited the Duke, a descendant of the Angevins who had once ruled Naples, to head the new government. Sir Kenelm encouraged him and, fortified with his knowledge of 'legal piracy', helped to organize his little fleet and explained the tactics by which he could elude any Spanish warship that might attempt to stop him. Some did; but all the same he reached Naples in safety, and even maintained himself there until the following April.

As to Digby, he lingered some six or seven weeks at Livorno, then proceeded to Florence where he met a number of agreeable people, and thence by way of Bologna to Padua, where he signed the

[39] *Brief Lives.*

[40] Letter from A. Contarini, Venetian ambassador in Rome, to the Senate. *C. S. P.: Venetian* (1647-52), 41.

[41] *C. S. P.: Venetian* (1643-47), 285-7. Cited by Gabrieli, 216.

[42] According to an anonymous letter among the Clarendon Manuscripts (30, p. 187) in the Bodleian. Gabrieli, 217.

Bidello's register at the University on April 14th.[43] If, as has been supposed, he sought an interview with the authorities in Venice, there would probably be a record of it. Crossing by one of the Grisons passes to Chur and Zürich, he was royally entertained by successive burgomasters who delivered high-flown orations and plied him with so much wine[44] that on arrival in Paris—by way of Lyon—he was greatly relieved to be able to drink water.[45] But the summer of 1648 was probably the most miserable of his life. One of his sons fell sick and died in Paris, while another, who was fighting in the Scottish army, was killed at Preston in August.

Not only did the defeat of the Scots mean that there was now no reasonable hope for the Royalist exiles in France, but that Sir Kenelm's very means of livelihood were imperilled. He owned a good deal of property in England; and there were times, too, when he wearied of exile. He never returned to Italy; but the efforts he had been making in Rome on behalf of his co-religionists he continued to pursue in the years that followed, and as these involved the relations between the English Catholics and the Holy See, it is not irrelevant to say a few words about them.

He appears to have written to London in September for permission to return home to see his mother and look after his estates, and a safe-conduct was granted him in November.[46] The weather may have delayed his departure. In January, 1649, Charles I was beheaded, and the violent revulsion of public feeling in his favour now seemed likely, if not absolutely to isolate the army, at least to render its position uneasy and hazardous. In these circumstances Cromwell and the Independents began again to look to the Catholics for support, and a number of exiles, including Sir Kenelm, received permission to return for a limited period.[47] It is even said that a Puritan cleric named Thomas Watson was actually sent to France to urge Digby to come home.[48] He can scarcely have needed urging. The Queen and her little court in the Louvre were desperately short of food and fuel, and Sir Kenelm himself, when he left Paris in February, was on the verge of starvation. After waiting over six

[43] See below, p. 117 for his son's sojourn in Padua.

[44] Du Bellay, a century before, had facetiously complained of the same thing ('*tant ils me firent boire*') in one of his sonnets.

[45] Letter to Dal Pozzo. Gabrieli, 221.

[46] E. W. Bligh, *Sir Kenelm Digby and his Venetia*. London, 1932, 257; *Calendar of Clarendon State Papers*. Oxford, 1872, I, 448. According to another account, however, he was invited and refused to go (Petersson, 234).

[47] S. R. Gardiner, *History of the Commonwealth and the Protectorate*. London, 1903, I, 96, 192. Gabrieli, 222.

[48] Petersson, 234.

weeks at Dieppe for a boat,[49] he crossed the Channel with Leonard Watson, one of Cromwell's agents, and later in the spring had an interview with Cromwell himself. The terms were clear. Catholic worship would be freely permitted if the Catholics disavowed the temporal claims of Rome and if they raised an army of 10,000 men for the service of the Commonwealth. The first condition seemed practicable; the second was beyond the power of Digby and his friends to fulfil.[50] And so the negotiations came to nothing. Cromwell and the other generals no doubt feared that any substantial measure of toleration would be bitterly resented by the public at large. Digby returned to Paris.

His venture, however, had not been fruitless. It must have been undertaken with the approval of the Queen who, at this time, showed much more practical sense than her son Charles. On the other hand Digby had presumably obtained some money, and had certainly secured the good will of a number of the Independents. They, with Cromwell, perhaps thought that he would serve as an unofficial intermediary between the government in London and the exiles in Paris. He was soon *persona grata* with Cromwell as well as with the Queen.

How can this extraordinary situation have arisen? Digby certainly had strong reasons to placate the Commonwealth. His assets in England were considerable; so too were his debts. And he may well have been influenced by the conception of civil obedience which his friend Thomas Hobbes, who was also in Paris, was to publish in 1651 in the *Leviathan*. Hobbes held that 'the obligation of subjects to a sovereign is understood to last as long and no longer than the power lasteth by which he is able to protect them'.[51] It was an attractive, if risky, opinion; and it attracted a good many people. Now in 1652 Digby heard that his property was in danger of being confiscated by the State. On the other hand, a new law allowed the Recusants until 1654 to redeem two-thirds of their property.[52] It was no doubt for this reason that Digby left Paris in January, 1654, and went privately to London. Here he attended to his financial affairs and—what is most significant—became a personal friend of the Protector.[53]

[49] Letter to Dal Pozzo, April 6th, 1649. *Archivio della Cisterna*, Lettere, cc. 102, 121. Gabrieli, 223.

[50] C. S. P.: *Domestic* (1649-50), 294-5. Cited by Petersson, 235-6.

[51] Ed. 1651, p. 21.

[52] Gabrieli, 227.

[53] It will be recalled that in April, 1653, Cromwell had walked into the House and dissolved Parliament, and that in December he had become Lord Protector. He moved into Whitehall Palace, took Hampton Court as his country residence and adopted the manner of a great noble.

His charm was no doubt very great; but Cromwell, a shrewd judge of men, must have seen far beyond this and into a soul of great integrity. Digby was given apartments in Whitehall Palace and frequently dined with the Protector. There is evidence in a letter from Sir Edward Nicholas, the Royalist Secretary in Paris (who remarked that 'Sir Kenelm Digby has become a great pensioner of Cromwell's'), that the Queen's Chancellor was working for a Franco-British alliance; and this supports the belief that Cardinal Mazarin had asked him unofficially to do so.[54] France was in desperate need of military assistance against the Spaniards; and the fact that Cromwell later signed a treaty, and sent over a powerful expeditionary force to help Marshal Turenne, suggests that Digby had had something to do with it. What is perfectly clear is that he continued to plead the cause of the English Catholics, and there is evidence that Mazarin had seconded, if not suggested, his representations. Cromwell himself would have gone a long way towards granting them tolerable conditions; but his Council was mostly against him, and public opinion violently opposed to him on this point. As he wrote personally to Mazarin:

I may not (shall I tell you I cannot?) at this juncture of time and as the face of affairs now stands, answer to your call for toleration . . .; although I believe that under my government your Eminency, in behalf of Catholics, has less reason for complaint as to rigour upon men's consciences than under the Parliament. For I have of some . . . had compassion, making a difference; and as Jude speaks 'plucked many out of the fire', the raging fire of persecution which did tyrannize over their consciences, and encroached . . . upon their estates. And herein it is my purpose, as soon as I can remove impediments . . ., to make further progress.[55]

The persecution was in fact sensibly mitigated; priests were no longer imprisoned or put to death. But Cromwell was even less free to do what he liked in the matter than Charles II was to be. He could not have established the system of complete toleration which Mary Stuart had promulgated in Scotland during one of the short intervals when Bothwell had restored her to power. Cromwell was, however, greatly in advance of his age, and he would certainly have done more, had public opinion been less hostile. Small wonder if Digby held him in such esteem.

Digby made his way back to France in the autumn of 1655. The next few years of his life were devoted mainly to scientific and

[54] Cf. *Clarendon State Papers*, II, 302. Petersson, 254.
[55] C. H. Firth, *Life of Cromwell*, I, 78-9.

especially medical research, and to travel. The Restoration enabled him to return home, and he was to be one of the founding members of the Royal Society.

CHAPTER V

Expatriates and Philosophers

IT seems probable, even certain, that most of the English and Scots who settled in Italy were Catholic refugees, like those who formed the personnel of the College in Rome where their young compatriots were trained as missionaries for the reconversion of Great Britain; a few also who were living in Florence in the time of Ferdinand I and Cosimo II. Few of the other wanderers and expatriates seem to have severed their connexion with the home-country. The Genoese Riviera was not then organized as an attractive resting-place for retired soldiers, scholars and other persons of taste and discernment: it was indeed one of the most perilous spots in western Europe, not so much because the Via Aurelia had fallen into utter disrepair and communications were precarious, but owing to the pirates from Tunis and Algeria who made descents on the Ligurian coast and carried off people as slaves to Africa.[1] An Englishman may sometimes, like the hero of J. H. Shorthouse's novel, have been strongly attracted to Italian Catholicism, only to find in the end that he was a Protestant at heart. Of the host of refugees who in the 1640's fled from Puritan and Parliamentary persecution, a majority decided to live in France, although a few like the poet Crashaw, and James de la Cloche, a son of Charles II, ultimately found their way to Italy. It would be interesting to know how many of the merchants resident in the great Italian ports married and settled permanently where their business-interests would tend to retain them: probably not a few. They could maintain in Livorno and Naples, and probably in Venice, a *train de vie* far more splendid than would have been possible at home.

Many young English and Scotsmen—younger sons of the gentry with no prospect of money or advancement or even a career in their own country—served in Italy and elsewhere as soldiers of fortune. There was a tradition for this kind of life, dating at least from the days of Sir John de Hawkwood,[2] the famous condottiere whose tomb

[1] This went on until the early nineteenth century, when the pirate strongholds were bombarded by British warships; and it was not stopped until the French conquered and occupied Algeria.

and marble monument are in Santa Maria del Fiore, where also his likeness has been immortalized by Paolo Uccello.

It might happen for other reasons that a native of Great Britain found Italy so much to his taste that he decided to make his home there. An expatriate of a milder stamp than Hawkwood was Sir Edward Carne, that engaging Welshman whose story, with those of other wandering Britons, has been chronicled by Mrs G. M. Trevelyan.[3]

As Henry VIII's ambassador to the Court of Rome he had been engaged in negotiating the King's divorce from Catherine of Aragon. Some years later, after the restoration of Catholicism in England, Mary and her husband King Philip sent him with two other ambassadors to Rome to renew the oath of obedience. Their task was not an easy one. Paul IV, a haughty and uncompromising prelate, had been exasperated by the confiscation of Church properties in England and by the distressing fact that Mary had not managed to restore them. What made things even worse from the diplomatic point of view was that Mary had heedlessly assumed the title of Queen of Ireland, a title to which she had no right.[4] So the Pope let the English envoys cool their heels for a month or so, and then soundly berated them for the sins of Henry VIII in regard to the Church estates. This was extremely embarrassing for Viscount Montague, the senior envoy, as almost his whole estate consisted of

[2] It is outside the scope of this study to outline the career of the 'first real general of modern times', as the historian Hallam has described Hawkwood. Born into a family of landed gentry in Essex—perhaps towards 1320—he commanded the White Company in southern France between 1359 and 1363, and from then until 1390 served various Italian princes and republics, and especially Florence, as a mercenary leader. He married, probably as his second wife, Donnina, daughter of Bernabò Visconti of Milan. His daughters made good and often distinguished marriages. One of them was the wife of John Shelley, M.P. for Rye, and thus apparently an ancestress of the poet. His son John came to England in 1404 and settled on the family estate at Hedingham Sibil. Sir John, who owned a good deal of property in or around Florence, had spent his last years in that city, and when he died, in March, 1394, was interred in the Duomo with the most distinguished honours. See the long article in the *D.N.B.*, IX, 236-242. The standard work is by Temple-Leader and Marcotti: *Giovanni Acuto*, Florence 1889; English version, London, 1889. He was known as 'Acuto' in Italy.

[3] Janet Trevelyan, 'Wandering Englishmen in Italy' in *Proceedings of the British Academy*, Vol. XVI. London, 1930, pp. 61-84. This charming and learned paper (the annual Italian lecture) is a selective survey of some characteristic figures. I am indebted to it for much of the information in the following pages about Carne, Tobie Matthew and Sir Robert Dudley.

[4] The whole affair is vividly described by Gilbert Burnet in *The History of the Reformation of the Church of England* (1679-81), cited by Mrs Trevelyan, *op. cit.*, p. 65.

Abbey lands.[5] He and Carne, however, answered His Holiness with all becoming humility, and the Welshman, not being personally involved, contrived to win his favour. He remained in Rome as lieger ambassador; and on Elizabeth's accession to the throne, he decided—for he was a Catholic and he loved Rome for its beauty and amenities—that he would like to stay. Now this placed him in a dilemma, because he owned considerable properties in Britain. The solution which he found has all the neatness of a Euclidean demonstration. Sir Edward first sought the Queen's permission to return home. She readily granted it. The Pope then refused to allow him to leave Rome, advancing cogent reasons for his action. Elizabeth, who was not yet as well versed in foxcraft as she was later to be, requested King Philip to intervene on behalf of Carne. Philip discovered the truth, but skilfully concealed it in replying to Elizabeth. And the upshot was that Carne remained in Rome and retained his property in England.[6]

But the religious or political refugee sometimes met with a tragic end. This was the fate of Sir John Cheke,[7] and also for a different reason, of Edward Courtenay (1526-1556), a son of Henry Courtenay, Marquess of Exeter. He had been incarcerated with his parents in the Tower, at the age of twelve, and there he remained until he was twenty-seven. He apparently learned Italian during this period, for round about 1548 he translated, under the title of *The Benefit of Christ's Death*, Antonio della Paglia's *Trattato utilissimo del Beneficio di Giesù Christo, crocifisso, verso i Christiani*, a work which, if it was not a Protestant treatise, had at least a Protestant character, and was banned in Italy. In 1553, when Mary came to the throne, she caused young Courtenay to be released, conferred on him the Order of the Garter and created him Earl of Devonshire. He probably had very engaging manners and, according to Michel de Castelnau, who was later to be French ambassador in London, '*il estoit l'un des plus beaux entre les jeunes seigneurs de son age*'.[8] Both Mary and the Princess Elizabeth looked upon him with more than friendly eyes, and Bishop Gardiner gave him to understand that the Queen might make him her consort. When, however, Mary married Philip of Spain—an unpopular alliance—Courtenay's friends suggested that he should propose to Elizabeth, and also that popular favour would place Elizabeth on the throne. A rebellion was planned in the early months of 1554, under the leadership of Sir Thomas Wyatt, the poet's son, and when this miscarried Courtenay was again thrown into the Tower. Some remnant of tenderness on the

[5] Burnet. [6] Janet Trevelyan, *op. cit.*, XVI, 64-6.
[7] A. Lytton Sells, *The Italian Influence in English Poetry* (1955), 83-4.
[8] *Mémoires*, p. 74.

Queen's part probably saved his head, as a year later he was simply condemned to exile. It was then, towards Easter, 1555, that on the advice of Cardinal Pole he decided to go to Padua, whither Sir John Cheke, a Protestant, had returned in 1554. He apparently arrived in September and somewhat later matriculated among the 'Giuristi' at the University. From here he must have visited Venice: De Noailles, the French ambassador, spoke of him with the warmest admiration.[9] Unhappily he either did not suspect the presence of enemies or else perhaps failed to take the necessary precautions: his sudden death, on September 18, 1556, which remains one of the enigmas of history, strongly suggests that he had been poisoned. He is one of the few Englishmen honoured with burial in the great church of Sant'Antonio.[10]

More fortunate was Tobie Matthew the younger (1577-1655), a son of Tobie Matthew, Archbishop of York. A gifted and independent-minded young man, he was blessed or, if you like, handicapped, by a remarkable zest for life and by expensive tastes which were constantly involving him in debt. The Archbishop, not a patient man, made scenes, and as the English atmosphere felt rather stuffy and confining, Tobie in 1604 went abroad. But instead of living quietly in France, which would have pleased his father and mother, he made for Rome, got in touch with Father Parsons of the English College and not long afterwards, in Florence, joined the Catholic Church. This step transformed his moral outlook, and he now turned over a new leaf. It seemed to him that his duty was to return to London as a confessor of the Faith, and in 1607 he did so. He explained his motives to the Archbishop of Canterbury and to Lord Salisbury, as Sir Henry Wotton records in a letter of August 3, 1607, in which Wotton bewails such a falling away to an 'idolatrous Church'.[11] There must have been something engaging about young Matthew's declarations and about his person. The matter, however, was considered serious, and if he had not had powerful friends, including Francis Bacon who was particularly fond of him, the worst might have ensued. What did ensue was imprisonment in the Fleet,[12] and finally banishment from the country. This was no hardship for a young man with money. One could wander about France, visit

[9] *Le plus beau et le plus agréable gentilhomme de l'Angleterre.*

[10] For Courtenay, see Giovanni Fabris, *Gli Scolari illustri dell'Università di Padova, Padua,* 1941, p. 9, and the *D.N.B.*, Vol. XIV, 1260-61, which says nothing about the suspicion of poison. This, however, is the most likely hypothesis.

[11] *Life and Letters,* ed. Pearsall Smith, I, 395.

[12] Where various friends, including the great Alberico Gentili, tried in vain to reconvert him.

Spain in perfect freedom, but first of all make one's headquarters in Florence, from where it was easier to contemplate the virtues of England than from a cell in the Fleet prison.

One cannot but be amused by the indignant letter which Wotton addressed to Lord Salisbury on this occasion (September 5, 1608). 'There is in that town [Florence],' he wrote, 'a certain knot of bastard Catholics, partly banished and partly voluntary resiants (sic) there, whereof Tobie Mathew is the principal; who, with pleasantness of conversation, and with force of example, do much harm, and are likely to do more, considering the correspondency they hold with the English in Rome.'[13] Wotton was afraid that they would seduce other Englishmen from the Faith. While in Italy, Matthew appears to have learned Italian thoroughly, and he was regarded by Bacon as such an authority on the English language that the author of the *Essays* had him read his works before they were sent to the printer. Towards 1615 Matthew returned home and ingratiated himself with King James. He now translated Bacon's essays into Italian, publishing the *Saggi Morali del Signore Francesco Bacono, cavagliero Inglese e Grand Cancelliare d'Inghilterra* in London in 1630. Mrs Trevelyan believes that Bacon wrote the essay on Friendship with Tobie in mind;[14] and it is certain that when Bacon was disgraced, his friend's loyalty did not change. Catholic as Tobie Matthew remained, he continued in favour with Charles I and it was not until years later that Parliament exiled him. He was a perfectly loyal Englishman, but travel and experience had opened his mind to the virtues of other Europeans. The preface to his collected letters contains a fascinating comparison or series of parallels, between the people of the United Kingdom and the three great nations of western Europe. Of the English, the Scots and the Irish he says:

> these three gallant nations of the world do carry a particular resemblance to the three gallant nations of Europe—the Italian, the French and the Spanish. For the Scottish nation hath it eminently with the French, the Irish as eminently with the Spaniard, and the English, in my opinion, with the Italian. I say not but that there are many differences . . . but yet that there is more sympathy with it than with the others . . .

And he explains that between the Englishman and the Italian there is 'a concurrence . . . of those most excellent qualities of being the most obligeable, the most civil and modest and safe, in all kinds, of

[13] *Life and Letters*, I, 434.
[14] Janet Trevelyan, *op. cit.*, p. 71.

4. *An audience with the Doge* See pp. 61, 63, 69
(From the original painting by Odoardo Fialetti at Hampton Court. Reproduced by gracious permission of Her Majesty the Queen.)

5. *Fra Paolo Scarpi* See pp. 62-6, 72

(From the picture by an unknown painter in the Bodleian Library. Reproduced by kind permission of the Librarian.)

all nations'.[15] The English, however, are eminent in their possession of 'a certain thing called Good Nature' and there is a 'bottomless mine' of this 'pure gold' in England.[16]

Before leaving Florence for London so quixotically in 1607, Tobie Matthew must have met or heard about Sir Robert Dudley who had recently arrived there. Less skilful in making the best of both worlds, Sir Robert (1576-1649)[17]—Comes Warwicensis, as he justly styled himself, and Duke of the Holy Roman Empire, by letters patent of the Emperor—was to carve out for himself a far greater destiny in one of them. He was the son and heir of the Earl of Leicester by Lady Sheffield whom the Earl had married in 1573.[18] Leicester had him educated at Christ Church, Oxford, and the young man early gave signs of that genius for mathematics and engineering which he afterwards turned to such remarkable effect. Before Leicester died (1588) he bequeathed to his son the Kenilworth estate and the other properties that would accrue to him on the death of his, Leicester's brother, the Earl of Warwick; and there is no doubt that Leicester regarded young Robert as the rightful heir to both Earldoms. During the 1590's Robert Dudley took part in an expedition to the West Indies and a little later, at Cadiz, was knighted by Essex. He then returned to England and married. He was now a wealthy man; but, harassed perhaps by the question of civil status, he attempted to establish his legitimacy in the Archbishop's court, with a view to claiming the title of Warwick that was now vacant. It would have been wiser to rest content with the Kenilworth and other estates he already held, because he had a cantankerous stepmother who constantly frustrated him and even trumped up, in the Star Chamber, a charge of conspiracy against him.[19] Outraged by these proceedings and probably also because he was estranged from his wife, he crossed the Channel in 1606, taking with him his mistress Elizabeth Southwell in the disguise of a page. They seem to have fallen in with a

[15] Cited by Mrs Trevelyan, p. 71.

[16] The passage curiously anticipates Louis-Beat de Muralt's book *Sur les Anglois et les François et sur les Voyages* (1721), with the closer and more detailed analysis of national character made by this observant Swiss officer. Muralt notes, a little drily it is true, that the English pride themselves on their 'good natured people'. He admires their gift for reticence and silence which he contrasts with the talkativeness of the French; but he warmly and very justly praises the French gift for friendship.

[17] For Robert Dudley, see Mrs Trevelyan, *op. cit.*, 72-77; *D.N.B.*, XVI, 122-24; and *Enciclopedia Italiana*, XIII, 251.

[18] By some extraordinary means his parents were able to shuffle out of this marriage, and each of them married again—probably a case of double bigamy—thus creating a legal tangle of which their son was to be the victim.

[19] Trevelyan, p. 72.

naval captain named Robert Elliott, an energetic Catholic, who induced the Pope to grant a dispensation permitting Sir Robert to marry Elizabeth; which he did, to the great scandal of Sir Henry Wotton, who, from his embassy in Venice, vindictively noted the part that Elliott had played in this affair.[20]

The wayward couple now settled in Florence and turned Catholic. What appears especially to have shocked King James was that Dudley had assumed the title of Earl of Warwick. He instructed Wotton to order the culprit to return to England and defend his action; and in May, 1607, Wotton sent George Rooke, a member of his staff, to serve this order upon Sir Robert.[21] On the latter's refusal to return, his lands were sold, the Kenilworth estate was acquired at a low figure by Prince Henry while the two other properties were seized by the Sidney family. *Les absents ont toujours tort.*[22]

George Rooke's mission of 1607 had not ended here. While still in Tuscany, apparently at Pisa, he was persuaded by the Signoria of the Republic of Lucca to pay them a visit. They were very anxious to get into their power a certain Alessandro Antelminelli, last surviving scion of a Luccan family of which the others had been pursued on a charge of treason, and tortured and executed. Antelminelli, of whom I shall speak later, had taken refuge in London where he adopted the name of Amerigo Salvetti. The authorities at Lucca now offered to pay George Rooke the sum of 'two thousand ducats provided that within the term of two years he delivered Salvetti [to them] on the beach at Viareggio'.[23] Rooke, considering this a good offer, referred it to Sir Henry Wotton. The latter deprecated a monetary transaction; but he had been much annoyed with his old friend the Grand-Duke Ferdinand for receiving and sheltering English Catholics; he was especially enraged against Captain Elliott, although the latter had done him no harm; and so he suggested to Tegrini, the Lucchese envoy who had come to Venice to see him, that they should kidnap Elliott, 'who is an inquisitive person and may readily be induced to come to Lucca'. On obtaining possession of Elliott, Wotton undertook to send to London to have Salvetti arrested; and the two men would then be exchanged.[24] It was to the credit of James and Salisbury, to whom this monstrous plan was communicated, that the latter professed ignorance of any such person as

[20] Letter to Lord Salisbury, Dec. 15th, 1606. *Life and Letters*, I, 373.

[21] *Ibid.*, II, 478.

[22] Dudley got nothing. Whether any of the money went to the wife and daughters he had deserted, we do not know.

[23] Cited by Mrs Trevelyan, p. 74. Wotton discusses this proposal in a letter to Lord Salisbury, Oct. 2, 1607 (*Life and Letters*, I, 401-2) and Pearsall Smith describes the affair in detail on p. 401, note 1.

[24] Trevelyan, 74; and Pearsall Smith, 401, note 1.

'Alessandro Interminelli', and refused to commit the King and himself to any dishonourable course of action;[25] and it was to the credit of Ferdinand that, having got intelligence of the scheme, he placed Elliott under strong protection. He furthermore commissioned both Dudley and Elliott, a skilful naval officer, to reorganize and modernize the Tuscan fleet, a task they set about with great efficiency.

It seems probable that Dudley, for a time, experienced a certain homesickness. More than one wanderer, no doubt, has 'sighed by Arno for [his] lovelier Tees'—or Avon. In 1612 he wrote and submitted to King James a treatise on the need for maintaining an up-to-date navy, and recommended the 'Gallizabras', a new kind of warship that mounted fifty cannon. The fact is that the exile was a most capable marine-engineer, and James would have been wise to respond favourably to this overture,[26] and to the letters which Dudley wrote him in 1613 and 1614. But he was prejudiced against him, for more than one reason no doubt; and so 'Roberto Dudleio, Comes Warwicensis', had to remain in Tuscany. Cosimo II[27] continued to employ him in shipbuilding and other kinds of work. Dudley bought himself a house in the Vigna Nuova in Florence, and it was here that Lord Herbert visited him and 'handsome Mrs Suddel' in 1614. He prospered. 'He was,' we read, 'a handsome personable man, red-haired and of admirable comport, and above all noted for riding the great horse, for tilting, and for being the first of all that taught a dog to sit in order to catch partridges.'[28]

The Grand-Duchess Maddalena, a sister of the Emperor, obtained for him by Imperial patent the title of Duke of Northumberland, and Urban VIII conferred on him and his posterity the title of Highness.[29] He now went from strength to strength. Ferdinand II, who succeeded his father Cosimo in 1621, commissioned him to drain the great maremma between Pisa and Livorno, and to dredge and enlarge the latter port. Of his great success in these enterprises we may judge from the anonymous life of Sir Robert:

About that time Leghorne, which was a small town, grew by his endeavours to a great city on a sudden, and at this day is acknowledged so to be . . . And I have heard from some living who have frequented those parts, that this our author Robert Dudley

[25] *Cal. of State Papers, Venetian*, Oct. 12, 1607.

[26] But the Court was extravagant and the government was becoming increasingly short of the funds which should have been spent on the navy. It was not until the time of the Commonwealth that England possessed navies capable of great operations far from home-waters.

[27] Grand-Duke from 1609 to 1621.

[28] Cited by Mrs Trevelyan, p. 76. [29] *Ibid.*, 75.

was the chief instrument that caused the said Duke not only to make it firm, but also to make it a scala franca, a free port, and of settling an English factory there, and of drying the fens between that place and Pisa. At which time also our author called and invited to that place many English merchants that were his friends and so enriched it that it is now one of the best harbours in Europe and bringeth in considerable revenues to the Duke.[30]

We shall find further evidence of this (if evidence were needed) in the narratives of travellers, but it may be noted here that, while he no doubt helped to bolster up the Tuscan economy at a time when a severe recession was beginning to prevail,[31] Dudley was especially opening a new and profitable market for British exports.[32] One wonders whether Mandeville had him in mind when he coined that notorious maxim: 'Private vices, public benefits'. Much as his past conduct was to be deprecated, it is impossible not to pay tribute to the genius and energy he displayed in the public service. The Grand-Duke rewarded him with a pension of two thousand sequins a year and the gift of a villa at Castello[33] near Florence. Dudley built himself a town-house, so that he now had plenty of room to bring up his children who before long had numbered thirteen. His eldest son, the Earl of Warwick, took to wife a daughter of the Duc de Rohannet; four of his daughters married Italian noblemen and most of his descendants became wholly Italian. But one of his granddaughters married the Duke of Shrewsbury when, in the days of Queen Anne, the latter was travelling in Italy, and she returned with him to England.[34]

Sir Robert wrote a number of books, but his great title to literary fame rests on the three volumes of the *Arcano del Mare* which were published in Florence in 1645 and 1646. This great work contained a treatise on oceanography, a treatise on naval engineering and all kinds of information about port-facilities and other matters useful to navigators; and it was illustrated with maps.

A life of Roberto Dudleio, written by himself, would have been a fascinating document. As some wit has remarked,

[30] Quoted by Anthony Wood, *Athenae Oxoniensis* (Trevelyan, 76).

[31] The silk- and woollen-weaving industries were dying out, and agriculture was suffering from heavy taxation and governmental interference. See J. Lucas-Dubreton, *La Vie quotidienne à Florence au temps des Médicis*, Paris, 1958, 323. Cosimo II was no great statesman and his successors were even more incompetent.

[32] See below, pp. 221, 229.

[33] The anonymous *Life* says 'the castle of Carbello', but the Enciclopedia *Italiana* (XIII, 251) gives it as the villa at Castello.

[34] Trevelyan, 76-7.

Lives of great men all remind us
We should write our lives ourselves,
And, departing, leave behind us
Two thick volumes on the shelves.

It is to be lamented that only one or two of the exiles in Italy seem to have followed this precept. Even in the pages devoted to Italy in Sir Edward Herbert's book and in Nicholas Ferrar's memoir, most of the stuff of daily life escapes us; we have other means of recovering a little of it—from the correspondence and the travel-books of the age. Now the student of Anglo-Italian relations in the Cinquecento is handicapped by the paucity of such records. The Seicento on the other hand offers a great deal of material respecting certain figures and an exasperating lack of it about others who are equally or even more interesting. The information we have is scattered among private letters and manuscripts, State Papers, diplomatic correspondence, not to speak of printed memoirs and other books; and there are in Aubrey's fascinating *Brief Lives* details about travellers in Italy which are not obtainable elsewhere.

Passing over the minor figures[35] and deferring a study of the poets and artists to a later essay, we meet with two outstanding political philosophers, men whose Italian experiences and studies contributed not a little to their divergent opinions: Thomas Hobbes and James Harrington.

Thomas Hobbes[36] (1588-1679) was, like his friend Kenelm Digby and many another distinguished Englishman, destined to spend a

[35] A minor but interesting personage was James Howell whose letters (*Epistolae Ho-Elianae*) are a source of information for the diplomatic history of the reign of James I. He was entertained by Wotton in Venice towards 1621 and he afterwards wrote a book entitled *The State of Venice* which contains acute observations on international politics. (See Wotton, *Life and Letters*, I, 60, 169, 179, 358, note 1.)

[36] There appears to be no critical life of Hobbes, and it would be difficult to discover more about him than is contained in the records of his age and of that which immediately followed. The best modern outlines are in Sir Leslie Stephen's long article in the *Dictionary of National Biography*, IX, 931-39; and in the same author's *Hobbes in the* 'English Men of Letters' series, London, 1904, ch. 1, pp. 1-69. The original sources are mostly in Hobbes's own autobiographies in Latin, prefixed to William Molesworth's edition of the *Opera Philosophica* (1681) for which see the 1839 edition, Vol. I, pp. xiii-xix (Life in prose), and lxxxv-xcix (Life in elegiac couplets); in the 'Vitae Hobbianae Auctarium', by Richard Blackburne, pp. xxii-lxxx; in the article by Aubrey in his *Brief Lives*, and in Aubrey's Life of *Mr Thomas Hobbes of Malmsburie*, which appeared in 1813 in an edition of the English works. This last tells us nothing of Hobbes' Italian travels; but the article in *Brief Lives* contains interesting details about them, and the *Vitae Hobbianae Auctarium* very precise ones.

large part of his life overseas. The pattern was usually the same: a few years in Italy and many years in France. In 1608, after taking his degree at Magdalen Hall, he became tutor to the young heir of William Cavendish, first Earl of Devonshire. He retained this position, which was really one of friend and companion, for the twenty happiest years of his life. In 1610 they travelled together in France, Germany and Italy. Hobbes, who was already a brilliant Latinist and a fair Greek scholar, now learned to speak French and Italian; and it is curious and significant to note that it was on this tour, and not earlier in England, that he 'resolved to become a scholar'.[37]

The following sixteen years or so were spent in England, where Hobbes acted as secretary to young Lord Cavendish and made his famous translation of Thucydides. Unhappily his patron, who had become second Earl on the death of his father in 1626, died in 1628. It was just before this, while living at Chatsworth, that Hobbes took one of his horseback tours of the Peak country and wrote the *De Mirabilibus Pecci Carmen*, a brilliant tour-de-force in which he describes Mam Tor, the horrors of Eldon Hole, the amenities of Buxton and the splendour of the Cavendish mansion and its gardens.[38] In 1629 he accompanied Sir Gervase Clifton's son to Paris in the capacity of tutor[39]; but in 1631 he was recalled home to become tutor to William Cavendish, the third Earl (1617-1684), the son of his former pupil and the kind patron who, years later, was to provide him with home, comfort and protection in his old age. The Earl was at this time a boy of fourteen. In 1634 Hobbes was commissioned to take him, as he had once taken his father, to France and Italy. This must have been a welcome opening. Already in 1633 he had been trying to obtain a copy of Galileo's *Dialogues* (1632), although in vain, since all the copies had been sold.[40] Now, however, he might have an opportunity of meeting the great man himself. He and his pupil appear to have lingered in Paris on the way out, but whether he was then first introduced to the brilliant circle of le Père Mersenne, we do not know. It was a circle of which, after

[37] Cf. The 'Vitae Hobbianae Auctarium' in *Opera Philosophica*, I, xxiv; 'Versatus autem aliquamdiu illis in regionibus [Gallia Italiaque] doctissimorum hominum copia florentissimis . . ., solidam demum sapientiam (qui verus est peregrinandi finis) secum domum retulit'. And see Leslie Stephen, *Hobbes*, 1904, 8-9.

[38] Leslie Stephen, *op. cit.* 14, and see especially J. H. Firth's charming and learned *Highways and Byways in Derbyshire* (London, 1905, ed. 1928), which is full of details about Hobbes, and especially his later years—pp. 152-3, 218, 222, 287, 298-302.

[39] He seems to have intended to visit Venice, but to have been prevented.

[40] W. R. Sorley, 'Hobbes and Contemporary Philosophy' in the *Cambridge History of English Literature*, VII, 284.

1640, he was himself to be one of the ornaments. He and Cavendish spent some time in Florence, apparently in 1635 and 1636, and here he made the acquaintance of Galileo who was living in the beautiful villa at Arcetri. It is at this point that John Aubrey's notes are so illuminating:

When he [Hobbes] was at Florence, he contracted a friendship with the famous Galileo Galileo (sic), whom he extremely venerated and magnified; and not only as he was a prodigious witt, but for his sweetnes of nature and manners. They pretty well resembled one another as to their countenances, as by their pictures doth appear; were both cheerful and melancholique-sanguine; and had both a consimilitie of Fate, to be hated and persecuted by the Ecclesiastiques.[41]

One may imagine the two philosophers gazing from the villa at Arcetri over the vine-clad hills—over a landscape that can hardly have changed in the last three hundred years—; or, after nightfall examining the moon or the satellites of Jupiter through the 'optic tube' in Galileo's observatory.[42] It may have been this encounter, more even than the subsequent conversations with Mersenne and Descartes, that turned Hobbes's mind in the direction of mathematics. It certainly kindled his interest in the scientific movement of which Galileo was then the leading spirit in Europe. And I think it persuaded him, if he still needed persuading, of the primacy of experiment in science, at a time when many, especially among physicians, set too much store by reading old treatises. Galileo in the *Dialogues* of 1632 had sung the praises of ignorance in respect of ancient authority:

Ignorance has been the best teacher I have ever had, since in order to be able to demonstrate to my opponents the truths of my conclusions, I have been forced to prove them by a variety of experiments, though to satisfy myself alone I have never felt it necessary to make any.[43]

I am tempted to derive from this period—from Hobbes's conversations with Galileo—that prejudice against books which was

[41] *Aubrey's Brief Lives*, edited . . . by Oliver Lawson Dick, London, 1950, 157.

[42] The University of Florence now has an observatory on the crest of the hill about a mile away in the direction of Poggio Imperiale, that is, nearer to Florence.

[43] *Dialogues*, 1632. Cited by R. T. Petersson in *Sir Kenelm Digby*, 1956, 121.

afterwards ascribed to him and which he has been represented as expressing to Saint-Evremond. Whether Saint-Evremond ever did go to Derbyshire, perhaps between 1675 and 1679, we do not know; nor do we know what historical value is to be ascribed to the apocryphical correspondence between Waller and the French exile, both of whom were friends of Hobbes; but there is, I think, an element of truth in the following dialogue, which like other parts of the same letter, is obviously based on a genuine knowledge of the Earl of Devonshire and of the old tutor of whom he was so fond:

'My lord Devonshire [said Hobbes] has more than ten thousand volumes in his house. I entreated his lordship to lodge me as far as possible from that pestilential corner. I have but one book, and that is *Euclid*, but I begin to be tired of him. I believe he has done more harm than good. He has set fools a reasoning.'

'There is one thing in Mr Hobbes' conduct,' said Lord Devonshire, 'that I am unable to account for: he is always railing at books, yet always adding to their number.'

'I write, my lord,' answered Hobbes, 'to show the folly of writing ...'

'But should you feel no tenderness for your own productions?'

'I care for nothing,' added he, 'but *The Leviathan*, and that might possibly escape by swimming.'[44]

Galileo and Machiavelli may not have been the only Italian influences on Hobbes. During his second visit to Italy the War of the Valtellina was in its last phase and the War of the Mantuan Succession was fresh in people's minds and probably in their conversation. Now in wartime men may be said to revert to the 'state of nature' which, according to Hobbes, was a state of war. In such conditions their lives are 'nasty, brutish and short'. But peace had continued to prevail in Tuscany under the despotism of the Grand-Duke, while within the territories of the Serenissima a paternal oligarchy, a great Leviathan who was Queen of the Adriatic, insured a state of tranquillity in which a reasonable man could live in a civilized manner.

To return to Galileo: one must remember, of course, that Hobbes was not the first Englishman to meet him, and perhaps not the last. Harvey and others had known him at Padua; and round about 1621-

[44] Cited by J. B. Firth, *op. cit.*, 300. See also what Leslie Stephen says of Hobbes' attitude to books and book-learning in *Hobbes* (1904), pp. 65-6. 'Descartes, like Hobbes, insisted upon, and exaggerated his ignorance of previous authors.'

1622 Kenelm Digby may have called on him at Bellosguardo.[45]

It seems likely that Hobbes and the Earl travelled back to Paris late in 1636; had they visited Padua they would almost certainly have signed the Bidello's register. Hobbes now entered the famous circle of Marin Mersenne and probably met Descartes for the first time. Mersenne, whom he particularly mentions in his Latin Life in verse, had translated Galileo's book on Mechanics.[46] In 1637 Hobbes and his pupil returned to England; but after Lord Strafford's execution Hobbes fled back to Paris; and here he remained until 1651, frequenting the members of the 'Académie Mersenne'[47] and also the colony of English refugees which became more numerous as the years went by. Lord Newcastle, who had been commander-in-chief in the north of England, had abandoned hope of the Royalist cause after the disaster at Marston Moor (July, 1644) and joined the Queen in Paris. He was a cousin of the Earl of Devonshire and this would explain why, as Aubrey records, Hobbes, Waller, Descartes and Gassendi were once entertained 'at the Marquess's table at Paris'.[48] Thus his friends were mostly Frenchmen and Englishmen; but his reputation—or rather, after the appearance of *The Leviathan* (1651), his notoriety—was immense.

His views on the limits of a subject's duty to a ruler who is no longer able to protect him, justified his making peace with Parliament and returning home in 1651; as indeed they justified the procedure of many other honest Royalists, like Devonshire himself. But the general doctrine he advanced was such that neither Royalists nor Republicans felt inclined either to avow or disavow it, as Leslie Stephen so acutely observes.[49] Anglicans and Catholics looked on him askance, but after the Restoration Charles II, who liked and was amused by Hobbes, protected him; and in 1669, when he was apparently with Devonshire in London, he received a visit from Prince Cosimo de'Medici and Lorenzo Magalotti, who mentions him with particular approbation. The unflinching logic of *The Leviathan* owes much to French and Italian thinking, but most of all no doubt to

[45] R. T. Petersson, *op. cit.*, 54, 322. Milton is believed to have visited Galileo in 1638. The old scientist had gone completely blind in the spring of that year. See Piero Rebora, 'Milton a Firenze' in *Il Sei-Settecento*, Florence, Sansoni, 265-268.

[46] Leslie Stephen, *op. cit.*, 22.

[47] For this period, for Hobbes' 'Objections' to Descartes' *Méditations* and Descartes' replies, and especially for the warm friendship that grew up between Hobbes, Mersenne and Gassendi whom he held in great regard for his 'sweet-natured' disposition, see Leslie Stephen, 32-41. It was during these years that he wrote and published *De Cive* and composed *The Leviathan*, of which he presented a manuscript copy to the exiled Prince of Wales in 1650.

[48] *Brief Lives*, ed. *cit.*, 309.

[49] *Op. cit.*, 42.

Hobbes' personality, his low view of human nature and his awareness of the political realities of the age.

A political theorist who was more deeply influenced by Italy than Hobbes had been, but unfortunately less effective as a writer, was James Harington, or Harrington (1611-1677), a young kinsman of the Lord Harington of Exton who had translated the *Orlando furioso*. It was at some time in the 1630's that he travelled in France and Italy with an eye to instruction in politics and the art of government. In Rome he declined to kiss the toe of His Holiness, a discourtesy which Charles I afterwards taxed him with. In Venice he was deeply impressed by *questo bel e stupendo governo* which had assured to the Republic political stability, prosperity, greatness and security for over a thousand years. That he, in common with so many of his contemporaries, regarded it as the best polity then existing, may be taken for granted; but he did not assume that it could be transplanted to other lands. One could simply draw inspiration from it. And herein one sees the beginnings of that sense of relativity which was being developed a little later by Saint-Evremond. In the years that followed his Italian journey Harington kept an eye on the course of events in England. He probably assented to the propriety of Cromwell's decision to get rid of Parliament and govern autocratically; because that was the only way in which England at that time could be governed. But he saw equally—what Hobbes perhaps did not realize—that it would not always be so, and even that it would not be so for long. Nothing in fact in England then seemed as though it would be so, for long. As compared with the enduring stability of the 'Serenissima', the upheavals and somersaults of English government showed up in alarming contrast. 'He was wont,' says Aubrey,

to find fault with the constitution of our government, that 'twas *by jumps*, and told a story of a Cavaliero he sawe at the Carnival in Italie, who rode on an excellent managed horse that with a touch of his toe would jumpe quite round. One side of his habit was Spanish, the other French; which sudden alteration of the same person pleasantly surprized the spectators. Just so, said he, 'tis with us. When no Parliament, then absolute Monarchie; when a Parliament, then it runnes to a Commonwealth.[50]

He had brought home from Venice a number of books on political theory, and it was probably during the 1640's that he studied and digested Machiavelli. English politics internal and external in the

[50] *Brief Lives, ed. cit.*, 126.

1650's verified some of Machiavelli's observations. But Harington noticed that the recent political changes had been the outcome of social changes—'the gradual shifting of the balance of property from king and lords to the commons', in Professor Sorley's words.[51] Harington did not agree with the thesis of *The Leviathan* (1651), and the ideal commonwealth he proposes for England in his *Oceana* (1656) was probably intended, in part, as a reply. A measure of equality among the citizens is to be assured by limiting the size of estates; among executive officials, by rotation in the offices to which they are elected. Laws are framed and discussed by the Senate, voted on by the people, and executed by the magistrates; because, as Harington observes, 'a popular assembly without a senate cannot be wise' and 'a senate without a popular assembly will not be honest'. This kind of constitution will work well in times of peace and prosperity; in times of stress only a great man can meet the emergency. 'A parliament of physicians would never have found out the circulation of the blood, nor would a parliament of poets have written Vergil's Aeneis.' For the rest, Harrington's commonwealth is a limited democracy, and the nobility are its natural leaders in war.[52] The inspiration of the *Oceana* is brilliantly composite. 'Machiavelli,' as Leslie Stephen says, 'is his great authority, and Venice . . . his great model.'[53] But these sources were used in the measure in which their lessons could be adapted to the then situation and character of the English people.

An odd and fascinating character of whom Aubrey records enough to make us want to know more, was James Bovey, who was born in 1622. He was only five feet tall. At the age of fourteen he had visited 'France, Italie, Switzerland, etc.'; but how long he stayed abroad we do not know. 'In all his travills,' says Aubrey, 'he was never robbed.' People esteemed him mainly as an expert in finance, political economy and law-merchant; but Aubrey also tells us that, like Hobbes, he was a wonderful linguist. The Seicento was indeed the age of the great English linguists: no European nation at that time seems to have possessed as many as England. It was no uncommon thing for a scientist or philosopher to be expert in Latin, French and Italian, and Hobbes, Finch and Evelyn were not exceptional in such attainments.

The Honourable Robert Boyle (1627-1691), youngest and most brilliant son of the Earl of Cork, learned to speak Latin and French as a child. He had the advantage of a Genevese tutor named Mar-

[51] 'Hobbes and Contemporary Philosophy,' *op. cit.*, VII, 299.
[52] *Ibid.*, 300.
[53] *Dictionary of National Biography*, XXIV, 434-5.

combes who, when Robert was only eleven, took him with his elder brother Francis to Paris and later to Geneva, where they stayed for nearly two years. It was here that his French became really fluent; here too that he had that experience which confirmed him in a life of piety, a piety as intense and inner as it was active and practical. Boyle says that he acquired 'as much Greek and Hebrew as sufficed to read the Old and New Testaments . . . A Chaldee Grammar I likewise took the pains of learning'. But this was in later years. From Geneva M. Marcombes and his charges proceeded to Florence, where they spent the winter months of 1641-42. Boyle now mastered Italian and began to study the writings of Galileo. The latter was still living at Arcetri when Boyle and his tutor reached Florence, but he died early in January, 1641/2 before the visitors' departure for Rome. In Rome Robert's French was so good that he passed for a French boy.[54] 'I have often times heard him say,' Aubrey tells us, 'that after he had seen the Antiquities and architecture of Rome, he esteemed none any where els.'[55]

His later life in England and his great contributions to science, especially to chemistry, are too well known to need repeating. Foreign scientists sought him out, and recorded their impressions. In 1667 Lorenzo Magalotti, then secretary of the Accademia del Cimento, was shown round his laboratory at Oxford[56]; and on May 18, 1669, as I will show elsewhere, Cosimo de' Medici, with Magalotti and others in attendance, visited him in London. On this occasion Boyle showed them various new apparatus and performed experiments for their benefit. He was, says Magalotti, reputed to be 'one of the brightest geniuses in England'.

It may seem curious that we should know so much more about the doings in Italy of British scientists, doctors and philosophers, than we know about the very many poets who went there, in addition to architects, painters, art-connoisseurs and other travellers—if one except those who actually wrote travel-books. The reason, however, is clear. The literary prestige of Renaissance Italy had been

[54] He was then barely fifteen.

[55] *Brief Lives*, ed. cit., 36. The Boyle brothers reached Marseille in the spring of 1642, intending to return home. Their father, who was then involved in difficulties in Ireland, had sent them £250, but the money never reached them. In this dilemma Marcombes took them back to Geneva, which was his native place, and they contrived to live on credit and raise enough money by the sale of jewels to get back to England in the summer of 1644 (*D.N.B.*, II, 1027).

[56] Stefano Fermi, *Lorenzo Magalotti scienzato e letterato* (1637-1722). Piacenza, 1903, 42; and Piero Rebora, *Momenti di Cultura Italiana e Inglese*, Mazara, 1952, 169.

succeeded by the scientific prestige of Padua, Bologna and Pisa. Not merely Fracastoro and Mattioli in Botany, Fabrizio and Santorio in medicine and biology, Galileo and later Torricelli in physics and related subjects, but a host of brilliant mathematicians and researchers had quickly placed Italy in the forefront of the scientific movement; and it was this that led many of the most progressive minds in England to cross the Alps. John Evelyn, John Finch and John Ray—all Fellows of the Royal Society—left, in one form or another, substantial accounts of their adventures. Robert Boyle, though still little more than a schoolboy, related his Italian experiences and his narrative stops only at the moment of his return by way of Marseille. Regarding Robert Dudley, Kenelm Digby and Thomas Hobbes we have a great deal of authentic information.

Now the number of poets and literati who travelled in Italy during this century was still considerable. Inigo Jones was in Venetia in 1594 and 1595, and again in 1613 and 1614, when he also visited Rome and Naples; Thomas Carew lived in Venice with his kinsman the ambassador in 1612; Sir Edward Herbert, in Florence, Rome and Padua in 1614 and 1615; Nicholas Ferrar, in Padua from 1614 to about 1617, when he ventured to Rome; Sir John Suckling (who invented the game of cribbage) travelled in Italy by the time he was eighteen[57]—perhaps towards 1627. Thomas Howard, Earl of Arundel and Earl Marshal of England, spent his latter days in Padua,[58] probably about 1644-45. Milton, as everyone knows, was entertained and even feted when he visited Florence, Rome and Naples, and again Florence in 1638 and 1639. Edmund Waller was first at Padua in 1644 when he dedicated a Latin poem to one of the professors, and again in January, 1646 when he matriculated. Andrew Marvell travelled in the peninsula in 1644 or 1645; Richard Crashaw sought refuge and solace in Rome in the early winter of 1646 and died at Loreto in August, 1649. Other visitors were Wentworth Dillon, Earl of Roscommon, in 1659; John Wilmot, second Earl of Rochester (October 20, 1664); and Edward Sherburne at some date between 1654 and 1659.[59] There are famous names here; but of what most of them did and saw we know very little, sometimes nothing, except in the cases of Nicholas Ferrar, Lord Herbert and John Milton. Of these and other poets, and also of Inigo Jones I propose to speak in a companion volume.

57 Aubrey, *Brief Lives*, ed. cit., 287.
58 *Ibid.*, 337.
59 Mario Praz in *Modern Language Review*, XX (1925), 290.

CHAPTER VI

The University of Padua

IN *The Two Gentlemen of Verona* Shakespeare speaks of young men going overseas,

> Some to the wars, to try their fortune there;
> Some to discover islands far away;
> Some to the studious universities.[1]

Of the studious universities Padua was not only the most popular—more even than Montpellier where, however, there was a good medical school, but it was also the focal point of any serious visit to Italy. Founded from Bologna in 1222, the 'Studio Patavino' had gradually out-distanced its parent. It became the State University of the Venetian Republic and was free from Papal control. This favoured the advance of research and the growth of Rationalism, even of a certain Scepticism, but always within the framework of Christian faith. The students were organized in 'nations', and there seems to have been a 'nazione anglica' from a date prior to 1331 when a distinction between English and Scots was formally recognized. In 1534, Horatio Brown tells us,[2] they were separated into two nations, but in 1603, on the accession of James I, they were reunited. From the later fifteenth century onwards a number of Englishmen who were later to win distinction in law, medicine, scholarship or the Church, had been educated at Padua.[3] Of these Sir John Cheke, Regius Professor of Greek at Cambridge, was among the best known. He lectured for a time in Padua, and the fact of his being a Protestant testifies to the liberal atmosphere of the place. For the English it seems to have been mainly a graduate school. Dr Caius had left Gonville Hall in 1539 to study at Padua before returning to settle in his former college, which now includes his name. There is no tablet of his arms either in the 'Cortile antico' of the

[1] Act I, scene 3.

[2] 'Inglesi e Scozzesi all'Università di Padova dall'anno 1618 sino al 1765,' in *Monografie storiche sullo Studio di Padova*. Venice, 1922. This is based on Codex 634 of the Biblioteca del seminario patavino.

[3] See the present writer's *The Italian Influence in English Poetry, from Chaucer to Southwell*. London and Bloomington, Indiana, 1955, pp. 82-84.

University or in the 'Aula Magna'; but this simply shows that he was not then 'a gentleman of coat armour'.[4] He took his M.D. at Padua in 1541. Francis Walsingham, who was later to become Elizabeth I's Secretary of State, is recorded as a student in the academic year 1555-56, and on March 22, 1556, he was made Counsellor of the English Nation.[5]

English Catholics who sought refuge in Italy gravitated naturally to Rome, but we have records of a one time Cambridge Don who took up permanent residence in Padua. This was Richard Willoughby, a Norfolk man. He had taken his B.A. in 1567, was elected a Fellow of Corpus Christi in 1571 and became a Proctor in 1578. He resigned in 1579 and went to Paris where he turned Catholic.[6] What he was doing in the 1580's we do not know, but in 1592-93 he was Counsellor of the English Nation at Padua,[7] and he later made the acquaintance of Galileo, who inscribed to him a copy of one of his works on astronomy, a copy now in the University Library at Padua. And there is still a tablet, bearing his name and the arms of his family, near Galileo's tablet in the Cortile antico.[8] He evidently remained in Padua, as he died there, apparently in the spring of 1617. Reporting the death in a letter of May 5, 1617, to Sir Ralph Winwood, Wotton describes him as 'an infectious Papist, of a still and dangerous temper', and adds other remarks in which there seems to be more of prejudice than real knowledge.[9]

But from the late sixteenth century onwards the majority of English students must have been Protestants.[10] By far the most famous was William Harvey. He had entered Gonville and Caius College in 1593,[11] he went to Padua in 1598 and studied there under Fabrizio d'Aquapendente (1537-1609),[12] Casserius and Galileo. Fabricius, as he is usually called, was studying biology in the modern spirit: he investigated the venous system, and also made researches

[4] G. H. Darwin, 'On Monuments to Cambridge men at the University of Padua' in *Proceedings and Communications of the Cambridge Society of Antiquaries*, Vol. VIII (1891-94), Cambridge, 1895, p. 338.

[5] I. A. Andrich, *De Natione Anglica et Scota iuristarum universitatis patavinae ab a. MCCXXII P. ch. N. usque ad a. MDCCXXXVIII*, Padua, 1892.

[6] G. H. Darwin, *article cited*, 339-340.

[7] Andrich, p. 43.

[8] Darwin, *art. cit.*, 341-43.

[9] *Letters, II*, 114.

[10] Some of them, and especially the visitors, were of exalted rank. Roger Manners, 5th Earl of Rutland, visited Padua in 1596, and it was perhaps there that he suffered the illness which is one of the few facts we know of his Italian sojourn—except that he willingly sought the converse of scholars. Roger Manners has the posthumous distinction (in common with Lords Derby, Oxford, Bacon and Southampton—and Queen Elizabeth herself) of being credited with writing at least some of the works of Shakespeare.

[11] G. H. Darwin, article cited.

[12] He taught for upwards of sixty years at Padua.

in muscular action and in embryology. In his book *On the Valves of the Veins* (1603) he maintained that the function of the membrane on the inside of the veins is so to slacken the flow of blood that the tissues may extract nourishment from it. He did not understand that the main function of the valves is to cause the blood to circulate from the heart;[13] but he had advanced some way to this understanding, which Harvey worked out, which he expounded in theory in his lectures in 1616 and explained in his book *On the Movement of the Heart and the Blood* in 1628. Even after this, however, proper diagrams or maps of the venous system seem to have been available only in the medical school at Padua, and it was from there that John Evelyn, and apparently Sir John Finch, brought specimens to England.

One should recall also that Padua had in 1545 established the first botanical garden in Europe: a model that was followed at Bologna, at Pisa and finally in Paris.

All this is not to say that there were not other very good universities in Italy. The Roman College, and the English College in Rome, were excellent for classical and philosophical studies. At Bologna notable advances were made in geometry—in calculating the volume of solid bodies—by Bonaventura Cavalieri (1598-1647), and in optics by F. M. Grimaldi (1618-1663), as we shall see elsewhere.[14] Pisa, which was the State University of Tuscany, became an important centre of research, and was to take the lead in biology towards 1660 when Borelli and Malpighi were professors there.[15] Galileo, who was a Tuscan, had been a student and then lecturer at Pisa before his appointment, in 1592, as Professor of Mathematics at Padua. But by this time Padua was more pre-eminent than ever. Its degree of M.D. was considered the best of its kind in Europe; and the University was also, thanks to Galileo and such great professors as Santorio (1561-1636), who invented the clinical thermometer and made an astonishing discovery in regard to 'insensible perspiration', in the forefront of scientific research.

It was here that Galileo made his most sensational, though probably not his most important, discoveries. In 1609 he constructed a telescope on the model of the as yet imperfect instruments which had been made in Holland and France; and this, in January, 1610, revealed a number of great 'marvels'—the satellites of Jupiter, at least forty stars in the Pleiades, and the extraordinary appearance of Saturn. Galileo, indeed, spent only eighteen years in Padua. Most

[13] A. Wolf, *A History of Science, Technology and Philosophy in the 16th and 17th Centuries*. London, 1935, 411.

[14] In a companion volume.

[15] See p. 121.

of his work was done near Florence and the results published in the *Dialogues* of 1632 and the *Discorsi* of 1638.[16] But is is not too much to say that in the early seventeenth century Padua was 'the intellectual capital of the world'.[17] No wonder if Wotton, seeing how many of his countrymen had been drawn to the University, remarked that 'our English swarme at Padua'. Virtually every traveller also called there, if it were only for a few days.

'Many-domèd Padua', as Shelley called it, has expanded in the course of the last half-century. Apartment houses and tall commercial buildings in stone have been raised in the area between the railway station and the Piazza Cavour. But further south, round the University and beyond, and also to the west and along the banks of the Bacchiglione, this city in red brick cannot have looked very different in the seventeenth century from what it looks today. The huge 'Salone' which separates the two markets, the tower of the old Municipio, Ezzelino's ancient castle, the Cathedral and the many churches, especially that of St Anthony—'il Santo'—, the even more beautiful Eremitani, where Mantegna's exquisite frescoes have been restored, the Scrovegni chapel, with Giotto's frescoes—one of the jewels of Italy—these and other buildings retain their medieval aspect. Arcades still line the old streets and many of the new ones. There are little *piazze*, unexpected corners in Padua, along the old canals and in such narrow *canti* as the Via dello Spirito Santo, where you might think yourself back in the Middle Ages. Doubtless, like most cities of the time, the streets were then dirty and ill-kept. The Prato della Valle was still marshy ground, for it was not until the eighteenth century that Andrea Memmo had it drained, causing a circular canal to be built in the centre, trees planted inside the circle and the wall adorned with noble statues of Paduan and other worthies.[18] But the surrounding countryside can hardly have changed at all. The vast plain covered with little farms and bounded to the west and south-west by the blue cones of the Euganean Hills, has always been admired. One imagines the fields then as now bright with scarlet poppies in June, while in the late autumn the lines of shimmering poplars spread over the landscape a delicate filigree of gold. It is an enchanted land that inspires in those who have lived there an affection as warm as do the hills of Tuscany.

Such then was the countryside, and the great city, whose University was then attracting many of the brightest intellects in Europe.

[16] See A. Rupert Hall, *The Scientific Revolution*. London and New York, 1962.

[17] J. W. Stoye, *English Travellers abroad* (1604-1667). London, 1952, 143.

[18] Cesare Foligno, *The Story of Padua*. London, 1910, 231.

Lectures were given in the building[19] still known as 'il Bo' or 'Il Bue', that is, the Ox, because it stood on the site of a former inn of that name. Here, behind the 'Cortile antico' whose walls are adorned with the coats of arms of noble students, was the 'Aula Magna' on the floor above, and behind that, on the ground floor, the 'Anatomick Theatre', the oldest of its kind in the world, where operations were performed and dissections demonstrated.[20] Galileo's observatory stood apart, near the present Via San Francesco. Ordinary degrees were conferred in the Bishop's Palace and doctorates in the Cathedral.[21]

The records of British students and visitors are scattered and incomplete.[22] The register of autographed names which was kept by the Bidelli of the English and Scottish 'nations' from 1618 onwards, was discovered by Horatio Brown in the library of the Seminario vescovile and published in 1922. This is the most complete. It records 2,038 names for the period 1618-1762, and of these the great majority belong to the seventeenth century. But all the visitors did not sign their names in the Bidello's register. Apart from this, there is an official register of those who matriculated in the Law School, that is, as 'Giuristi'; and there must have been a register of those matriculating as 'Artisti', a category which of course included the mathematicians; but it has been lost. Many celebrated names figure in one or both of the registers. Of the movements of some of these men in Italy we know little or nothing; of others a great deal.

It seems to have been usual, on arriving in Padua, to put up at the principal inn, which was the 'Stella d'Oro' in the Piazza della Paglia, or Straw Market. This market occupied the site of the present Piazza Garibaldi which you pass through today on your way from the station to the city-centre. It was within three or four minutes of the University and the Municipio. The 'Stella d'Oro' was apparently a high-class inn and relatively comfortable in winter, as the principal room contained, according to Coryate, a 'stove', that is, a heating apparatus on the Swiss or German model.[23] Peter Mundy stayed there at the inclusive charge of five lire a day, that is about 2s. 4d. in the English currency of the time.

If you were merely visiting Padua and then proceeding to Venice,

[19] It has now been enlarged and is officially the 'Palazzo Centrale', to distinguish it from the 'Liviano' and the scientific laboratories which are in other parts of the city.

[20] It is still there.

[21] Fynes Moryson, *Itinerary* (1617). Ed. Glasgow, 1907, I, i, 73.

[22] Some are in the University Archives in the Palazzo Centrale, some in the Library of the Cathedral. I also consulted the Museo Civico.

[23] *Coryats Crudities* . . ., 1611, 153.

you would hire a boat which left from the canal behind the University and took about seven hours. If on the other hand you intended to study in Padua, you engaged a room in a lodging-house which must usually have been a private house that accommodated one or two students. You could buy your own food, cheaply enough in the market—the same that exists today—and a small boy would carry it home for you for a soldo. A private room of this kind, in the 1590's, cost a zechin a month, or less, according to Fynes Moryson. 'The Hostesse dresseth your meat in the bargaine for your chamber, and findes you napkins, tablecloths, sheets, and towels,' and also keeps your food, even to the bread you leave, in your cupboard or hers. Food was not expensive. Six eggs, for example, cost eight soldi, butter fourteen soldi per lb., apples two soldi per lb. Fish also was inexpensive. A whole turkey could be had for six or seven lire. Moryson bought one lb. of mutton for five and a half soldi, one lb. of veal for eight, and a fowl for two lire. It must be explained that twenty soldi made a lira, and ten lire a zechin.[24]

Fynes Moryson describes the above system which was probably followed by most Italian and foreign students, except the Germans who, not liking the trouble of buying their food, preferred to be served *en pension* in a boarding-house or an inn. This cost from eight to ten silver crowns per month.[25]

In the early seventeenth century the student population was probably greater than fifteen hundred, which was Coryate's estimate.[26] Gentlemen were allowed to wear swords, but not to carry firearms; whereas in most Italian cities, at least in the north, all weapons had to be surrendered at the gate-house on arrival, to be recovered only on departure.[27] In Padua, however, a certain number of students contrived to keep pistols surreptitiously, and John Raymond tells us that round about 1646-47, when he visited Padua, there were two factions which carried on a most deadly vendetta at night and even endangered the lives of anyone who happened to be out of doors.[28] For the rest, there was occasionally a duel, with swords, and when the outcome was fatal the survivor was simply

[24] Fynes Moryson, *Itinerary*, I, i, 69-70. A lira seems to have been worth about 5½d., and a zechin to have been the equivalent of about 4/6 in the currency of the late sixteenth century. The life of a student in lodgings in Padua was probably then very comfortable, agreeable and not too expensive. An Englishman could apparently live and travel in Italy on £100 a year, but this, owing to the travel, would involve severe economy and most people must have spent more.

[25] *Ibid.*, I, i, 69.

[26] *Crudities*, ed. 1611, 154.

[27] Richard Lassels, *An Italian Voyage, or a Compleat Journey through Italy* . . . (1670) 2nd edition, London, 1698, 15.

[28] *Il Mercurio Italico* . . ., London, 1648, 210-18. See below, p. 216.

banished, a punishment which Fynes Moryson considered inadequate.[29] In January, 1608, Sir Julius Caesar's son Julius—a grandson of Queen Elizabeth's physician Giulio Adelmare—was killed by a man named Brochetta who had hurt him in the fencing school. Julius had afterwards waylaid Brochetta with a pistol, missed his aim and been run through. Sir Henry Wotton sent George Rooke to Padua to demand justice, but as Julius had been breaking the rule in carrying a firearm, the authorities merely banished Brochetta.[30]

Given the general state of public opinion then obtaining, the University regulations were not unreasonable, although the police-system must have been inadequate. But it was inadequate in Italy as a whole. In Rome and elsewhere the police were extraordinarily handicapped by the number of churches and convents where malefactors could take refuge.[31] Padua was, however, a fairly safe place to live in, and safer than most except perhaps Florence, Siena and one or two other places in Tuscany. The amenities were considerable. The arcades that lined the streets afforded shelter from the sun in summer and rain in winter. Communications with Venice, by way of the Brenta Canal, were well organized and agreeable. The rich plain that was watered by the Brenta and the Bacchiglione and of which almost every square yard was already under cultivation, assured an abundance of delicious food. The mere sight of it inspired enthusiasm. Coryate quotes the Emperor Constantine Paleologus as saying that, if he had not always read that Paradise was situated in the East, he would have supposed 'it could not be in any other place of the world, but only in Padua'.[32]

One has a thrill, when perusing the register of students and visitors, to note the name of some great English or Scottish lord, or distinguished writer or scientist.[33] Thus Charles Cotton[34] signed the autograph register on November 18, 1632; John Donne, the poet's son, in 1634; and 'Orlando Lytton' on March 14, 1637. This must have been Sir Rowland Lytton of Knebworth, a son, presumably, of the 'William Litton' who, years before, in December, 1609, had

[29] *Itinerary*, I, i, 73.
[30] Wotton, *Letters*, ed. Pearsall Smith, I, 410 and note 3.
[31] We know that this was one of the greatest abuses in eighteenth-century Italy (see Maurice Vaussard, *La Vie quotidienne en Italie au XVIIIe siècle*. Paris, 1959, 137-9) and may assume that things had been no better in the seventeenth century.
[32] *Crudities*, 130.
[33] Although Nicholas Ferrar's name does not appear (for the good reason that the Bidello's register only begins in 1618), we know that he lived at Padua from about 1614 until 1617.
[34] Not the poet and friend of Izaak Walton, but his father.

carried a letter from Lord Salisbury to ambassador Wotton in Venice. 'He is a gentleman that hath brought an excellent good mind into this country,' wrote Wotton, 'and one that without doubt will carry it home again, and will enrich it abroad with the best observations. He is at the present in Padua, where he bestoweth his time (as I hear all say) exceeding industriously.'[35] We know less, unfortunately, about Orlando, and very little indeed about the Lytton family prior to their alliance with the Bulwers.[36] John Evelyn signed the register on July 29, 1645, the day before he matriculated as a 'jurist'. Edmund Waller matriculated on January 25, 1646, and signed the Bidello's register the same day. Kenelm Digby, a son of the famous Sir Kenelm, signed on July 16th, 1646, but did not matriculate until April 14, 1647. The name of Thomas Killigrew, the dramatist and future theatre-manager, appears on July 14, 1647, and he notes that this was 'the 7 Journey', which possibly means that it was his seventh visit to Padua, though the expression is obscure. He was travelling in Italy at the time to raise funds for the exiled Prince of Wales.[37] The names of John Finch and Thomas Baines appear on October 19, 1652; both matriculated as 'Giuristi' in 1654, and in 1656 Finch was elected Prorector and Syndic of the English nation. Edward Browne, the eldest son of Sir Thomas Browne, signed the register on February 27, 1665. He is said to have 'spent some weeks . . . studying Anatomy' and to have greatly admired the neatness of the demonstrations carried out by a certain Marchetti, who had worked under Finch.[38] A different class of persons, and more literary, is represented by 'Roscomon', the fourth Earl, Dryden's friend (June 3, 1659), and 'Rochester', the second Earl (October 26, 1664).

Apart from the above, the names of a number of famous men who were presumably not students, occur: that of Sir Henry Peyton (1620) who commanded the English fleet in the Adriatic; of Sir Isaac Wake, ambassador to Venice (July 9, 1624); of James Graham, Earl of Montrose, the great soldier and poet (July 9, 1624); of 'Petrus Killigrew', probably Sir Peter Killigrew, known as 'Peter the Post' because he had acted as an intermediary in carrying messages between King and Parliament and had contrived to keep on good terms

[35] *Life and Letters of Sir Henry Wotton*, ed. Pearsall Smith, I, 477-8. William Lytton was a son of Sir Rowland Lytton, and his son was presumably a Rowland.

[36] The Lyttons derived their name from the village in the Peak Forest where they were settled in the eleventh century. Sir Robert Lytton, who had fought for the future Henry VII at Bosworth, acquired the Knebworth estate, and the family appears to have moved there towards 1580.

[37] See above, p. 47.

[38] Norman Moore, *Medicine in the British Isles*, cited by A. Mallock, *Finch and Baines* . . . Cambridge, 1917, 18. See below, p. 121.

with both. His name occurs in November, 1654, and again in August, 1655. William Juxon, one time Bishop of London,[39] was in Padua on July 21, 1655; and William Sancroft, who was to become Archbishop of Canterbury in 1678, on March 8, 1660. John Graham of Claverhouse, another name renowned in history, signed the register on March 18, 1671.

Most of these seem to have been visitors. Of the regular students the most important group were the physicians and anatomists. Padua, wrote Lassels, who had probably been there more than once, is 'famous for the Study of Physick, as many of our thrice worthy Physitians in England can testify'.[40] A study of the *Roll of the Royal College of Physicians*[41] shows that during the sixteenth and seventeenth centuries some fifty-seven Fellows of the College had studied in Padua and that many had taken their degree there. William Harvey, whose work in medical research we have already touched on, and who was afterwards to act as a doctor in the Royalist army, had taken his M.D. at Padua in 1602.[42] Laurence Wright, who was later to become Oliver Cromwell's personal physician, had matriculated at Padua[43] and was Counsellor of the English nation in the Faculty of Law in 1615. Sir Thomas Browne may have studied here; his son Edward certainly did, as we have seen. Among the many English physicians associated with the medical school, at least seven were distinguished enough to be afterwards knighted. In this group Finch and Baines stand in a class to themselves.[44]

[39] It was he who had ministered to Charles I in the days preceding his execution and who accompanied him on to the scaffold. He became Primate in 1660.

[40] *An Italian Voyage* . . . ed. 1698, 262.

[41] By William Munk. London, 1878, I, 125. And see J. W. Stoye, *English Travellers Abroad* (1604-1667). London, 1952, 225-7.

[42] As his diploma, now in the archives of the College of Physicians, expresses the pleasure of the University on the occasion of his degree, one may assume that he had been liked and even admired at Padua.

[43] W. Munk, *Roll of the College of Physicians*, I, 181.

[44] Of many other students and visitors, not mentioned above, we have only sparse information. Sir John Harington, a son of the famous translator of Ariosto, appears to have stayed in Padua during the winter of 1608-9. He was accompanied by his tutor, Mr Tovey. In Venice he was received by the Doge, visited the new fortifications in Friuli, worked hard at Greek and Latin, and wrote letters to his father in Latin and Italian. Sir Thomas Puckering, another young man with a tutor in attendance, stayed here for a time in 1613, after earlier visits to Florence and Venice. Sir Edward Herbert spent some weeks in Padua, attending lectures. After Thomas Howard, Earl of Arundel, had made his tour of Italy with Inigo Jones and Thomas Coke, the Countess brought her sons to Venice and took a villa near Padua so that they could study there. These were James Howard and Henry Howard, who afterwards succeeded to the title. They signed the Bidello's register in 1620 and appear to have remained until 1623 with Tunstall acting as tutor and

What emerges from a survey of the records is that, whereas in earlier times many people had gone to Padua to study Law or the classical languages, the University was now attracting especially the scientific-minded; and it so happens that the students of whom we know the most belonged more or less to this class. It was not always a clearly defined one. John Finch was something of a connoisseur of art and John Evelyn was interested in everything from anatomy to landscape-gardening. But while artists and archaeologists studied in Rome, and sometimes in Florence, and those who wished to learn good Italian lingered in Siena, the men curious of scientific research spent a greater or shorter part of their time at Padua.[45] This, as we shall see, was notably true of John Ray, perhaps the greatest botanist of the century, who studied for some months (1663-64) at the University of Padua prior to his botanical exploration of Italy and Sicily.

John Evelyn (1620-1706) is the type of a class fairly common in the Seicento, men of wide intellectual interests who, without being professional scientists like Boyle and Newton, contributed to the formation of the new culture. His *Diary*, which has just been re-edited and annotated by Dr E. S. de Beer, is a valuable source for the history of his times. In it he recorded everything he considered of interest in his continental travels—and he made a point of seeing everything; he inserted additional information from the best books he could find on the cities he had visited; and later, after his return home, he further amplified it with notes from such travel-books as Richard Lassels'. In Padua he lived for some time, in 1645 and 1646, studying Botany and Physiology and taking with him on his departure a plan of the venous system which he afterwards presented to the Royal Society.[46]

But the prominent Englishmen most closely associated with the University in the middle years of the century were Finch and Baines.[47] John Finch (1626-1682) was a son of the Recorder of London and, like Evelyn, a man of wealth. He studied for a year or two at

Thomas Coke attending to business arrangements and correspondence (J. W. Stoye, 129-130). The interests of such students, and of visitors like Thomas Carew and Edmund Waller, must have been literary and social. So too perhaps were those of 'Johannes Vaughan Cambrobritannus' (June 9, 1638), and of 'Thomas Vaughan Cambro-Brittanus' (sic), whose name I find in the register as signing on August 7, 1659, and who was probably the twin-brother of Henry Vaughan, the Silurist.

[45] At least until the middle 1650's when the University of Pisa was perhaps beginning to take the lead.

[46] See pp. 188-210 below for Evelyn's experiences in Italy.

[47] See Archibald Mallock, *Finch and Baines: a Seventeenth-Century Friendship*, Cambridge, 1917. The following sketch is based mainly on Dr Mallock's admirable monograph.

Oxford, and then, after apparently taking part in one of the battles at Newbury, entered Christ's College, Cambridge. It was here, in 1647, that he met Thomas Baines who was to become his 'fidus Achates'. Baines was a native of a small Cambridgeshire village. Whether he was a man of greater character, if not ability, than Finch cannot be decided; but the latter depended very much on him. In 1651 they received permission to go to France, and from France they proceeded to Geneva and descended into Italy by way of the Simplon (1652).

During the sojourn in Italy Finch corresponded regularly with his sister Anne, who was married to Viscount Conway. He sent her two 'Bologna dogs'—a sort of lap-dog—named Julietto and Vittoria; related some of his observations on Natural History, such as those relating to the hibernation of bears in winter; and generally reported on the progress of his studies. He and Baines seem to have reached Padua about mid October, 1652,[48] and here they studied under Molinetti,[49] a distinguished anatomist who occupied the chair that had once been held by Aquapendente. There exists in manuscript a short treatise on the circulation of the blood which Finch wrote at Padua,[50] but whether this was his doctoral dissertation I do not know. Wealth, in addition to character and ability, must have made him popular. It is probable that he signalized his election as Pro-rector and Syndic of the English by some generous gift or donation to the University, as I find, in Part I of Favaro's *Saggio di Bibliografia,* that an oration was delivered in his honour and in his presence in the Cathedral on November 1st, and another on November 25th, and both these were printed. The title of the second reads as follows:

Portentum Aegyptium de D. Catharina V. et M. Panegyris habita in aebidus eidem sacris a Hieronymo Bernabo Genuensi. Illustrissimo ac Generosissimo D.D. Ioanni Finchio Nobili Anglo, Patavinae Iurisconsultorum Universitatis Pro-Rectori ac Syndico Meritiss. nuncupato. Die XXV Novembris. M.DC.LVI—Patavij, ex typograph. Camerali.[51]

One must admit, after making allowance for the superlatives of Italian courtesy, that this was praise. Tablets with Finch's coat-of-

[48] They signed the register on October 19th, but did not matriculate until 1654.

[49] John Ray, the botanist, records 'Antonius Molinetus' as lecturing 'Ad theoricam ordinarium medicinae' in 1663 and 1664.

[50] Mallock, p. 15.

[51] *Saggio di Bibliografia dello Studio di Padova* (1500-1920). Parte prima, no. 264.

arms still exist in the Cortile Antico and in the Aula Magna, where there are also three small tablets to Baines.[52] Both men took their M.D. in the autumn of 1657, and Finch at least must have acted for some time as demonstrator and probably lecturer. Before leaving Padua in 1659 he appears to have acquired one of the 'anatomical tables' of the venous system, the one which William Harvey, who was physician to Anne Conway and related to the Finch family, is supposed to have brought from Padua, but which Dr Mallock has reason to think was really brought over by Finch.[53]

It was about this time—in 1657—that the Accademia del Cimento, the members of which had been associated for some years past, was officially established in Florence under the patronage of the Grand-Duke Ferdinand II.[54] The latter was interested in scientific research and was furthering its progress at the University of Pisa, but it was his brother, Prince Leopold, a man of wide culture and great intelligence, who was the soul of the movement and the real animator of the Cimento. This famous academy was not strictly the first of its kind in Europe. The Filomati of Siena and the Lincei of Rome had been founded earlier. But in the 1650's it was by far the most distinguished. Its more notable proceedings were to be recorded by Lorenzo Magalotti and published in 1668 under the title of *Saggi di Naturali Esperienze*, and afterwards translated by Richard Waller and published in England for the Royal Society in 1684.[55]

Now Finch's skill in dissections had become so widely known that in 1659 Ferdinand II appointed him Professor of Anatomy at Pisa. Although he had here, among his colleagues, men of the greatest ability—names famous in the history of Science, like Marcello Malpighi the biologist and G.-A. Borelli the physiologist—Finch's reputation rose so high that a local poet composed three epigrams in his honour, the first of which concluded with the couplet:

> *Nempe hominem nunc findere scite, ac fingere primum*
> *Divinae monstras nil minus artis opus.*

'Thou showest that it needs no less of divine art to split a man skilfully (scite) than to fashion him in the first place'; or, better perhaps,

[52] Baines was not a noble. G. H. Darwin, art. cit. in *Proceedings . . . of the Cambridge Society of Antiquaries*, VIII, 343-4, reproduces Finch's tablet in the Aula Magna and one of Baines's.

[53] Mallock, 83-4. This is of course conjectural. Harvey may have returned to Padua and obtained one himself. The register (see Horatio Brown, *op. cit.*, 23) records a 'Guglielmo Hervy nobile Inglese' as signing on June 21, 1629, but whether this was the famous physician one is not sure.

[54] This Ferdinand was a well-meaning but undistinguished person—very inferior as a man and a ruler to his grandfather, Ferdinand I.

[55] Mallock, 22-3.

'to take a body to pieces than to put it together'[56]—an extravagant compliment.

It must have been on account of the Restoration that Finch and Baines returned home late in 1660. They had not seen England for nearly ten years. On December 5, 1660, they signed a document along with other 'savants' who were 'resolved to form a society for promoting experimental philosophy'; and Charles II, who had Medici forbears and was impressed by the foundation of the Accademia del Cimento, caused the Great Seal to be affixed to the charter of the Royal Society in 1662. In March, 1661, both Finch and Baines were elected Fellows of the College of Physicians, and on June 20th they received the M.D. of Cambridge in consideration of their degrees at Padua. It was just prior to this, on June 10th, that Finch had been knighted.

In the autumn of 1662 they returned to Tuscany, where they probably spent more time in Florence than in Pisa. Finch was now on terms of great intimacy with Prince Leopold. To him he wrote accounts of his experiences in Rome and Naples, where he and his friend were travelling in the autumn of 1663. The letters relate more particularly to their conversations with Cardinal Ricci, a Roman Mathematician whose society they found charming; and with Tommaso Cornelio, a Neapolitan Mathematician and Physicist who had apparently thought out a means 'of compressing of the air by elastic force'. At Naples they wandered on the slopes of Vesuvius, without, however, reaching the summit, and they also visited the 'Grotto dei Serpenti' without seeing the snakes whose ministrations were popularly supposed to cure dermatitis. Finch, for a scientist, seems at times to have been rather credulous, but even he doubted the efficacy of this treatment, if one may so call it. People suffering from skin-trouble, he informed Prince Leopold, dose themselves with opium and then creep into the cave, which is low and narrow, and lie still: 'it is said that they, after being licked by the serpents, come out cured of any skin disease'. But Finch thought that any such cures should be ascribed to the great heat of the cavern.[57]

On returning to Pisa, in December, 1663, Finch resumed his professorial duties; but he and Baines again visited England in the following year, and in March, 1665, Charles II appointed him as English Resident in Florence. Baines, as usual, accompanied him to his new post. For the first few days they were entertained by a gentleman whom we shall meet later, a gallant and interesting

[56] There is, of course, a sort of pun on 'findere' and 'fingere', with their exactly opposite meanings.

[57] Letter of December 10th, from Pisa.

Anglo-Florentine who was Bernardo Guasconi in Tuscany and Sir Bernard Gascoyne in England. They must also, about this time, if not earlier, have been acquainted with Lorenzo Magalotti,[58] the energetic secretary of the Cimento, who was to visit London in the winter of 1667-68, and again in 1669, and to establish close relations with Sir Henry Oldenburg, then secretary of the Royal Society.[59] Sir John Finch remained in Tuscany until 1670, assisting or keeping a fatherly eye on young Englishmen who visited Italy, such as his own nephew Daniel Finch, son of the Solicitor General; or trying to settle any political difficulties that arose. One of these was due to the Pope's efforts to stop the celebration of the Anglican service in the Residency, as he had already suppressed it at Livorno. One may note in this connexion that Ferdinand II was more subservient to the Papacy than his grandfather, the ex-Cardinal, had been.[60] In matters purely political, however, Sir John's duties cannot have been onerous. He probably made some of the arrangements for the extended visit which the Grand-Duke's son, Prince Cosimo, escorted by Magalotti and a number of other gentlemen, paid to England in 1669; but Tuscany was an ally, and relations with Great Britain were not only amicable but extremely cordial.

It was during this period that Finch came into touch with Carlo Dolci (1616-1686), the great religious painter who on rare occasions turned his genius to portrait-painting. Dolci was commissioned to paint both Finch and Baines, and these portraits 'when seen in England . . . made such a sensation that many noblemen and gentlemen of that nation, on their way through Florence, had their portraits painted by him'.[61] Finch also purchased from Dolci a copy of his 'Erodiade', which he presented to Charles II and a copy of his 'Davide' and one of his 'Maddalena' which he gave to Queen Catherine.

In 1670, after his return from an extended journey through Spain, Portugal, England, the United Provinces and France, Prince Cosimo became Grand-Duke on the death of his father. Piety, continence and patience were his saving graces; but for the rest he had no ability, nor was he of a person or character to inspire affection. His relations with his wife were deplorable. Marguerite-Louise d'Orléans hated Italy and disliked her husband. She was a clever, even brilliant

[58] It seems certain that they knew each other, though I have not found any record of their meeting.

[59] To be studied in a later volume.

[60] See J. Lucas-Dubreton, *La Vie quotidienne à Florence au temps des Médicis*. Paris, 1958, 324; and more particularly Umberto Dorini, *I Medici e i loro tempi*.

[61] Filippo Baldinucci in *Notizie de' Professori del disegno* (1717), cited by Mallock, p. 52.

young woman, but a frightful termagant and her behaviour grew more and more deplorable.[62] Much of this was public knowledge, and it may explain why Finch was not now quite happy in Florence and why, towards the autumn of 1670, he and his friend returned to London. It was recognized that they were inseparables; and when Finch was made ambassador to Constantinople, Baines—who had recently been knighted—went with him. They could not resist the temptation to travel by way of Genoa and Florence, and to take ship from Livorno. But sad days were in store. Anne Conway, to whom her brother had been greatly devoted, died in 1679, and 'honest Dr Baines' passed away at Constantinople in 1681.

Finch had no wife or children to lean on. He was now broken in spirit and his health seems also to have been giving way. He was back in Florence in March, 1682, and after purchasing a number of pictures he sailed to England. His first move here was to make for Cambridge, drawn thither by memories of youth and because it was now the one haven of refuge from the sea of life—that sea on which he had lost everything but fame and wealth, which, in the last resort, are no substitute for happiness. And his welcome could scarcely have been warmer. The Fellows and Scholars of Christ's met him at Trumpington, and on reaching the College he was received with the greatest distinction. Here he founded a Fellowship. He died on November 18th. Both he and Baines (whose body had been embalmed and brought over from Turkey) were regarded as among the great benefactors of the College, and a noble monument was erected a few years later in their honour.[63]

During most of his career Finch had been in close touch with the Cambridge Platonists, who owed much of their inspiration and learning to the Florentine neo-Platonists of the fifteenth century. Christ's College was, after all, their headquarters. Henry More had probably been his tutor in undergraduate days and was, in any case, a great personal friend both of Finch and Anne Conway.[64] Ralph Cudworth was Master of the college at the time of Finch's last visit.[65] It would be interesting to know whether he was himself a neo-Platonist. Cartesianism would certainly have been more in keeping with his scientific interests; and More, who had been largely instrumental in popularizing Descartes' philosophy in England, may

[62] J. Lucas-Dubreton, *op. cit.*, 327-8. She later returned to France where, however, she behaved so scandalously that Louis XIV, who was her cousin, had her confined in the Convent of Saint-Mandé.

[63] I am indebted to my one-time supervisor and old friend Professor B. W. Downs, sometime Master of Christ's College, for drawing my attention to the importance of Finch and Baines.

[64] Mallock, p. 3.

[65] *Ibid.*, p. 78.

well have directed his mind in that direction; but this is a matter of conjecture.

Both Finch and Baines—'fidissimus J. Finch Achates', as he has been called—were more important figures than the above outline may have suggested. Finch was not merely a well-to-do man—owner at one time of Kensington Palace—in high favour at Court and the brother of an influential minister of state; he was also one of the most skilful anatomists of his age, and, thanks to his studies and demonstrations in Padua and Pisa, one of the prime movers in the formation of the Royal Society. Dr Mallock recalls that on May 20, 1663, he and his friend were elected Fellows at the same time as John Evelyn, Kenelm Digby, Dryden, Wren and several others. By acting as a link between English and Italian scientists, by the many Italian treatises on medicine he had in his library, by his activities as a diplomatist, and even by the large number of paintings he brought home, of which at least nine were by Carlo Dolci, he contributed far more than all but a few of his compatriots to promote in England a greater appreciation of the Italian genius in science, as well as in the pictorial arts.

PART II

Italy as seen by the English

6. *The Cortile antico in the University of Padua* See p. 114

Photo: A. *Lytton Sells*

7a. *The Rotonda near Vicenza* See pp. 166, 216

Photos: A. Lytton S

7b. *The Roman Gate, Turin* See p. 164

CHAPTER VII

Daily Life and the Daily Round

IT would be possible to reconstruct from the travel-books a composite picture of the Italian scene as it appeared to visitors between about 1593 (Moryson) and 1659 (Mortoft); and this would accord with a method often employed by historians. But the Italian scene was constantly changing; it was never quite the same, any more than other scenes, from decade to decade. And one not only does more justice to individual travellers by treating them separately, but one may also hope to come nearer the truth by presenting the successive Italies which each of them contemplated. It is not, however, to be expected that they should describe Italy as we should see it, could we go back and view it through modern eyes. Our authors were less critical than their eighteenth-century successors. Travellers like the Comte de Caylus, the Président de Brosses, Arthur Young and others have left information more specific in some ways than the writers we are to study. There was much that such good observers as Fynes Moryson, John Evelyn and Richard Lassels took for granted, because the material conditions and comforts of life in Europe as a whole were not what they are today. A few general remarks touching matters which our travellers either do not treat of, or only just touch on, may not therefore be out of place.

The story of Italy in the Seicento is one of a continual economic recession accompanied by a decline in the moral stamina, though probably not in the private morals, of the country. The political and military weakness, apparent until recently in modern Italy, has been due to three centuries of foreign occupation and oppression and also to poverty. A certain degree of wealth is necessary for the maintenance of the military virtues. In the seventeenth century the glory of the medieval Republics had departed; but this is more apparent to modern historians than it was to travellers at that time. It is certain that the effect of Spanish rule in Lombardy and southern Italy was to depress, discourage or demoralize every stratum of society.

Genoa and even Venice had lost a great part of their foreign trade. The textile industries on which much of Lombard wealth and practically the whole wealth of Florence had been founded, were decadent and incapable of meeting English and Dutch competition; and this was probably due to excessive taxation and lack of enterprise on the part of the governments concerned. Protective tariffs do not appear to have assisted native industries, and as the peninsula was divided into numerous states and principalities, each with its tariff-barriers, material prosperity suffered. For the artisans and the peasants the standard of living seems to have been going down, except in Venetia and Piedmont. When, after 1713, the Austrians had replaced the Spaniards, there was an improvement, and the age of the benevolent despots ushered in far better times; but in the Seicento the Spaniards were not greatly interested in promoting the well-being of their subjects, and economic distress continued to take its toll.

Between 1550 and 1600 the population of the peninsula appears to have gone down from 11,165,000 to 10,080,000,[1] and it probably declined further during the seventeenth century. M. Maurice Vaussard, in a brilliant study of eighteenth-century Italy which has just appeared, records that the city of Venice numbered 150,000 souls in 1586, but only 137,000 in 1780; that Milan had a population of 120,000 towards 1690[2] and no more than 130,000 in 1790, and this in spite of the notable industrial expansion of Milan and Lombardy in general during the eighteenth century. The plague of 1630 had killed 85,000 people in Milan,[3] and 7,000 out of a population of 70,000 in Florence.[4] Even as late as 1765 the population of Florence was only 78,000.[5] Naples, however, was a very large city, with a population of 259,932 in 1606.[6] and this may well have remained more or less constant throughout the century.

One cannot, however, generalize with confidence about seventeenth-century Italy, because the many estates into which it was divided presented a great variety of conditions. The Duchy of Savoy, with its centre in Piedmont, and the Venetian Republic, states which were entirely independent, seem to have enjoyed considerable economic well-being. Venetia was governed by the most capable and enlightened aristocracy that has ever existed and maintained for so long the independence and integrity of a republic. Nobility and

[1] J. Lucas-Dubreton, *La Vie quotidienne à Florence au temps des Médicis*. Paris, 1958, p. 311.

[2] Milan had had a population of over 200,000 in the early sixteenth century, but there were only about 100,000 people there in the early seventeenth.

[3] M. Vaussard, *La Vie quotidienne en Italie au XVIIIe siècle*. Paris, 1959, pp. 17-18.

[4] Lucas-Dubreton, *op. cit.*, 323.

[5] Vaussard, 95-6.

[6] G. C. Capaccio. *Descrizione di Napoli ne'principii del secolo XVII*, ed. Capasso, 1882, 23-24 (cited by De Beer Evelyn's *Diary*, II, 325, note 4).

peasantry were here on friendly terms, and in fact nothing like the class-war then existed in Italy. Florence, which had been well-governed by Ferdinand I, fared less and less well under his successors. The later Medici were men of little capacity or character; Giangastone (reigned 1723-1737), the last representative of the house, was a degenerate; and Tuscany suffered in consequence.[7] The city of Rome was well governed by the Popes, although the administration of the Papal States was not particularly good, and the police-system in Rome itself was largely ineffective owing to the great number of churches and other sanctuaries for malefactors. On the other hand Rome was, as regards its buildings, the most modern and up-to-date of the cities of Europe, and nowhere else was the government so humane and nowhere was every class of the community so intelligently cared for.[8] In addition to this Rome was a wonderfully agreeable place of sojourn and the most brilliant artistic centre in Europe.

If well-to-do people lived in luxury, they also provided employment for a host of domestics[9] who would otherwise have been left to starve; and while such persons would today be mostly employed in industry and commerce (except in times of trade-recession), it does not follow that they then suffered as servants from any sense of indignity or were less happy than modern shop-assistants, office-clerks or factory-workers. On the contrary they identified themselves with the houses they served and basked in the wealth and glory of their masters. To be the servant of a great lord who took a personal interest in one's welfare was no less dignified and happy a situation than to be the employee of some industrial corporation or governmental concern of which the chief executives are inevitably unaware of one's existence. The seventeenth century was less frigidly impersonal than the twentieth.

It is probable that many Italian cities, as regards their structural appearance, did not look very different from what they do today. Such places as Venice, Vicenza, Verona, Siena, Pisa, much of Florence, and many others, seem scarcely to have changed in that respect; but prior to the industrial revolution all these cities had a more countrified appearance. The traveller approaching along the highway would see ox-drawn wagons lumbering along, well-dressed gentlemen proceeding on horseback, ladies in gaily-painted coaches—in place of railway assembling yards, petrol stations, rattling lorries and frantic automobiles. On the other hand, city-streets were badly

[7] Lucas-Dubreton, 323-331. [8] See below, pp. 196, 229-30.

[9] M. Vaussard, p. 96, notes that, in 1760, 10% of the working population in Venice were domestic servants. The situation elsewhere in Italy, and also in the Seicento, may well have been similar.

paved as a rule,[10] and the refuse which must have been quite malodorous in hot weather was only cleared at irregular intervals. Some of the work now effected by scavenger-services was then left to the torrential rains to deal with.

To guess just what 'commodités' (if one may use the word) existed before the nineteenth century, is difficult and perhaps impossible. The best hotels probably afforded some. But modern hygiene was non-existent. The condition of streets, porticoes and even stairways of good houses in Naples appears to have been horrifying;[11] and the combination of squalor with external splendour was far more marked here than in northern Italy. The north was better heated in winter than central and southern Italy. In Rome and Naples most houses and palaces were apparently not heated in any regular way during the cold weather.[12] Not that they are in much better case even now.

Travellers from England and France, where windows at this time were generally glazed, must often have been surprised by the comparative rarity of glass in Italy, at least as late of the mid-seventeenth century. Fynes Moryson remarks that in Naples in 1594 'the windowes are all covered with paper or linnen cloth'[13] and this appears to have been usual in most cities, except in Florence, Genoa and of course in Venice. In Florence, as early as the fifteenth century many of the better-class houses appear to have had glazed windows. But Venice was the home of glass-making, an art in which it still retains the primacy. 'And howsoever glasse be common with us on this Side the Alps,' says Moryson, 'yet it is certaine that the glassemakers of Venice, dwelling in the Iland Murano, have a more noble matter, and thereof make much better glasse than we can.'[14]

It was not safe, in big cities, to venture into the smaller thoroughfares at night. Little lamps burned before the statues of the Virgin or of saints, statues which were quite numerous[15] and many of which stood in niches on the house-walls; but it seems doubtful whether any regular system of street-lighting, such as existed in London by the 1660's, was introduced into Italian cities before the mid-eighteenth century.[16]

Of the better known centres, Milan, Bologna and Rome are no doubt those which have been most radically transformed. The huge apartment-houses which have sprung up in Bologna since the last

10 Except in Genoa and Naples, where most visitors were impressed by the excellence of the paving (see e.g. Evelyn, *Diary*, II, 353).

11 Vaussard, 23.

12 But one could have a fire lit in one's room if one so desired.

13 *Itinerary*, I, ii, 112.

14 I, ii, 89.

15 Vaussard, 23.

16 In 1765-66, Lalande (cited by Vaussard, p. 101) records that the thoroughfares in Venice were lighted with 3,000 lanterns.

war are especially conspicuous. Milan, as we see it today, with its industrial regions spreading for miles in every direction, was then a small provincial capital with a rural approach. The industrial development of Lombardy only began in the eighteenth century. Rome was a mere fraction of the great city of the ancient Republic and the Empire. Little more than half the area enclosed by the Aurelian wall was occupied in the seventeenth century, and this was the portion, mainly on the lower ground, that was bounded by the Capitoline and Palatine on one side, by the Tiber and by the Pincian Hill on the other; although much of the Trastevere was not unlike what it is now. The rest seems to have been occupied by market-gardens and waste land where goats and cattle browsed. The region round the Piazza di Spagna, where Evelyn lodged, was already the quarter favoured by visitors; from this piazza a winding path led up the slope to Santa Trinità de'Monti, the great stairway not having yet been constructed; but if, from the top of this slope, you walked left along the edge of the Pincian, you came to the Medici Villa, now the French Academy, which had been built by Ferdinand I of Florence. The population of Rome towards 1640 seems to have been about 114,260, according to Lanciani:[17] it was a smaller place than Venice, and much smaller than Naples.

The character of Italians probably varied from region to region even more than it does today. The Venetians were a good-mannered, even-tempered and eminently reasonable sort of people; the Piedmontese rather grave, though in other respects not unlike the French; the Tuscans very charming and hospitable, but mercurial too and no longer as ebullient as in the days when they had governed (or misgoverned) themselves. Among the upper classes in Tuscany crimes of violence were a thing of the past, or at least they had been since the hair-raising vengeance which Veronica Cibo had taken upon her husband's mistress in December, 1638—one of the most lurid affairs in the annals of Italy. Venice too was an orderly city. But in central and southern Italy tempers were apt to be volcanic, and here the common folk were not unready to draw the knife on small provocation—and to use it. There were, however, pockets of violence even in the north, where Brescia had already acquired a reputation for the frequency of murders committed there and on the road to Verona—a reputation it still maintained in Stendhal's time.

Everyday life, on the other hand, afforded a great deal of gaiety and many simple pleasures. The religious festivals and the beautiful processions that accompanied them; other festivities such as horse-racing, provided entertainment for all classes. Private morals seem

[17] R. Lanciani, *The Ruins and Excavations of Ancient Rome*, 1897, p. 94.

to have been improving. The Italians were then, as now, a happily constituted people, hard-working and cheerful, not given to gluttony or drunkenness, sober and contented with their lot. But in Lombardy and Tuscany the more intelligent members of the upper class were inevitably depressed by the loss of political freedom.

If until recent years general historians have neglected the social history of seventeenth-century Italy, this is because such factors as political, military or economic power have determined the course of their studies. From that point of view France, England, Spain and the United Provinces have seemed more important. But civilization is more than politics and economics; and to shrug off Italy as merely 'decadent' at this time is to ignore her contributions to the arts of peace. If she then gave birth to no more than two or three writers of the first rank, she was still producing competent engineers, fine architects and sculptors, distinguished and original painters, and above all great doctors, mathematicians and scientists.

The historian who attempts to evoke a past age in its entirety must always, I suppose, weigh the advantages of the analytic method against the synthetic. The latter has the advantage of presenting a sort of continuum and coming nearer to what the reality may have been like; but, in order to avoid a bewildering confusion, the former sometimes imposes itself. The tableau, or outline of a tableau, indicated above, generalized and rather abstract as it may be, is less like a picture than a diagram. There is cogency in Mérimée's ironical observation that what interests him in history is the anecdotes he finds in the memoirs: these alone have the breath of life. There is cogency in Renan's plea for the part that imagination and conjecture may play in filling in the gaps and silences left by the 'documents'. Scientific history (if history can be scientific) conducts us through a museum where we inspect rows of plaster casts—not flesh and blood, but something which has never existed outside a museum. We can never know, of course, just what the past was like. And, though we bow respectfully to the claims of 'documentation', we recognize that Sainte-Beuve was right when he stressed the importance of the anecdote, and used anecdotes so effectively in his literary portraits. (There are places in his *Port Royal* where we feel present, there in the flesh so to speak, seeing and listening to the good nuns and the holy Solitaries). So, when we turn to Italy in that same age, it is the individual traveller, when he forgets to be learned and informative, and simply tells us of his personal feelings and adventures—it is he who causes the past to live once again for us.

CHAPTER VIII

Conditions of Travel: Foreign Exchange, Transport, Hotels

I HAVE attempted in previous chapters to give some account of those Englishmen, students for the most part, expatriates and philosophers also, who[1] left no formal or detailed account of their experiences. But a fair number of journals or travel-books were composed and some of them published at the time. A few like Evelyn's *Diary*, which, however, was not printed until 1818 and then not in full, are monuments of information. But it is perhaps the amateur books of travel written by adventurous young men with no professional axe to grind, that best give us the *sensations d'Italie*—sensations which make them interesting, and valuable too, as documents for the historian. The books by Fynes Moryson, Tom Coryate, George Sandys, William Lithgow, Francis Mortoft, Sir John Reresby and John Raymond enable one in imagination to accompany their authors on an exciting adventure. The most original and in some ways the best informed English observers of the Italian scene were Moryson, Raymond and Lassels, and their works were probably the most influential.

There were of course guides to foreign travel. Even in *The Compleat Gentleman* Henry Peacham gives advice on the subject; but James Howell's *Instructions for Forreine Travel* (1642) was a formal guide to the subject and in some demand for a time. There also existed guides to individual countries.[2] The principal works relating to Italy were J. H. von Pflaumern's *Mercurius Italicus*, of which a second edition appeared in 1628—a well compiled guide-book in Latin and the Baekeker of the age; and François Schott's *Itinerarii Italiae rerumq. Romanorum . . .* (3 vols., 1600). Of the latter the Latin version was reprinted more than once, as was the Italian translation of 1610, a version presented as by 'Scotto' or 'Scotti'. Finally there were books devoted to Rome, of which the best were P. Totti's

[1] With the exception of Robert Boyle.

[2] For the Netherlands, L. Guicciardini's *Descrittione di tutti i Paesi Bassi* (1567), and for France, Claude de Varennes' *Le Voyage de France* (1637).

Ritratto di Roma antica (1627) and *Ritratto di Roma moderna* (1638). For Naples one could consult G. C. Capaccio's *Neapolitanae historiae . . . Tomus primus* 1607)[3]; the other guides to Naples appeared only in 1685 or later. All these works were used by one or other of the English authors, but they also consulted and sometimes borrowed from their predecessors. Thus Fynes Moryson became a sort of authority as, after 1670, did Lassels.

Montaigne had been the perfect traveller. He enjoyed being on the road and seeing new places and strange customs. His *Journal de Voyage* (he toured in Germany and Italy in 1580 and 1581) would certainly have been used as a sort of guide by English tourists, had it been available; but it was not printed until late in the eighteenth century. The Sieur de Villamont's *Voyages*, relating his experiences between 1588 and 1592, were, however, probably familiar to some of them. This adventurous Frenchman had climbed the Roche Melon (11,605 feet) above Susa in 1588. In 1591 he was in Padua and Venice and he gives a good account of travel by waterway in north Italy.

No one probably then thought that there might be an art of writing the travel-book or that such books would one day, in the hands of a George Borrow or of some great Alpinist like Edward Whymper or H. W. Tilman, become a genre as artistic as the novel sometimes is. Hence most of the seventeenth-century works on travel are in effect diaries or itineraries.

Not that Italy was by any means the goal of every traveller who went abroad for study or experience. Prior to the outbreak of the Thirty Years' War a certain number of young men studied at Wittenberg, Heidelberg or some other German university. German inns, however, were not distinguished for their amenities and, as Moryson remarks, the so-called hosts were apt to be churlish. Still, it was not unusual in those early years to cross Germany on one's way to Italy, particularly before 1595 while Henri IV was struggling against the Catholic League and the Spaniards, and when the Englishmen in France were the soldiers assisting him. After that, and with the establishment of order in France, it became easier and more agreeable to travel that way; and moreover, for a prolonged sojourn, France was the most accommodating of the European countries because it was near at hand, many of the inns were good, and there was other

[3] Dr E. S. de Beer, to whose great learning I am indebted for this account of the guides to specific countries, gives full bibliographical notices of these guides at the end of Vol. II of his edition of Evelyn's *Diary* (Oxford, 1955, pp. 569-579). One notes that the big guide-books were usually in Latin or Italian.

accommodation suited to almost every taste. Thus the more Protestant-minded could place their sons, even young boys, in the family of a Calvinist pastor who would lodge and board them, and give them an excellent education. A nobleman travelling in France would often stay in the houses of the Protestant gentry, still quite numerous, or of some great lord like the Duc de la Trémouille whose daughter Charlotte had married the Earl of Derby. The student could study in the Medical School at Montpellier or the Law School at Orléans. And there were probably always a large number of Englishmen staying in Orléans, Blois, Saumur (where there was a Protestant Academy) or some other town in the Loire valley, to improve their French. Catholic refugees were of course equally comfortable in a country which, for many years, was to remain the most tolerant in Europe. During the Interregnum also the majority of the Royalist exiles settled in France, especially in Paris where the active and benevolent Sir Richard Browne busied himself on their behalf; and only minorities in the Netherlands and in Italy.

But for travellers in general, Italy came next in popularity to France; and if, as the years went by, Englishmen continued to take more pride in speaking good French than good Italian, they still took some pride in the latter, as we shall see from John Raymond's testimony and from Magalotti's.

How was one to reach Italy? What official and monetary arrangements had to be made? What were the modes of transport to Italy, and in Italy? What was the accommodation like? And what were the perils of the way?

It was necessary first to obtain a passport, and this usually specified the goal and purpose of the journey and the length of time during which the traveller would be abroad. It also fixed the amount of currency he might take: in the early years of the century this seems to have varied from £10 to £20, or more if one had servants.[4] One could take a larger sum by permission of the government, but it was inadvisable to carry much money owing to the danger of theft. For these reasons, as Fynes Moryson explains at length, the traveller carried bills of exchange or letters of credit; and if he were going far afield he might take both.[5] The bill of exchange seems to have been invented in the thirteenth century by the Florentine and Lombard merchants who had agencies in Genoa, as an improvement on the older written contracts which were used by the Genoese and Vene-

[4] E. S. Bates, *Touring in 1600*. Boston and New York, 1911, pp. 343-3.
[5] Moryson, *Itinerary*, I, iii, 277-9.

tians.[6] It was a *lettera di pagamento*, serving to transfer credits between the merchant-banker in Italy and his correspondents or branches in other parts of Europe, including England. During the fourteenth century it had become generally current as a means of settling accounts[7] and also, one may safely surmise, for the use of travellers all over western Europe; so that by the sixteenth century it must have been the normal means by which one financed a journey in foreign parts. We know for example that when Rabelais was in Rome in 1548 as physician to the Cardinal Du Bellay, he negotiated a bill of exchange issued by Thomas Delberne et Compagnie of Paris and payable by their correspondents, Benvenuto Oliviero & Co., in Rome.[8] An English traveller would therefore deposit a substantial sum in specie with a 'merchant' in London. This, in the seventeenth century meant a goldsmith;[9] and one should add that, after the withdrawal from England of the great Italian bankers[10] who had financed Elizabeth I and advised Sir William Cecil on monetary matters, all English banking was in the hands of goldsmiths prior to the foundation of the Bank of England. The traveller then, after paying down a sufficient sum in cash, would draw bills of exchange (which were also called 'letters of advice') negotiable by the 'merchant's' or rather goldsmith's 'factors' or correspondents abroad,[11] for example in Paris, Lyon, Geneva or an Italian city, such as Genoa, Livorno and Venice. These bills were issued in triplicate. The traveller took one copy, and the two others were sent ahead by post or messenger. Bills were drawn 'at sight', 'at usance' (Italian 'usanza'), half-usance, or double-usance. If 'at sight', it meant that the money was to be paid at once, but this was only practicable for cities near at hand. 'Usance' meant a month for countries near at

[6] Raymond de Roover, *L'Evolution de la lettre de change: XIVe-XVIIIe siècles*. Paris, 1953, pp. 18, 25-48, 112 and passim. Very little was known of the early history of banking, or at least of this fundamental branch of it, prior to M. de Roover's brilliant researches.

[7] *Ibid*., 24, 25.

[8] Rabelais' formal receipt for *trente deux escus d'or en or* is reproduced by A. Heulard in *Rabelais: ses voyages en Italie, son exil à Metz*. Paris, n.d. (c. 1892), p. 263 and from this, by E. S. Bates, *Touring in 1600*, 342. Mr Bates describes the financing of travel on pp. 342-7. Moryson is our principal source of information as regards England.

[9] R. Ehrenberg, *Capital and Finance in the Age of the Renaissance*. Trans. H. M. Lucas. London, 1928, 347, 353.

[10] Especially the Genoese financiers Benedetto Spinola (see De Roover, 66) and Orazio Pallavicino, who was naturalized and knighted. The great international firm of Affaitidi et Cie, whose principal office was in Antwerp, had had a London branch (see Pierre Jeannin [i.e. J. P. Clébert], *Les Marchands au XVIe siècle*. Paris, 1957, p. 87).

[11] Moryson, *Itinerary*, I, iii, 277.

hand, but three months for Venice,[12] and probably two for Livorno. The rate of exchange was calculated in London, where the merchant-bankers met once a week at the Royal Exchange.[13] The European exchange-rates fluctuated greatly and erratically towards the beginning of the seventeenth century.[14] The commission varied from 5 per cent to 15 per cent per annum, but 10 per cent was usual.[15]

There might, however, be delay in negotiating one's bills of exchange, especially if the duplicate or 'letter of advice' had not arrived, or if it did not contain a description of the payee—which, however, it occasionally did. In these circumstances, one sometimes carried 'letters of credit'. The letter of credit required the correspondent of the London banker to furnish the traveller with what sum he required from time to time, and the correspondent then reclaimed payment from London. Moryson advises a substantial deposit with one's London 'merchant' before leaving, rather than be faced with an unexpectedly heavy debt on return; and he himself used letters of credit in Dantzig and Venice. The commission was usually not more than 10%.[16] But one has the impression that letters of credit were used only for long journeys or protracted sojourns, and mostly by well-to-do men; and that most seventeenth-century travellers carried only bills of exchange.[17]

[12] *Ibid.*, and p. 278.

[13] Moryson says 'the Burse', and it may have been familiarly known by this French name. The Royal Exchange had been founded by Sir Thomas Gresham on the model of the Antwerp Exchange. Gresham, who had a house in Antwerp and vied with Spinola and the great Italian bankers in his understanding of the money-market, had re-established English financial credit in the 1570's and stabilized the pound sterling (see Ehrenberg, 252-5; P. Jeannin, 86-7, and especially R. de Roover, *Gresham on Foreign Exchange*, Cambridge, Mass., 1949).

[14] Moryson, I, iii, 276. The rate was determined by the free play of the money-market, as it had been in the later Middle Ages (R. de Roover, p. 50), and it varied between the 'specie-points', that is the upper and lower rates between which it was more profitable to use bills of exchange than to transfer actual currency (De Roover, 57-8). The banking-centres were extremely sensitive, as they are now, to any war or revolution; and no government could control the operation of these natural laws. A skilful financier could, at the most, prevent fluctuations that were too violent, as Gresham had contrived to do (De Roover, 61); at one moment he had had to transfer gold from London to Antwerp, to settle the debt (p. 67). In the period that interests us, the European rates seem to have been quoted in relation to the *écu* of Lyon (Lyon giving the 'certain' to Europe), just as today they are quoted in relation to the £ sterling (De Roover, p. 53).

[15] *Ibid.*, 278. Mr J. W. Stoye in *English Travellers Abroad* (1604-1667). London, 1952, 193 note 1, cites from Harleian MS. 943, fo. 119, a bill of exchange negotiated in Venice in 1651. This was payable within three months from the date of issue.

[16] Moryson, *Itinerary*, I, iii, 278-9.

[17] See Bates, *op. cit.*, 346.

Having made these arrangements with a goldsmith in London, the traveller might then insure his life. Very little appears to be known about this system, but it certainly existed because it was illegal in France and the Netherlands, and was everywhere regarded as immoral. The risk was calculated, for western Europe, as roughly four to one against a safe return.[18] Another system which became very popular towards 1600 was to 'put out' a large sum before leaving the country, on the understanding that, if one returned, one would be repaid at 300%. This seems to have been the rate for Italy; for the Holy Land (much further and more dangerous) 500% was obtainable.[19] If, therefore, one came back safely the advantage was considerable, as E. S. Bates points out: one might cover all expenses and make a handsome profit into the bargain. So many people hastened to abuse the opportunity that the practice appears to have been discouraged and discontinued.[20]

The next step was to decide on the mode of transport. One could go by ship to Genoa, or Livorno; but apart from the discomfort and danger of storms, there was even greater peril from the Barbary pirates in the Mediterranean. The sea-trip from Marseille to Genoa was risky, as Evelyn discovered. Most travellers therefore went overland—once they had crossed the Channel. But the crossing might be, and fairly often was, a very slow business. In bad weather it sometimes took a week or more. The charge from Dover to Calais at the beginning of the century was 5/-; from Gravesend to Flushing 6/8.[21] But there were many additional charges and expenses, and also, as travel took so much longer than it does now, a journey to Italy was then far more costly than it is today.[22] It was also dangerous. One might be robbed and killed by soldiers, as armies were usually ill-paid or paid in arrears;[23] Highwaymen and bandits might or might not be more merciful. Conditions in France during the wars of religion, which were over at this time, had been frightful; in Germany during the Thirty Years' War (1618-1648) they were indescribable. It is recorded in correspondence preserved in the Montagu Papers that in 1639, 'it is an ordinary thing in Brandenburg country to eat man's flesh'.[24] One avoided Germany. But if one travelled by way of France and Switzerland (which was well governed and the safest country in Europe, there was far more than

18 E. S. Bates, 327.

19 *Ibid.*, 326. But even this might be calculated at 300%.

20 *Ibid.*, 327-8, 326.

21 *Ibid.*, 328.

22 *Ibid.*, 335-5.

23 *Ibid.*, 348.

24 *Montagu Papers*, p. 124 in *Historical Manuscripts Commission*, London, 1900, 45. Cited by Bates, 350.

a sporting chance of arriving safely in the earthly paradise, and it is unlikely that more than a very few travellers came to grief by the way.

Northern and central France were not of course so very unlike England. But to cross the Alps into Italy was to enter a world where everything was novel and dazzling. The fragile loveliness of Spring when the mountains turn suddenly from grey to pale green, and earth puts on a vesture of almond- and peach-blossom; the splendour of Autumn when the hand of an artist paints the vineyards purple and crimson and gold—exactly how far our ancestors were sensitive to all this we do not know; but one finds more than one indication, in Raymond and Lassels for example, that they were not indifferent to nature; and, besides, Italy offered other wonders in abundance.

Not that, in the early years of the century, and even as late as 1648, every part of Italy was equally accessible to Protestant Englishmen. One was not exactly welcomed in Lombardy until after the Peace of the Pyrenees. Nor, prior to 1590 or 1592 was it advisable to visit Rome, except in disguise. Sixtus V (1585-1590) took a severe view of heresy. But Clement VIII (1592-1605) was a mild and relatively tolerant pontiff. It is true that for many years and until the accession of Charles I and his marriage with a Catholic princess, Protestants continued to regard Rome and southern Italy as dangerous ground; but they probably exaggerated the danger. If one refrained from expressing anti-Catholic opinions, and showed a decent respect for Catholic beliefs and customs, one was not likely to be molested. It was, however, unwise to spend Easter in Rome—in those days—because a close enquiry was made, from house to house, as to those who were communicants.[25]

The Roman attitude was understandable. Protestantism in England and Scotland was militant and aggressive. Rome cannot but have been shocked by the torture and execution of Catholic priests, and it was natural that in the capital of Christendom, the successor of St Peter should exact respect. As E. S. Bates puts it in his admirable book on *Touring in 1600*, 'whether or no the high officials at Rome were faulty in dogma or in virtue, they were usually both men of the world and gentlemen';[26] and they could be really kind, good Samaritans in a very true sense, to an Englishman in distress.[27] They were not prepared however to stand nonsense, or what they re-

[25] Bates, 110-112. [26] *Ibid.*, 112.

[27] A seaman named William Davis, a Protestant, who fell sick in Rome in 1598, was tended in hospital without charge and given money to assist his return to England. His narrative was printed by Awnsham Churchill in A *Collection of Voyages and Travels*, Vol. VII (see Bates, 112).

garded as such. They took a particularly severe view of the Protestant tutors whom Scottish, and sometimes English, noble families sent abroad in charge of their sons, to preserve them from the wiles of the Jesuits; and on such—if the reigning pontiff was not a Clement VIII, but one of his immediate successors—the Inquisition was apt to pounce.[28]

But to the sporting-minded—and that is, to most Englishmen—there was a spice of attraction in such perils. And then Rome exercised a greater fascination over the minds of the Protestants than it probably does even today, because here were the great memories of the early Church, here too those older vestiges of the Republic and the Empire which their studies at school and University had endeared to them. Little wonder if Wotton, Moryson and Nicholas Ferrar all ventured into Rome.

The reign of Charles I ushered in better times for travellers and removed most of the danger which had hitherto existed. Not only was the Papacy grown more indulgent, but it looked with a not unfriendly eye on this cultured and tolerant prince. Urban VIII who pursued, as far as he dared, an anti-Spanish and anti-Austrian policy, was far from desiring to annoy foreign Protestants.[29] Milton, Evelyn, Raymond and others all travelled openly in the Papal States. In the days when Cardinal Barberini and the staff of the English College extended hospitality to Protestants, it was almost imperative to proceed from Florence by way of Siena to Rome, to spend at least Holy Week in the Eternal City, to inspect the marvels of Naples, especially the Grotta del Cane, and perhaps make an attempt on Vesuvius; to look in at Loreto; and to arrive in Venice for Ascension when the Doge sailed out on the 'Bucentoro' and cast the symbolic ring into the Adriatic. One then returned home, except between 1618 and 1626,[30] by one of the Grisons passes to Chur and Zürich, or after about 1636 more frequently by the Simplon and Geneva.

There was no standard way of entering Italy. Prior to the outbreak of the Thirty Years' War, it had been not unusual to come by way of Vienna and over the eastern Alps. Coryate crossed the Mont Cenis and entered Italy by Turin. After about 1636 travellers seem to have preferred taking ship from Cannes to Genoa, or approaching by way of Zürich and the Bernina. The Simplon route from Geneva

[28] When young John Harington was touring Tuscany with his tutor Tovey, they avoided passing by Bologna (in Papal territory) precisely for this reason (Stoye, 127); but John Mole, Lord Roos's tutor, was caught about this time, and he died still in prison thirty years later (Bates, 54).

[29] Even Innocent X, who succeeded him in 1644 and was pro-Spanish, does not seem to have wished to molest Protestant visitors.

[30] That is, during the war of the Valtellina.

was also open at this time. When entering Italy and also when passing from one state to another, the traveller had to produce a bill of health ('bolletino di sanità').

The modes of travel in Italy were various. Poor men like Coryate and Lithgow went mostly on foot. In general, however, one hired a horse at one of the Posting-Houses to ride from city to city; or one joined with three or four other travellers to take a coach. In certain districts it was most desirable to travel well-armed and in company. The Papal States and the borderland between those states and the Kingdom of Naples were infested with bandits, and these were and remained quite dangerous regions well on into the nineteenth century. Another mode of travel was to arrange with a Vetturino,[31] who was a kind of courrier and travel-agent, to organize the itinerary, the hiring of horses and vehicles and the payment of hotel expenses (exclusive of wine and extras). As he was responsible for all these items one knew the basic cost in advance. The *Vetturini* are said to have been familiar with the bandits, and to have been able to protect their parties from attack.[32] But arrangements with a Vetturino were mostly practicable only for a rapid 'giro d'Italia'. In many parts of northern Italy, where the Po and some of its tributaries were navigable, it was often easier and safer to travel by water, and such travel was well organized.[33] One could go from Turin to Milan, Bologna or Venice in this way; or from Milan, of course. There was a daily service between Mantua and Ferrara. The lock-system, first developed in Holland, was gradually improved there and in France and Italy, and in Evelyn's time there were a number of locks on the Reno, which linked Bologna and Ferrara. The Brenta canal, nearly empty and stagnant until recently, was then a busy waterway.

Apart from private lodgings and boarding-houses, there were probably one or two or even more good *alberghi* in the great cities. Moryson, in the light of experience, advises those who are staying only for a few days to put up at the best; and few names except those of the best can now be traced. At Turin the 'Rosa Rossa' was popular: Richard Symonds stayed there in 1649 *en pension* for three lire of Turin—probably about 2/6—a day.[34] In Milan the 'Three Kings' was the best known; in Brescia the 'Albergo del Torre'; in

[31] Stendhal used this mode of travel in the early 1800's.

[32] I owe this information to Professor Agapito Rey.

[33] Shakespeare was familiar with all this, though whether he knew of it from the Italian merchants in London or from Villamont's *Voyages* or from common hearsay, we do not know.

[34] See *Travels of Peter Mundy in Europe and Asia*, 1608-1667. Edited by Sir R. C. Temple. Hakluyt Society, I, 235.

Verona, the 'Cavaletto', where Montaigne had lodged and where Peter Mundy, John Evelyn and John Raymond were also to put up.[35] In Padua, as already mentioned, the 'Stella d'Oro'[36] enjoyed a great and no doubt deserved reputation. The main living room, which was presumably the dining-room, was well-heated in winter, as Coryate tells us.[37] In Venice in the middle years of the century, one was well advised to put up at the 'Aquila Nera' near the Rialto, where 'honest Signor Paulo Rhodomants', as Evelyn describes him,[38] could be trusted to look after you. It was the 'Danieli' of the time, though not so agreeably situated. But there had been, and probably still was, a 'Leone bianco' in Venice, and also a 'Sirena Ostriata',[39] with no doubt the picture of a scarlet mermaid hanging over the doorway. Whether it was a house of good repute I cannot say. But Venice possessed many other hotels, such as the 'Luna', bastie comme un palais', according to Villamont (c. 1590) and the 'Cavaletto', both of which were near the Mole; and the 'Specchio' and the 'Storione' which were at the Rialto.[40] In Ferrara the 'Angel' was 'a very noble Palace', and the more notable in Evelyn's eyes, as there were 'not many fine houses in the Citty'.[41] Now if you were faring along the Adriatic coast, you might ask for a room at the Duke of Urbino's inn just outside Sinigaglia. Here were forty bedrooms, each with its own door and none with more than two beds, and five or six salons nobly decorated where you might sit and converse after meals.[42] This place must have been the equivalent of some of the 'palaces' at Cortina d'Ampezzo, now regarded as the pride of the Italian hotel-industry. It was not the only State-hotel. At Radicofani, on the frontier between Tuscany and the Papal States, Ferdinand I had built a fine hostelry which was maintained by his

[35] J. Raymond, *Il Mercurio Italico* . . . London, 1648, 232. Cf. the *Diary of John Evelyn* . . . edited by E. S. de Beer, Oxford, 1955, II, 485.

[36] Peter Mundy says: 'Wee . . . lodged att the Starr in the Piazza de la Paglia, at five livers per man per daye.' That is, about 2/4 or 2/6 in the English currency of the time.

[37] *Crudities*, 1611, p. 153. See below, ch. X.

[38] *Diary*, ed. cit., II, 429.

[39] Bates, 252. But Bates's excellent chapter on European inns in general describes the accommodation available at the beginning of the century, and especially at the time of the Innkepers' International Congress at Rothenburg in 1610.

[40] E. Zaniboni, *Alberghi Italiani e Viaggiatori Stranieri:* sec. XIII-XVIII. Naples, 1921, 35-76. This is the only book I have found on the Italian hotels that existed prior to the early nineteenth century. In the mid eighteenth century the 'Louvre', the 'Mezzaluna' and the 'Regina d'Inghilterra' were all first-class houses (p. 78). When Musset and George Sand stayed at the 'Danieli' (originally the 'Albergo reale') it was new.

[41] *Diary*, II, 428.

[42] Lansdown MS., p. 720, in the British Museum. Cited by Bates, 241.

successors; and many persons travelling between Siena and Rome seems to have taken a meal, if they did not actually put up there.[43] Rome offered ample choice: the 'Two Swords', the 'Orso' and the 'Vasa d'Oro', which seems to have been a luxury-hotel. The curtains hanging above the sumptuous beds were of silk and cloth of gold.[44] In the time of Montaigne one could stay there for twenty *scudi* (silver crowns) a month, or, according to Mr Bates, about £35 in English currency.[45] In the mid-seventeenth century, it was probably far more expensive.[46] But most Englishmen visiting Rome appear to have lodged in a guesthouse, like Monsieur Petit's in the Piazza di Spagna. In Naples, however, you would probably go to the 'Three Kings', which did you splendidly: full pension, wine included, for about a crown a day in the 1640's,[47] that is, something like 5/6; or, because this was very expensive, you might try the 'Aquila Nera'. Turning north again, and reaching Livorno, where bills of exchange and letters of credit could be negotiated, an Englishman would normally be lodged by one of the English merchants; for others the 'Buon Amico' offered accommodation. In Florence, as in Lucca, all the *alberghi* were in the same street and closely supervised by the State.[48] The 'Chiavi d'Oro'[49] was probably the best known in Florence; but the well-to-do citizens were very hospitable, and it was not difficult to find private lodgings. Milton is believed to have been entertained at the Palazzo Gaddi, of which the building still stands in the Via del Giglio, although the gardens behind it, the 'Paradiso dei Gaddi' as they were called, bounded on the north by the Via del Melarancio, have unhappily disappeared.[50]

Any description of the appearance of hotel-rooms and the material amenities—or lack of amenities—which they afforded is largely conjectural. Few travellers thought of saying much about what was generally taken for granted. Small country-inns and even second-class *alberghi* must have been very rough, though less so than in Germany where food, drink and primitive shelter seem to have been the only considerations.[51] But a first-class albergo in Italy was very

[43] Cf. Raymond, 58; Evelyn, II, 207-8.

[44] Bates, 240.

[45] Zaniboni lists many other hotels in Rome, such of the 'Orca', the 'Lupa', the 'Asino', the 'Scudo', etc.

[46] *Ibid.*, 338-9.

[47] Evelyn, *Diary*, II, 325 and note 5.

[48] Bates, 271.

[49] *Ibid.*, 277.

[50] The whole block, or rather triangle, has been built over.

[51] Bates, 242-3. In some German inns, everyone was expected to sleep in the main living-room where they had eaten; they lay about round the 'stube' and endured excessive heat, not to speak of the proximity of undesirable neighbours. One French traveller said that you 'might as well try to sleep in a market-place on market day' (Bates, 242).

attractive;[52] though whether it was better than similar accommodation in England, we do not know.[53] It was probably more refined: the tables were set out with clean white napery, and brightened with flowers and fig-leaves. Italians have always had an eye for beauty. Glasses filled with wine stood ready, placed in water to keep them cool in summer.[54] The host and waiters were smiling and assiduous, and altogether it was very inviting. It gave the wayfarer a sense of the high fitness of things.

He might not, as in France and Flanders, be offered a glass of wine or beer by a pretty maid on alighting from his horse;[55] Italians being less preoccupied with their stomachs than we northerners are. And one imagines that, after he had seen to the accommodation for his horse (which was the first consideration for a decent and intelligent traveller), he would ask to be shown his room. He would usually have a room to himself, or, if the place was busy, and the room was a *camera a due letti*, he might share it with one of his friends or with a stranger whose company he felt he could endure for a few nights. He would rarely, if ever, in a good *albergo*, have to share a bed.[56] And the bed would be provided with sheets and coverlet. It was not, as in Germany, where you were compelled to share a bed, and where your companion might be anything[57] from a margrave to a pedlar.

We will suppose that the traveller now goes down to lunch—or dinner. Few Italians probably took much at midday, but the English, the French and the Germans would be in evidence, and in the evening too, when everyone had a meal. The fare varied a good deal from region to region and it was more sparing than in northern countries, but prepared more attractively. Butter, cheese and no doubt poultry were available in most places, with various salads. In North Italy veal and mutton were the staple dishes. Whether the Milanese were already serving veal cutlets in batter, the Bolognese with toasted cheese, and the Florentines with rosemary, I have not been able to ascertain. Fynes Moryson is the great authority on food, finance and hotels in Italy and most other countries except Spain, and from him, we know that in Padua and Venice one could get mutton, veal, pullets, turkeys, pigeons, eggs and various kinds of fish, including

[52] In Venetia, windows were already glazed in the 1590's, but at Bologna, according to Moryson, they were covered with paper, partly oiled (*Itinerary*, I, ii, 93). The use of glass must, however, have become general, in better-class houses, in the course of the Seicento.

[53] Bates, 244-5.

[54] *Ibid.*, 260.

[55] *Ibid.*, 255.

[56] *Ibid.*, 241.

[57] *Ibid.*, 242. In German inns, where everyone did not sleep in the 'Stube', the bedroom was often a dormitory.

cockles and 'shalops which they call holy cockels';[58] and of course fresh fruit and salad. Were these 'scallops' really *scampi* or *canestrelli*, which are now a specialty of Venetia?—rich in phosphorus and excellent for the metabolism. Beef was not in favour here, for the good reason that butchers were forbidden by law to kill an ox until the poor beast was too old to work. But if you happened to pass by the Lake of Garda, you would find the trout delicious. The food in Tuscany does not seem to have been very different from that of Venetia. When Moryson was in Florence, he bought lamb, mutton, capons, pigeons and a great variety of fruit, which Signor Bevigliano, host of the 'Chiavi d'Oro', caused to be served to him, as he did not take the more expensive *table d'hôte;*[59] but it appears that boar and kid's flesh were the specialties of Tuscany.[60]

Breakfast in Italy, and indeed everywhere on the Continent, was a trifle: a glass of wine and a few small cakes perhaps. An Englishman would save some meat and bread from supper and eat it when he got up next day. The Venetians had brought coffee into western Europe in the later sixteenth century, and there were coffee-houses in Venice after 1640;[61] but it is doubtful whether much coffee was drunk in Italy before the eighteenth century. In the Spanish possessions, and perhaps at Genoa, hot chocolate was probably coming into vogue: the Spaniards imported the cocoa-beans from Mexico. China tea had been spoken of as far back as 1559 by Giambattista Ramusio in his travel-book. The Dutch were the first to import it, towards 1610.[62] A French physician recommended it in a thesis of the Faculty of Medicine and after 1660 it became fashionable in France,[63] and was considered rather smart in England, even a year or two before the Restoration. But the English were mainly coffee-drinkers at that time, and coffee-houses were numerous in London long before cafés were well-established in Paris. Tea never seems to have acquired any vogue in Italy. But a specialty of Italy which some of the travellers may have noticed was the *gelato*; it must have been popular in Rome, Naples and especially in Sicily. It was a Sicilian, Francesco Capelli, known familiarly as Procope, who established the first real café in Paris, in 1689[64] (more than

[58] *Itinerary*, I, i, 70.

[59] *Ibid.*, I, ii, 154-5. Full pension at the 'Chiavi d'Oro' in 1594 was ten crowns a month.

[60] Bates, 259.

[61] *Enciclopedia Italiana*, Milan, 1937, VIII, 258, 262.

[62] *Encyclopaedia Britannica*, XXI, 861-2.

[63] G. Mongrédien, *La Vie quotidienne sous Louis XIV*. Paris, 1948, 85-6. Tea was for some time very expensive.

[64] *Dizionario enciclopedico italiano*. Rome, 1958, IX, 808. It was in the Rue de l'Ancienne Comédie and became very famous as a meeting-place for literati in the eighteenth century.

thirty years after the first coffee-houses had appeared in London) and who also introduced the manufacture of ice-cream.

A pleasant feature of the good inns in Italy was the excellence of the appointments. Not only were the plates of silver—as indeed they were in France and England by the middle of the century—but the drinking vessels were of Venetian glass, and Italy was the only country in Europe where a fork, as well as a knife and spoon, was regularly provided.[65] Fynes Moryson and Coryate both noted the use of forks in Italy.[66]

At the beginning of the century one could probably live in comfort in Italy, and even travel a little, on £60 or £70 a year; towards 1650, £120 or £130 would have been adequate.[67] The cost of living seems to have been lower than in France and England.

[65] Bates, 265-7.

[66] The fork was in use among the higher nobility in France, but not among the well-to-do bourgeoisie, even those who kept a maître-d'hôtel and a large domestic staff, except perhaps in the last years of the century (Mongrédien, 97-8). In England, the fork was still apparently unknown when Magalotti visited London in 1669.

[67] These figures are based on Fynes Moryson's expenses in 1594, and Evelyn's in 1644 and 1645. Evelyn had one or two servants, purchased expensive articles and took lessons, all for less than £300 a year.

CHAPTER IX

The Travel Books:
I - Fynes Moryson

AMONG the writers of travel-books, priority and place of honour belong to Fynes Moryson (1566-1630). None of his successors, except perhaps Raymond, seem to equal him for freshness of outlook, liveliness of style and the variety of personal observations which he gives. His *Itinerary* did not appear until 1617, some years after Coryate's *Crudities* and two years after George Sandys' *Relation of a Journey*; but his travels in Italy antedated theirs by many years and his sojourn there was far more prolonged.

He was a son of Thomas Moryson, M.P. for Great Grimsby, and was educated at Peterhouse where he took his B.A. in 1584 and was elected to a Fellowship towards 1589. Now the statutes of the College permitting two members of the Society to travel, and Moryson's father having apparently agreed to finance a tour abroad, Fynes left England on May 1, 1591[1] and, after visiting many parts of Germany, the United Provinces, Poland, Bohemia and Austria, arrived at Treviso in Venetia at the end of October, 1593. He tells us at this point of the regulation requiring all visitors to Italy to present a health-certificate, or *Bolletino di Sanità*[2]; a certificate also being required when one passed from one Italian state into another. The great heat at the end of October compelled him to take off the 'woollen wasecoat' which he had bought at Dantzig. The horse he was riding and for which he had given eighteen gulders (about £3) in Cracow was less easily disposed of, when he reached Padua. This was truly astonishing, because 'horse-meat was very deere' in that city. The reason was, that the dealers had discovered he was obliged to sell his horse and agreed together to offer him lower and lower

[1] *An Itinerary: Containing His Ten yeeres Travell through the Twelve Dominions of Germany, Bohmerland, Sweitzerland, Netherland, Denmarke, Poland, Italy, Turkey, France, England, Scotland and Ireland.* Ed. Glasgow, 1907, 4 vols. Part I, Book I, p. 2.

The references in this chapter are to the Parts, Books and pages of the first edition (1617), which are given in the margins of the 1907 (Glasgow) edition.

[2] I, i, 68.

prices. In the end, however, he sold the horse for twenty silver crowns, or about £5,[3] to a fellow-countryman who was going to Germany: one of the few deals on record which seems to have been advantageous to both parties.

Moryson spent November and December in Padua, 'in which famous University I desired to perfect my Italian tongue'; and for the purpose of conversation he stayed at a large pension at '8 silver crownes[4] the month' inclusive; but later, in Venice, he paid only four crowns for a room and purchased his own food, which the landlady then prepared for him.[5] His description of Padua is rather brief but as regards the University he mentions that, apart from the study of law, mathematics and music (he should have added medicine and the natural sciences), one could learn to ride, fence and dance under excellent masters. There were eight colleges (presumably, hostels) for poor students, but lectures were given in the central building which 'was of old a publick Inn, having the signe of an Oxe, which name it still retaineth.'[6]

From Padua Moryson proceeded to Venice by taking the horse-drawn boat along the Brenta canal to Fusina, where, at the lock-gates, the passengers disembarked and had a meal. This mode of transport was considered more convenient than the coach:

For the boat is covered with arched hatches, and there is very pleasant company, so a man beware to give no offence: for otherwise the Lumbards carry shirts of Male, and being armed as if they were in a Camp, are apt to revenge upon shamefull advantages. But commonly there is pleasant discourse, and the proverb saith, that the boat shall bee drowned, when it carries neither Monke, nor Student, nor Curtesan . . ., the passengers being for the most part of these kindes. I remember a yong maide in the boat, crossed her selfe whensoever an old woman looked upon her, fearing she should be a witch, whereat the passengers often smiled, seeing the girle not onely crosse her selfe for feare, but thrust her crucifix towards the old womans eyes.[7]

How long Moryson stayed in Venice is not clear: probably three weeks or so. As Venice with its model form of government was the

[3] I, i, 69.

[4] Rather less than £2. In the 'Table for small coins' which precedes the narrative, Moryson says: 'The silver Crowne almost five shillings English, is given for 7 Lires of Venice; two Lires make a Justino: 20 Soldi a Lire: one Lire and 4 Soldi a Mutsenigo.' He also gives details of coins and values for other Italian States.

[5] I, i, 69-70.

[6] I, i, 73.

[7] I, ii, 75.

most admired of all Italian cities, Moryson's 'comments' on it are remarkably thorough,[8] containing as they do an account of its history and topography, a description of St Mark's and its treasures, a survey of the six quarters, or rather 'sextaries', and their churches; and of course of the Doge's Palace, the prisons, the ghetto, and the private palaces; lastly, the names of the principal noble families. In the private houses of the latter, the windows of the larger rooms are open to the air, he tells us, 'but the lodging chambers have glasse windowes, whereof the Venetians brag, glasse being rare in Italy, where the windowes are for the most part covered with linnen or paper.'[9] The interesting observation about glass-windows is obviously his own, and a few of the other details. He no doubt visited all the more important of the buildings described; but the historical information was apparently taken from Leandro Alberti's *Descrittione di tutta l'Italia,* an admirable guide-book that had appeared in 1550, and of which I surmise that Moryson procured the Latin translation, either the first edition (1566) or the 1588 reprint. And this was probably his authority for most of the other cities he visited.

On February 3, 1594 (N.S.)[10] Moryson set out by boat for Ferrara, and proceeded by way of Bologna, Rimini and Ancona to Loreto; thence across the Apennines to Rome. Here he saw so many English priests that he feared he might be recognized by some one or other who had been at Cambridge with him; and so, having 'agreed with a Vetturine at Rome, for forty foure Giulii to give me a horse to Naples, and to pay for my diet and horsemeat', he left almost at once (March, 1594) for Campania.[11] Although he had not been identified and denounced to the Spanish viceroy, it was still a risky enterprise to venture into enemy country, and it must have required considerable nerve to make the round of a number of churches, which he certainly did. In 'the Church of the Monkes of Saint Olivet' he especially admired the lifelike images of Ferdinand I and Alfonso II of Aragon (more attractive in death than they had been when living). 'Perhaps I have seene a more sumptuous monument, but a more beautifull did I never see.'[12] He even penetrated into the garden of the viceroy's palace, where he admired the cage of singing-birds. He noticed that in all the houses, most of them of four storeys, none of the windows were glazed.[13] But he can scarcely have inspected the sights of Naples with an easy mind. He did not attempt to climb

[8] I, ii, 76-90.
[9] I, ii, 89.
[10] I, ii, 90. Moryson insists on the 'new stile' here, 'as the Italians begin the yeere the first of January'.
[11] I, ii, 102-3.
[12] I, ii, 110.
[13] I, ii, 112.

Vesuvius, and his remarks about it are inaccurate.[14] His tour of the country beyond Posilipo was probably rather hurried in places and even perfunctory. He appears to have seen most of the celebrated ruins, classical sites and natural marvels. At the Grotta del Cane he and his companions tried the experiment with the dog, and were unnecessarily cruel. From Cape Misenum they walked along the shore to Cumae, and from there pushed as far as Linturnum, a good sixteen miles from Naples. Here there was only one 'base Inne'. The food was poor, the lodging worse: they could hardly get clean straw to lie on, and they passed a sleepless night. Moryson evidently kept a brief record of this arduous excursion, and afterwards, at home, filled in the historical and other details from Leandro Alberti's guide, which in fact he frequently acknowledges.[15] He could scarcely have done otherwise. But his account of the region is naturally less vivid and personal[16] than that of Sandys, who came here in peace-time, nor does he illustrate it with the delightful woodcuts that Sandys obtained.

Back in Naples, Moryson and 'the other passengers' (some of whom may also have been heretics) made a fresh agreement with the *vetturino* for the return to Rome: not a very favourable one, but it was a matter of Hobson's choice, if I may use the anachronism. In Rome once again, feeling that he could not count on maintaining an incognito much longer, he showed great intelligence in calling upon Cardinal Allen, the head of the English College, in stating who he was and in seeking the Cardinal's protection.[17] This was wise because, since the defeat of the Armada, Allen had changed his policy and was actually protecting English visitors; judging, no doubt rightly, that there was more likelihood of winning over heretics by kindness than by the measures he had previously favoured. Allen did in effect promise his protection; but Moryson feared to trust himself among

[14] 'This Mountaine Somma is most high . . . where is a gulfe casting out flames . . .' After mentioning the catastrophe of 79 A.D., he adds: 'It brake out again the yeere 1538 . . .' (I, ii, 110). Vesuvius and not Somma was the higher at that time, and it was very little active, except through a few vents in the upper part of the crater. The latter was then a deep gulf, luxuriant with grass and trees (see below, p. 176). The eruption of 1538 was by the Lago Lucrino, and it threw up the Monte Nuovo: it does not seem to have affected Vesuvius.

[15] He refers to it simply as 'Leander'.

[16] I, ii, 113-121. For this reason I defer a more detailed commentary to the chapter on Sandys. The latter not only did not labour here under the same difficulties as Moryson, but he had the advantage of being able to use Capaccio's up-to-date description of Naples and probably one or two other recent books. When Evelyn visited the region (1645) and described it, he used Sandys', and several other works, but not apparently Moryson's.

[17] I, ii, 121.

the crowd of English Catholics who would probably have tried to engage him in controversy. So he quietly and secretly, in company with 'two honest Dutch gentlemen' (German Calvinists), took a lodging near the Vatican,[18] where they would be least likely to be supposed living, and from here he visited the sights of Rome. Before leaving, he had the temerity to call upon Cardinal Bellarmine, introducing himself as a French Catholic; but immediately afterwards he departed on horseback, with his German friends, for Tuscany.

They reached Florence on Easter Sunday, and the next morning Moryson set out alone on foot for Pisa.[19] Here he spent a fortnight, very happily, meeting another English gentleman, 'Mr T. H.', and apparently conversing with the professors at the University.[20] He then returned on horseback to Florence. His impressions of the city were far more favourable than those of Wotton, who had been there a little earlier and said it was inhabited by devils. According to Moryson Florence was not only 'a most sweet City' but 'the Citizens are much commended for their curtesie, modesty, gravity, purity of language, and many virtues.'[21] He desired nevertheless to settle for a time near Siena and there study at the University and learn Italian really well; only, as there were many English and Germans at Siena, he thought it prudent to feel his way, and linger at first in the inn at San Casciano.[22] Here he met a certain Nicolao della Rocca, for whom he conceived great esteem and affection. In a letter of July 23, 1594, to 'T.H.', his English friend at Pisa, he related the adventures of a compatriot named 'W. M.', who had visited Rome in the guise of a Switzer. He had just returned to Florence when he was followed by a message from the Inquisition ordering his arrest; but a friend at the Grand Duke's court having warned him of this, he 'presently tooke him to his heeles towards Paduoa, in such haste, as hee seemed to flie over the Apennine without wings. And now (God be praised) hee is in safetie . . . I cannot hold from laughing, when I imagin . . . what large steppes he makes over the rockey Mountaines.'[23]

Moryson appears to have gone back to Florence early in August, in order to draw money, after which he took horse to Siena[24], and here he seems to have remained, studying Italian and enjoying the social amenities of the place, for upwards of three months. Although,

[18] I, ii, 141

[19] I, ii, 144.

[20] I, ii, 146. Galileo was at this time in Padua.

[21] I, ii, 147.

[22] 8 miles from Florence, on the road to Siena.

[23] I, ii, 159. It appears from this letter that both he and 'T.H.' had been reading the *Orlando furioso*.

[24] I, ii, 162. From here he wrote, on August 10th, to Nicolao della Rocca, admitting that he was an Englishman and that his German incognito had been adopted owing to England's being at war with Spain.

oddly enough, he does not speak of the stupendous Torre del Mangia,[25] or 'Lily Tower' as it is more elegantly styled, he does mention the 'statue of mixt mettal' which 'strikes the houre of the clock' and from which the tower derived its name; but he thought the Duomo, whose party-coloured marble seems so strange to modern eyes, 'the fairest church in Italy'. Finally, on November 18th, he rode to Lucca, stopping on the way at Castel Certaldo to see Boccaccio's grave; then again to Pisa; and then to Lerici, after inspecting the marble quarries at Massa Carrara and marvelling at the beauty of the men and women in those parts.

At Lerici[26] Moryson and some other travellers hired a felucca for Genoa. The voyage was to prove eventful. High seas drove them upon the rocks of the great headland beyond Portofino and they were obliged to clamber on hands and knees to the top of that mountainous promontory, and then to walk many miles to the nearest village. Early next morning they went forward on foot to Genoa, passing on the way a village which had recently been sacked and burned by Barbary pirates; the latter having carried off as a slave to Africa a young bride who had been married the day before[27]—one of many examples of the slave-raids that were conducted for centuries from north Africa.

Moryson's description of Genoa is relatively brief, but his admiration corresponds with that of later travellers. True, he quotes the proverbial saying about *uomini senza fede, donne senza vergogna,* etc., but it is clear that he himself found nothing to complain of. The costs of food and lodging were moderate. Private palaces were open to visitors, in return of course for a gratuity to the servant. He did not 'thinke that any City in the world hath so faire a streete' as the Strada Nuova. The thoroughfares are narrow, 'the Pallaces are stately built of marble, and the other houses of free stone, five or six stories high, and the windows are glased, which is rare in Italy. The streetes are paved with flint . . . Now in the very moneth of December, the markets were full of summer flowers, herbes, and fruits . . .' Owing to the steep hillside on which Genoa is built, transport was effected not by coach, but by 'horse litters' and 'seggioli', the latter being in effect sedan-chairs, furnished with glass windows and curtains, and borne by two porters.[28]

From Genoa, Moryson set out, still on foot, for Lombardy. It was a tiring journey over the mountains and he was not sorry to find

[25] I.e. The Tower of the Swaggerer, the latter being the figure which, something like 'I Mori' in the Torre del Orologio at Venice, came into action to strike the hours.

[26] Where he saw the Cardinal de Joyeuse who was waiting for a boat (I, ii, 165).

[27] I, ii, 166.

[28] I, ii, 166-168.

himself in 'the fruitful plaine' of the Milanese when, on the third day, he reached Voghera. Here he sat at supper with an English merchant who was posing as a German—a frequent subterfuge at this time (Wotton had already adopted it)—but whose true nationality Moryson quickly penetrated.[29] The inn where he put up at Pavia, though of good appearance, proved 'common to the baser sort' and the ruffians who came in late to drink so alarmed him that he resolved 'to lodge ever after in the best Inne, and of best fame'. After a 'short stay at Milan, for the danger of my abode there', he hired a horse to carry him to Cremona, where he was naturally most impressed by the 'Tower'. This, he tells us, 'is built of bricke, and hath foure hundred ninetie and two staires in the ascent.'[30] The 'Torrazzo', which is the bell-tower of the Cathedral, is still in fact the pride of the city.

Moryson does not speak of any relief he felt on leaving Spanish territory and riding into the Duchy of Mantua, but it is clear from the precautions he had taken when entering Milan, from the way in which he had made himself as inconspicuous as possible, that the consequences of detection would have been serious. In Mantua which was still independent he was safe enough; and here he visited 'the Dukes stately Pallace . . . compassed with water, where in the Giants Chamber I did see most faire pictures'.[31] After describing the extraordinary privileges which are enjoyed in Mantua (and in Savoy) by the Jews and which they 'have gotten by bribing . . . through the unsatiable avarice, of our Christian Princes', he mentions the interesting and curious fact that 'It is unlawful to weare a sword without licence of the Magistrate, either at Milan, Cremona, Mantua, or almost in any citie of Italy; only at Venice and Paduoa, and the cities of that State, strangers may wear Swords, and onely the wearing of Pistols or short gunnes is forbidden'.[32]

He was back in Padua on December 14th, and it was probably soon after this that he obtained at the University the certificate of matriculation which served as a passport through the territory of the Republic and exempted him from the payment of tolls and dues. This was the second winter he had spent in Padua. It gave him the

[29] I, ii, 169.

[30] I, ii, 172. It was built in the thirteenth century and is about 484 feet high.

[31] The 'Sala dei Giganti' is one of the great saloons in the Palazzo del Te, which was magnificently decorated with frescoes by Giulio Romano and his pupils. The paintings in the Giants' Room are not to our mind as attracitve as those in the charming 'Sala dei Cavalli' and the 'Sala di Psiche', but they are astonishing for the virtuosity displayed in the technique of perspective and *trompe l'oeil.*

[32] I, ii, 173.

opportunity of going to Venice to draw money from his account there;[33] but not needing to draw it all, and finding, as he says, no 'Merchant of Venice' who could transfer the balance to Paris, owing to the chaos then prevailing through the civil war, he decided to have a credit opened for him in Geneva. Once he went on foot to Arquà to see Petrarch's house and tomb, pausing on the way at Abano where he marvelled at the heat of the medicinal springs. Finally he purchased a horse—unfortunately a stallion—and on March 3, 1595 (N.S.), he rode off to Vicenza, admiring as he went the richly cultivated plain, the lines of pollarded elms supporting the vines, with the corn growing between them. He scarcely lingered in Vicenza, except to see Palladio's famous theatre—though not the Rotonda—but pressed on to Verona. Here the splendid churches, the girdle of walls and the ancient amphitheatre greatly impressed him, as did the 'nobility of the Citizens, who are indued with a chearefull countenance, magnificent mindes, and much inclined to all good literature'. Moryson combined a knowledge of ancient and medieval history which would do credit to Baedeker,[34] with a great capacity for enjoying all the good things that came his way. He speaks in this connexion of Catullus, of the Lombard and other barbarian kings who had the honour of being killed at Verona, of the Scaligeri and of the poet Guarini; and dwells with particular relish on the local wines, and notably on the 'Retian', which was 'praised by Pliny, and preferred to the wine of Falernum by Virgill'. It was a red dessert wine, sweet and 'thicke'.[35] And it is pleasant also to read that on the southern shores of the Lago di Garda he not only enjoyed the excellent fish, but—a thing rare among the travellers I have studied—the beauty of the landscape, his journey being 'in a most sweet plaine, rising still higher with faire distances'.[36]

Between Brescia and Bergamo, the country was pleasant but the temperature, even at this season, such that he 'could hardly indure the heat'; and now, as he was on his way to Geneva, he decided not to take the direct route by the Simplon, which would involve passing through the Milanese, but to find his way alone to Chur, first over the Bergamasque Alps into the Valtellina and thence through the country of the Grisons—a bold enterprise for one unaided by a guide. Moryson had always taken great care of his horses and he rarely fails to tell us how much he paid for their fodder; but this one proved troublesome and dangerous as well as expensive, because all

[33] He had presumably deposited a letter of credit during the previous winter.

[34] He may have used one or two books in addition to Alberti's, and he also gathered information by word of mouth.

[35] I, ii, 175-176.

[36] I, ii, 177.

the travellers he passed were riding mares and on the mountain-tracks he was obliged to dismount and lead his stallion by the bridle; in spite of which 'he was so fierce, as I could hardly keepe him from falling down most steepe mountaines, or from being drowned in the snow, which made me repent the buying of him, though otherwise he was richly worth my money'.[37]

But this is to anticipate the excitements of Alpine travel in the Spring of 1595. From Bergamo he had taken the road running north-east to Lovere,[38] at the head of the Lago d'Iseo, where he had his horse 'shod with eight sharpe and three blunt nailes'—a wise precaution in view of the tribulations ahead. The next day he rode up the Val Camonica, passing under the gigantic precipices of the glacier-crowned Adamello, of which he says nothing, and arrived towards nightfall at Edolo, where he slept. And now began the ascent to Aprica (which he calls 'Auryga') 'and now I beganne to freeze, for cold'. It was by this route, some thirty years later that the Venetians were to bring troops and artillery to the aid of their allies in the Grisons. The Venetian frontier lay just beyond Aprica, and from here Moryson descended to Tirano on the Adda and began the long ascent by Poschiavo to the Bernina Pass. The upper Engadine was of course still deep in snow, and the horse gave him frequent occasion for alarm. He saw many avalanches falling, and when near a place he calls 'Lanzi'[39] and some fifteen miles from Chur, heard 'more than a hundred Woolves howling', apparently 'busie about a prey'.

The rest of his journey by way of Zürich and Lausanne to Geneva, and his tribulations in war-time France, do not concern us. Suffice it to say that he was able to draw money in Geneva,[40] and sewed it in the quilting of his doublet; while the money he received at Metz from the sale of his horse was cunningly secreted in his baggage. Thus when some disbanded soldiers robbed him of the former, he still had something to fall back upon.[41]

Moryson reached London in May, 1595, some two months after leaving Padua; but in November of the same year he with his younger brother Henry set out on a journey to Jerusalem. They travelled by way of Innsbruck, then over the Brenner to Trent, and so on to Treviso and Venice, where they left their swords, daggers

[37] I, ii, 178-179.

[38] Which he calls 'Louer'.

[39] I, ii, 179. Perhaps Landquart (certainly not Ilanz). This suggests that instead of crossing the Albula and going down by Filisur and Thusis, he descended the Prätigau by way of Klosters.

[40] Here he 'had great contentment' in conversing with Théodore de Bèze whose 'affabitie and gravity . . .extorted reverence' and whom he accompanied to Church (I, ii, 181).

[41] I, ii, 185.

and European clothes with a merchant from whom they would collect them on their return. Having then fallen in with some pleasant Frenchmen they all took berths on a Greek ship sailing for the East.[42]

Fynes Moryson was one of the most intelligent and informative of our travellers prior to the eighteenth century, or even the nineteenth. His narrative is more readable than Evelyn's and less burdened with erudition. The great knowledge he had acquired of Germany and parts of eastern Europe enable him to place in better focus his picture of Italy—

Italy worthily called the Queene of Nations, can never be sufficiently praised, being most happy in the sweet Ayre, the most fruitfull and pleasant fields, warme sunny hils, hurtlesse thickets, shaddowing groves, Havens of the Sea, watering brookes, baths, wine and oyle for delight . . .[43]

Not, however, that he is uncritical. The laws and government of the Swiss Confederation inspire higher praise than those of other countries, and he notes how safe it is to travel in Switzerland.[44]

Very little seems to have escaped his observation. He describes buildings, though rarely in much detail, mentions relics and occasionally pictures and statues. He is perhaps deficient in a feeling of art, but this defect is compensated by the compendious nature of his narrative and by its proportion and balance. He kept an account of practically everything he spent, and if he has a fault it is in giving too many details of the price of commodities, the charges at inns and the cost of board and lodging in hired chambers. Yet even this is of great value to the economic historian. Only a complete analysis would do justice to his book: it is concise, well written, shrewd, sober, and yet full of human touches and flashes of fun.

Chapter V of the third Part of his work[45] contains an account of the geographical aspects of Italy, of its agriculture and commerce, of the diet of the people and of the inns.

Modes of travel, being partly a matter of taste, are treated of in the *Itinerary* proper, in Part I. Moryson himself usually bought a

[42] I, iii, 198-207. He explains the great desire he had had 'from my tender youth' to see 'forraine Countries' as due, not to any need for liberty, of which he had had plenty at Cambridge, but in order to improve his understanding by means of experience.

[43] III, ii, 105.

[44] III, iv, 261.

[45] This is contained in Vol. IV of the Maclehose reprint of the *Itinerary* (Glasgow, 1908).

horse and sold it later; but sometimes he hired a horse from one of the Post Masters or from a carrier, and sometimes he went on foot, or by river-boat. He notes, as regards diet, that 'the Italians generally compared with English or French, are most sparing'; but when they do make a feast it is sumptuous. 'A stranger may live in Italy with less expence, than in Germany, where he must beare the charge of his consorts excessive drinking.' The nature and quantity of food eaten in different parts of Italy of course vary; but except for the Milanesi who 'live plentifully', it is moderate in the extreme. 'The Padoans sup with halfe a peniworth of fish. The Venetians live sparingly,' and so on. 'The Florentines are of spare diet, but wonderfull cleanlinesse. Those of Lucca keepe golden mediocritie in all things.'[46] In cities where there are many Germans, who do not like the trouble of buying their own food, one can eat at an ordinary and pay by the week or month. Moryson, as we have seen, found it advantageous to purchase his 'vittles' and have his landlady prepare them: this seems to have been a regular custom in Venetia[47] and Tuscany. In places where there are boarding-houses, 'they eate at a common table, but each man hath his owne meat provided, the Hostesse dressing it, and serving each man with his own napkin, glasse,[48] forke, spoone, knife, and ingestar or glasse of wine, which after meate are severally and neately laid up by the hostesse'.[49]

If, however, the traveller, arriving in a strange city, intends to spend only a day or two, he should select the best inn available. The hosts are excessively courteous and sometime extortionate, but this, Moryson points out, was excusable because they were mulcted and almost 'devoured' by licenses and taxes. Charges in Florence, however, were reasonable. Moreover one could eat 'al conto', that is, à la carte, and by having a little bread and wine during the day and taking a good supper at the ordinary, manage very well. Italian inns generally, and Florentine inns in particular, offer clean and attractive dining-rooms, the tables spread with white linen and adorned with flowers, while each guest is provided 'with a forke of silver or other mettall', because 'they touch no meate with the hand'—one of the first mentions of the fork in English literature, the thing being then unknown in England and not coming into use with us until, I

[46] III, ii, 113.

[47] 'The very Gentlemen of Venice,' who claim pre-eminence above all others in Italy (having 'the singular title of Clarissimi), carry home what they buy to eate, either in the sleeves of their gownes, or in a clean handkercher' (III, ii, 114).

[48] Pewter was still in general use in England; but our windows, unlike most windows in Italy, were glazed—though not with plate-glass.

[49] III, ii, 116.

think, the end of the seventeenth century.[50]

Taking the country as a whole and with due allowance for the attractions of Venetia,

In the State of Florence, and especially at Sienna, a stranger may live more commodiously, then in any other part of Italy, because the inhabitants are most curteous (so as at Sienna they admit strangers to converse and dance with the chiefe Gentlewomen of the Citie), and because the language, especially at Sienna, is held the most pure, as also for that victuals are very cheape, and strangers neede not stand in feare of being murthered, as in Lombardy they doe.[51]

Moryson gives the impression that the amenities of Tuscany and Venetia, if not of other regions, were the most elegant and best adapted to personal idiosyncracy of any in Europe. They were certainly the most refined. But he insists elsewhere that there is no hospitality like English, and no inns where you can get better service for man and beast than an English inn—where you can eat in the public room or be served in your bedroom, as you wish.

In his account of Italian 'Husbandry' Moryson praises the economical use that is made of the land in fertile Lombardy and Venetia by the variety of fruit- and nut-trees that are grown, by the sowing of corn between the lines of olive- or almond-trees, or of the elms that support the vine-plants, and by the rotation of crops.[52] The discussion of Industry leads him to commend the Italian nobility for being exempt from the prejudice of taking part in it:

Not onely the Gentlemen, but even the Princes of Italy openly professe to be Merchants . . . and onely permit the retailing of their goods to men of inferiour sort . . . And by this course they keepe the Patrimonies discending from their Ancestors, and daily increase them (while our Gentlemen prodigall in expence, and ashamed to make honest gaine, destroy their families).[53]

He explains in this connexion that the silk-trade is a source of considerable wealth to the Tuscan nobility, and he describes the habits of the silk-worm and the technique of its cultivation.

[50] When Cosimo II of Tuscany visited London in 1669, the fork was still not in use on the tables of the nobility or even apparently at Court.

[51] III, ii, 115.

[52] III, ii, 109.

[53] III, ii, 111.

8. *The Lago di Agnano, near Naples* See pp. 178, 196

9. *Title-page of the first edition of George Sandys: A Relation of a Journey*

There were in Fynes Moryson[54] the makings of a radical—of the Tory kind. Elsewhere, in describing the preparations which he and his young brother Henry made in the autumn of 1595 for their journey to Jerusalem, he inveighs warmly against the 'droit d'aînesse'. Henry had used most of his patrimony to finance this venture. It was a custom at that time, as already mentioned, for a man about to travel to places from which the chances of return were extremely doubtful, to pay £x to some friend or kinsman on the express understanding that if he died abroad they should retain the money but that if he returned they should repay him £3x.[55] While considering this a fair arrangement, as it probably was, Fynes deprecated the legal situation which had given rise to it. Speaking of his brother who had paid out £400 on these terms, he remarks:

I say he had thus put out the most part of his small estate, which in England is no better with Gentlemens younger sonnes, nor so good, as with bastards in other places, as well for the English Law most unmeasurably favouring elder brothers, as (let me boldly say it) for the ignorant pride of fathers, who to advance their eldest sonnes, drive the rest to desperate courses, and make them unable to live, or to spend any money in getting understanding and experience . . .[56]

Add to this of course the prejudice against a gentleman's taking a hand in trade, and one understands why so many thousands of young Englishmen were virtually compelled to become soldiers of fortune, serving under the French, the Dutch or the Venetians. But not only was this prejudice rare in Tuscany and northern Italy, though it existed in the south, but the Italians had a better eye to the future in other ways. They more often put 'their money in stable things, to serve their posteritie', rather than into their stomachs.[57] It is fair, however, to add that Moryson considers English habits are improving, albeit slowly, and that in spite of the above remark—for he has a sense of *nuances* and frequently qualifies his observations—he defends his countrymen against the charge of gluttony.

He was decidedly a Protestant, without fanaticism but not with-

[54] Was he a younger son? I have not been able to ascertain. One of his brothers, Sir Richard Moryson, was four or five years younger than he; and Henry must have been younger still. When Fynes, who had been robbed in Lorraine, was stranded in Paris without money in April, 1595, he was fortunate in meeting the Danvers brothers who knew Sir Richard and who, though nearly penniless themselves, procured for Fynes the means of obtaining enough cash for his purpose (I, ii, 195).

[55] See above p. 140. The rate of interest might be even higher. The bitterness of Fynes's remarks is understandable. Both he and Henry fell sick of dysentery when in Syria and Henry died there.
tery when in Syria and Henry died there.

[56] I, iii, 198. [57] III, ii, 113.

out a touch of disrespect for Catholic beliefs. He plainly disbelieved the miracle of the House of the Virgin at Loreto, which he discusses at great length. Yet he showed considerable outward decorum[58] on this and other occasions, behaving in Rome much as the Romans did. The religious situation as it affected Protestant visitors, he places in clear focus. The Milanese and the Kingdom of Naples, governed as they were by Spanish viceroys, were extremely dangerous; the Papal States quite dangerous unless the visitor placed himself under the protection of the English College; Tuscany relatively safe, and the Venetian territories perfectly safe—provided of course that one showed no disrespect for the Catholic Church. It is clear that Venice was more tolerant than Elizabeth's England, or James I's, or than the Commonwealth.

One takes leave of Moryson—an attractive soul—with real regret. After his sorrowful return from the East in 1597, he paid a visit to Edinburgh (1598) and then, taking shelter with his sisters who were married to Lincolnshire gentlemen, began to arrange his travel notes. In July, 1600, he resigned his Fellowship at Peterhouse. He seems now, as at other times, to have been anxious about his financial future, which suggests that the father's estate had gone to the eldest son, though who the latter was we do not know. However that may be, Richard (born c. 1571) who had a good position in Ireland and later became Vice-President of Munster, suggested that Fynes should try his fortune there. He therefore in November, 1600, joined Richard in Ireland and served under Charles Blount, the Lord Deputy, until 1606. (His experiences there, in the time of Tyrone's rebellion, are described in Part II of his book.) He then continued to work on the narrative of his travels, and one gathers that, prior at least to 1617, he had 'enjoyed, though no abundant, yet a competent estate, and more plentiful then in my former dayes' (I, ii, 100). After this we do not even know where he lived—probably with one of his sisters. He died on February 12, 1630 N.S. (D.N.B.).[59]

[58] But not real decorum. By the shrine at Loreto stood an iron alms' chest covered with a grating. When his fellow-travellers threw in a handful of small coins, Moryson, observing that some of these remained on the top of the grating, secretly purloined them (I, ii, 100). But in describing this exploit he felt it necessary to explain and excuse himself and to add: 'yet after that, God of his mercy preserved me in my long and dangerous travell'. The best that can be said of a trick sufficiently harmless and trivial is what Mrs Trevelyan remarks: 'I suppose it satisfied his primitive sporting instinct' (*Wandering Englishmen in Italy*, *op. cit.*, 68).

[59] Moryson appears to have devoted many years to writing a history of all the countries where he had travelled, but in the end he destroyed this manuscript and confined himself to composing the narrative of travel which we now have. It was first written in Latin, then translated into English, and remains, as we have seen, one of the most valuable documents of the age.

CHAPTER X

Thomas Coryate

THOMAS CORYATE (1577-1617) appeared, outwardly at least, as fantastic as Fynes Moryson was cool and level-headed. 'He carried folly . . . in his very face,' wrote Fuller. 'The shape of his head had no promising form, being like a sugar-loaf inverted.' It contained none the less a great deal of Greek and Latin, and its owner had, besides, many likeable and even estimable qualities. Unfortunately he lent himself to ridicule. His father had been rector of Odcombe in Somerset, and the very name of 'Od-combe' carried irresistible suggestions to the wits whose society Tom frequented at the Mermaid in Bread Street. For a time he had been connected with the Court, but on May 14, 1608, he left Dover for a walking tour of the Continent, which took him through France, northern Italy, the Grisons, Switzerland and the Rhineland. On his return home he dedicated his shoes, or what remained of them, as a votive-offering in his father's church.

Coryats Crudities Hastily gobbled up in five Moneths travells in France, Savoy, Italy . . . Newly digested in the hungry aire of Odcombe . . . and now dispersed to the nourishment of the travelling Members of this Kingdome was published in 1611. It is half travel-diary, half guide-book. He had consigned to it not merely his personal experiences but everything he could discover about the cities and regions in question; and he also copied and inserted all the Latin inscriptions he saw: 654 pages, not counting the letter of dedication to Prince Henry and some hundred pages of 'panegyrick verses', mostly facetious, by sixty notable wits and writers. To analyse such a work is difficult.[1] There is a vast and pedantic amount of historical lore and detailed description of buildings and works of art; but it was Coryate's observations on men, women and manners, and especially his misadventures, that entertained his readers.

[1] There is an excellent analysis by Piero Rebora: 'Un eccentrico viaggiatore inglese del primo Seicento' in *English Miscellany*, Rome, 1951, No. 2, pp. 85-93. I take this opportunity of expressing my sense of obligation to Professor Rebora who gave me a copy of this article and a good deal of other material relating to the seventeenth century. I have examined the *Crudities* anew, in the Maclehose, Glasgow, edition of 1905, 2 vols., and my references are to the first, 1611, edition, of which the pagination is indicated in that of 1905.

For the journey between Lyons and Turin he made arrangements with a Vetturino, who provided horses; but on the descent from the Mont Cenis (June 11th) he walked for some seven miles down the steep, winding track, marvelling to see the amount of traffic, both of foot-passengers and baggage-mules.[2] He was also, when approaching Susa, struck by the altitude of the Roche Melon which the guide told him was fourteen miles high.[3] After spending a day in Turin, he took the coach for Novara, and a few days later was in Milan. The view from the roof of the Duomo inspired transports of admiration. This was indeed 'the garden of Italy':

The territory . . . was so plesant an object to my eyes, being replenished with such unspeakable variety of all things . . . that it seemeth to me to be the very Elysian fields . . . For it is the fairest plaine . . . that ever I saw . . . insomuch that I said to myselfe that this country was fitter to be an habitation for the immortall Gods than for mortall men.[4]

There was a certain temerity in passing through the Milanese because, though England and Spain were no longer at war, the Viceroy was still apt to be unpleasant. Young Lord Cranborne who visited Milan this same year met with a frigid, if not alarming, reception. Even the humble Coryate narrowly escaped violence from a Spaniard; and he speaks of the 'extreme hatred' that existed 'betwixt the Milanois and the Spaniards' who manned the citadel;[5] the Milanesi having by no means forgotten their former freedom and prosperity.

From Milan he travelled on horseback by way of Cremona and Mantua to Padua, which he reached on June 20th. During his three days in Padua he slept and ate at 'the signe of the Starre . . . being a very faire Inne', and here he was greatly impressed by the 'Stove', a mode of heating he saw nowhere else in Italy, though it was common in Switzerland.[6] Everyone in Padua seems to have assisted him, not only the compatriots he met, a Dr Moore and a Mr Willoughby, 'a learned student in the University',[7] and George Rooke who was

[2] Which was to be expected, since this was one of the principal routes, if not *the* principal, between the old capital at Chambéry and the present capital at Turin.

[3] Ed. 1611, pp. 79-80.

[4] *Ibid.*, p. 99.

[5] P. 105.

[6] P. 153.

[7] Pp. 156-7. Pearsall Smith (*Wotton*, II, 114) identified this 'Mr Willoughby' with Richard Willoughby whom Wotton described to Sir Ralph Winwood as 'an infectious Papist' (Letter of May 5th, 1617). But this Willoughby was already in 1608 an elderly man and can hardly have been described as a student.

attached to the embassy in Venice; but a Frenchman and an Italian scholar from Vicenza who helped him to interpret the difficult inscriptions. It was Willoughby who showed him what were considered the principal sights of the place; but one notices here, as in the observations of many other travellers, that these did not include the Scrovegni Chapel with the frescoes by Giotto or the Church of the Eremitani with Mantegna's masterpieces. Coryate was impressed by the Botanical Garden where the plane-tree (then unknown in England) and the Pistachio-tree caught his attention;[8] but he confesses he neglected to visit the 'Colleges' of the University and saw only the outside of 'Il Bo'.[9]

Leaving Padua about June 23rd, he travelled by boat down the Brenta canal to Fusina, whence 'I saw Venice . . . which yeeldeth the most glorious and heavenly shew upon the water that ever any mortal eye beheld'.[10] And in Venice he remained until August 8th. The description of the city occupies one hundred and thirty pages of his book, and this is indicative of the fascination which the place then exercised over Englishmen. Though it is not possible that he saw everything, it is unlikely that, with George Rooke to guide him, he missed much. The new bridge at the Rialto, St Mark's, the Doge's Palace, even the great paintings of Tintoretto, all and much else are described and admired. He tells us about the 'Chapineys', shoes worn by ladies of rank, so high that the wearer had usually to be supported on each side by attendants.[11] But what most amused Coryate's readers was the part descriptive of the courtesans, especially 'their nobler Cortezans', and the picture he solemnly inserted of himself most respectfully meeting 'Margarita Emiliana'. This was perhaps the lady of whom he wrote that in her Palace he 'did . . . heare her talk, observe her fashion of life, and yet was nothing contaminated therewith, nor corrupted in manner'. We can take him seriously in this matter, whatever his friends may have thought. She was probably, like some of the ancient *hetairai*, a woman of culture and decorum. He even tried to convert her, though without the success that Paphnutius had had with Thais. He also visited the Ghetto and tried to convert the Jews. 'Many vehement speeches' were passing 'to and fro' between himself and a Rabbi, when a crowd of some forty or fifty gathered round, whose attitude became so alarming that he began to edge away towards the bridge over the canal. Worse might have happened, had not Sir Henry Wotton been passing at that moment in his gondola and sent his secretary 'who conveighed me safely from these unchristian miscreants'.[12] The 'Observations of

[8] Coryate, p. 149.
[9] P. 153.
[10] P. 157.
[11] P. 282.
[12] Pp. 236-37.

Venice' conclude on a graver note. The Republic was being supported at this time in its struggle with the Papacy by England and France, and it gave Coryate 'great . . . comfort' on the day he left to see displayed in the Piazza San Marco a large portrait of James I; and at the Rialto Bridge another picture of James with Queen Anne and Prince Henry on one side and Henri IV of France on the other —'a thing that ministered singular contentment unto me'.[13]

Back in Padua on August 9th, he was invited to dinner by Lord Wentworth[14] and two days later was in Vicenza. In this 'faire citie' (Coryate would not have exaggerated if he had called it the most splendid small city in the world) two young men took charge of him and one of them spent almost the whole day in showing him the sights[15]—the Piazza della Signoria with its 'Tower of a marveilous heigth . . . but so exceeding slender that I never saw any Tower in all my life so high of such a slendernesse'; the Villa Valmarana on the spur of the Colli Berici; the Rotonda which then belonged to Count Capra and to which visitors were admitted (Coryate was somewhat aggrieved that the cellarer here did not offer him wine);[16] and Palladio's Theatre where the Russian ambassadors to Rome had not long before been entertained.[17]

On foot between Vicenza and Verona he was overtaken by a thunderstorm and soaked 'to the very skinne'. In Verona the Roman amphitheatre came near monopolising his attention:[18] here as elsewhere he was more interested in ancient history than in the medieval chronicles that fascinated Shakespeare. But he did visit the famous Giardino dei Giusti, whose terraces dominate the town and afford the loveliest panorama—a 'second Paradise', writes Coryate . . . 'a passing delectable place of solace'. He was not apparently impressed by the beauty of the Lake of Garda but he was—between Brescia and Bergamo—by the 'abundance of goodly Vineyards' where the grapes were ripe and

> passing faire and sweete. For I did oftentimes borrow a point of the law in going into their Vineyards without leave, to refreshe myselfe . . . Which the Italians like very good fellowes did winke at, shewing themselves more kinde unto me then the Germans did afterward in Germany . . .[19]

[13] P. 289.

[14] If this was Sir Thomas Wentworth, fourth Baron Wentworth and first Earl of Cleveland (1591-1667), then he was a very young man at this time.

[15] P. 304.

[16] P. 303.

[17] P. 299.

[18] Its great size alone is impressive. It seats 22,000 people and is in regular use today for the production of opera in July and August.

[19] P. 341.

It so chanced that he reached Bergamo at the time of the great fair; the inns were packed and it was only through the good offices of a priest that he was allowed 'to lye upon straw in one of their stables at the horses feete'. On preparing to leave for the Grisons he was referred to a Dominican friar who had been chaplain to the Venetian embassy at Chur. This friar, who saw at once that Coryate was English, strongly advised him to avoid the Spanish fort at the head of the Lake of Como, since, if arrested there, he would be handed over to the Inquisition.[20] And it seems clear at this point that, like Moryson before him, he was advised to take the road up the Val Camonica, which led directly from Venetian territory into that of the Grisons.

The road across the Bergamasque Alps was infested by brigands of whom, fortunately for Coryate, some thirty had been captured a few days before. At an inn where he slept,[21] he encountered an Italian Protestant from Chiavenna who had lived for some time near Cambridge in the service of Sir Horatio Pallavicino, the famous banker. This man 'spake pretty good English' and treated him to 'a cup of excellent wine'.[22] On the next day he descended into the Valtellina and so out of Venetian territory. The remainder of his journey by way of Chiavenna[23] and the Splügen concerns us less.

Though not a well-balanced man, Coryate was a scholar and an open-eyed observer. Speaking of the help he received from the two gentlemen of Vicenza, he adds: 'For surely many Italians are passing courteous and kinde towards strangers . . . Therefore I will ever magnifie and extoll the Italian for as courteous a man to a stranger as any man whatsoever in Christendome'.[24] He seems to have conversed in Latin with most of the gentlemen he met, and he noted in this connexion that everyone in Italy and elsewhere on the Continent pronounced the long i (as in *Vita, Amicus*) as 'ee'. He concluded that this had been the Roman pronunciation and determined to use it himself.[25] Even Natural History appealed to him. He speaks of the swarms of butterflies in Savoy; of the mosquitoes, 'those angry flies called cimices which . . . did very much offend me' in Bergamo. 'They will shrewdly bite a mans skinne.'[26] The material amenities of Italy are noted in detail. Thus one was required to use a fork in order to hold the joint while one cut off one's portion. A man who

[20] Pp. 350-52.

[21] Probably at Edolo or on the Aprica Pass.

[22] Pp. 355, 359.

[23] Note that, unlike so many—perhaps the majority—of travellers, he did not take the Bernina route; and that it was possible to reach Chiavenna without being stopped by the garrison at Fort Fuentes.

[24] P. 304.

[25] P. 353.

[26] P. 352.

held the meat with his hand was regarded as transgressing 'the laws of good manners . . . seeing all mens fingers are not alike cleane'.[27] The use of the fork was probably then confined to Italy and perhaps some parts of France. Coryate acquired a fork and took it home with him. Travelling to Cremona he observed the extensive use of fans and 'umbrellas', that is, sunshades. These 'will cost at the least a duckat', he tells us. They 'are made of leather something answerable to the forme of a little canopy, and hooped in the inside with divers little wooden hoopes . . . They are used especially by horsemen, who carry them in their hands when they ride, fastening the end of the handle upon one of their thighs . . .'[28]

Apart from an occasional naïveté and a certain extravagance in the amount of historical information, the *Crudities* is an attractively written book and really informative. But it was a mistake to call it 'Crudities'; a mistake to arrange a title-page covered with little 'emblems' which were really illustrations of episodes on the journey, such as Coryate in a gondola being pelted with eggs by an indignant courtesan from an upper window (one wonders whether this ever really happened); and a bigger mistake to invite men like Donne to write panegyrics for him. Never has a book been introduced with so many dubious compliments, not to say positive insults. There were verses in English, Latin, Greek, French, Italian, Spanish, Welsh and 'Utopian'. Some were kindly enough, others humorous. But those who mocked Coryate were less wise than they thought. When Donne called him a 'great Lunatique' he said a foolish thing; and when Prince Henry, to whom the book was dedicated, financed its publication, he did a wise one.

Poor Coryate! He afterwards exhausted himself in a journey, largely on foot, to Turkey, Egypt, Palestine and India, and died at Surat in December, 1617.

[27] Pp. 90-91.
[28] P. 112.

CHAPTER XI

George Sandys

MOST if not all our travellers had received a classical education and were interested in the vestiges of ancient Rome and the ancient world in general; but none so keenly as George Sandys. A son of Edwin Sandys, Archbishop of York, he had been born in March, 1577/8, and had studied at St Mary's Hall, Oxford. He was still a young boy when his father died, and it was perhaps his mother's death in 1610 that decided him to undertake a tour of those lands which ancient history had invested with glamour; and one observes that he says virtually nothing in his book about regions of which the interest was merely medieval or modern. It seems clear from his dedication of the book to Prince Charles that he had intended to visit only the isles of Greece, Constantinople, Egypt and Palestine, lands once the most glorious and sacred, but since 'the wild beasts of mankinde' have 'broken in', waste and overgrown, so that the cities have been made desolate, the temples subverted, 'nobilitie extinguished and no light of learning permitted'. He has related what he saw of their present condition in order to show the mutability of all worldly things, in the 'assurance that as there is nothing unchangeable saving God, so nothing stable but by his grace and protection'. A tour of southern Italy seems to have had no place in his original plan and, as we shall see, it was only by chance that he went there at all.

A *Relation of a Iourney begun An: Dom: 1610. Foure Books. Containing a description of the Turkish Empire, of AEgypt, of the Holy Land, of the Remote parts of Italy, and Islands adioyning* appeared in London in 1615[1] and was frequently reissued.

After travelling across France and north Italy, Sandys begins his narrative at Venice 'whence we departed on the 20 of August, 1610, in the *Little Defence* of London'.[2] He sailed down the Adriatic and, embarking on the *Great Exchange*—another English ship—at

[1] iv + 309 pages, with a list of Errata on the verso of p. 309. Printed for W. Barett. I have used the fourth edition (1637), but this is a reprint from the same blocks. The Errata have been omitted (and generally ignored in the text).

[2] P. 1.

Zacynthus, was taken round the Peloponnese, across the Aegean to visit Chios and the site of ancient Troy; thence to Constantinople which he describes in the latter part of Book I. From here, towards the end of January, 1610/11, he sailed in the *Trinitie* of London, via Rhodes to Alexandria; and after visiting Egypt (Book II), set out in March with three other Englishmen and three friendly Italians, one of whom was a priest and another a doctor, for the Holy Land. This he describes in detail, reproducing a large number of clear and admirable woodcuts of the holy places.[3] On April 8th he boarded the *Trinitie* (a ship that inspired confidence) and sailed up the coast to Sidon and Tripoli, intending then, it appears, to return by sea to London. One has the impression that he had had enough of travel in the Levant and among the infidels: 'Now shape we our course for England. Beloved soile . . . The Summer burns thee not, nor the Winter benummes thee.'[4]

But Providence was soon to revise his plans. After touching at Cyprus and at Candia in Crete, the *Trinitie* was forced northward by contrary winds, and then saw five sails approaching which had the appearance of warships. Happily they turned out to be English, and so to provide an escort; but now a great storm arose, they were fearfully tossed about, and the Captain who had intended to touch at Messina, decided to put in at Malta instead. On June 2nd they entered the harbour at Valetta, although they were not allowed to land for security reasons, as the war-galleys of the Knights of Malta were about to make a descent on the Barbary coast.[5] On the 6th the English vessels had permission to sail, but, says Sandys—'But no intreaty could get me aboord; choosing to undergoe all hazards and hardnesse whatsoever, then so long a voyage by sea, to my nature so irkesome.' Understatement could scarcely be more impressive. And so now he was left alone, 'without provision, and not knowing how to dispose of my self'.

'*Ogni male non viene per nuocere.*' But for this appalling contretemps, Sandys would never have seen the wonders of southern Italy.

It would be difficult to get lost on Malta. Very soon arrived an official who conducted our hero to a sea-side cave where he was to shelter for the night before being taken to the Lazaretto for the thirty or forty days of quarantine not unnaturally required of people arriving from the East. He had not been long meditating on this prospect when a number of things began to happen so extraordinary that he did not at first believe them to be real. First came a felucca which landed two old women who proceeded to spread on a rock a Turkey carpet, and on this a tablecloth on which they laid out

[3] Pp. 140-200.
[4] P. 218.
[5] P. 226.

tempting viands. Next came another felucca, carrying a 'Gallant' with 'two Amarosaes, attired like Nymphs'. These were Greek courtesans, the old persons were their mothers, and the gallant was a 'French Captaine . . . of much regard'. And so far from being annoyed by the Englishman's presence, they 'came and intreated me to take a part of their banquet', which he did. They next, 'in pity of my hard lodging, did offer to bring me into the City by night'. As this was an offence punishable by death, he seems to have demurred; and while they were still urging him, the official who had previously taken charge of him returned with a Maltese whose father was English. The Frenchman nevertheless promised to use his influence on Sandys' behalf; after which he put to sea with his charmers. True, their behaviour shocked the Archbishop's son not a little, though he found it reassuring to be back among these kindly Christians.[6]

The Frenchman was as good as his word. He next day sought an interview with the Grand Master of the Knights Hospitallers, and to such effect that the Council 'granted me Pratticke. So I came into the Citie, and was kindly entertained in the house of the aforesaid Maltese; where for three weekes space, with much contentment, I remained'.[7] Heaven protects its own.

To reach England with the minimum of sea-travel meant crossing to Sicily, and thence to Calabria. So on June 24th (1611) towards sundown he embarked in a felucca with five rowers; who, after assuring themselves that no Barbary pirates were in the offing, plied their oars steadily through the night. Next morning brought them in view of the rocky south-east corner of the great island;[8] but as it was held very dangerous to visit the interior, Sandys decided (the sea probably being calm) to continue trusting to the felucca; and he consoled himself, at least in his book, by a fairly ample excursus on history, ancient and medieval, with numerous quotations from Lucan and Ovid which he translated into rhyming verse with great felicity. He landed, however, at Syracuse, where he noted the presence of a Spanish garrison, and again at Catania, which he considered more 'ancient than beautiful'. It was tempting from here to make an ascent of Etna; but this would have required time and also—a more cogent reason—would have meant traversing a forest full of banditti. Next day, however, as the felucca rowed up the coast he had a good view of the mountain, of the fertile lower slopes, of the belt of woodland, and of the upper part 'almost covered with snow: yet smoaking in the midst like many conjoyning chimnies; and vomiting intermitted flames . . .'—a moment, it would seem, of unusual activity.[9]

[6] P. 227.
[7] Pp. 227-28.
[8] P. 234.
[9] P. 242.

The wealth and bustle of Messina greatly interested Sandys and, laying aside for a moment his Lucretius and Virgil, he notes that

Here live they in all abundance and delicacy, having much more than enough of food, and fruits of all kinds; excellent wines, and snow in the summer to qualifie the heat thereof, at a contemptible rate . . . the meanest artificers wife is clothed in silke: whereof an infinite quantity is made by the worm . . .[10]

Crime, however, is rife: 'no night doth passe without murder'; and so numerous and expert are the thieves that the gentlemen of Messina put all their money into the 'common table' (a kind of civic safe-deposit) and draw it out 'upon their bils' as they need it; just as we do in these latter days. Apart from this, however, life in Messina is pleasant, spectacular and—to English eyes—slightly improper. The great parade of the nobility every evening along the sea-front, the men on horseback, the ladies in 'large Carosses', is indeed a gallant sight; but they also have 'play-houses, where the parts of women are acted by women, and too naturally passionated'—a custom as yet unknown in England and which (to make it worse) 'they forbeare not to frequent upon Sundaies'.[11]

After spending three days in Messina, Sandys left on July 1st in another felucca, with two Spanish soldiers belonging to the Reggio garrison. A larger vessel apparently had them in tow for a time. When some few miles up the coast of Calabria, they were caught by a very strong current, the rope snapped and they were in great difficulties—which lent force to the fable that Virgil speaks of in the *AEneid*, about Scylla and Charybdis. Even so, however, they reached Scylla in safety, and Sandys expresses scepticism regarding the peril of the straits, observing that, in any event, the current does not now drive you on the 'divers little sharpe rocks' at the foot of the cliff.

He next describes the AEolian Islands which, however, he does not seem to have visited. Lipari had been attacked and depopulated by the Turks in 1544. Vulcano, where a terrible eruption had taken place in 1444, now merely smokes from one vent; but Stromboli burns 'almost continually like a beacon'. He stayed one day at Scylla:

My *Spanish* comrads were very harsh to me (for in these parts they detest the English . . .), but when upon their demand I told them that I was no Lutheran, they exceeded on the other side in their

[10] P. 245. He adds that 8,000 bales of raw silk are produced annually, and 5,000 exported to Naples, Ostia, Livorno and Genoa.

[11] Pp. 245-46.

curtesie. One of them had bin in the voyage of eighty eight; and would say that it was not we, but the winds that overthrew them.[12]

One supposes he was discreet enough not to argue the point.

The voyage up the coast of Calabria was anything but comfortable, and he was lucky in having soldiers as companions. Maybe he had elected deliberately to travel with them. It would seem that he knew and could speak Spanish, for otherwise one does not see how he could have conversed with them—unless they spoke Italian—or have learned so much about the country. To travel overland would involve the risk of being murdered, he tells us; or at least of being stung by a tarantula, of which there was 'great store' in those parts. The sting of this creature produces the most varied and alarming symptoms: some it renders sleepy, others wakeful; this man will be quarrelsome, another will grow merry and leap over tables. The best effect is when it makes the victim 'dance indefatigably' and so expel the poison. All this made it seem wise to stick to the felucca.

Not that this mode of travel was exempt from peril and discomfort. The towns where one could buy food were all perched for safety on the heights above the coast, while at intervals along the shore stood watch-towers and little forts for protection against the Barbary pirates who lurked among the islands. Down here were hostelries of a sort; but after sampling the one at Castiglione where the churl of a host expected them to bring in their own food and draw their water from a mile away, they decided in future to haul up their boat under shelter of one of the forts, and to sleep 'in our clothes on the sand'. To Sandys, a gentleman accustomed to properly cooked meals, the food seemed rather miserable, consisting, as it did, mostly of tunny, onions, cucumbers and melons; but he adds that mulberry trees abounded and that you could gather as much fruit from them as you liked.[13]

On July 6th they landed at Paola before rowing on up the coast, no doubt past the site of Paestum; but he makes no mention of that ancient city, though he must have known about the twice-flowering roses. The three temples stand on the plain some way back from the sea, and would be difficult and perhaps impossible to discern. The place in any event was a swampy and malarious wilderness, and the temples were only rediscovered in the eighteenth century. On July 8th the felucca set a course across the bay of Salerno, making

[12] P. 249.

[13] P. 250. 'More silke is made in Calabria then besides in all Italy,' he says, and adds that in the mountains they gather manna which falls at night like dew on the mulberry leaves. He later speaks of manna being brought to Naples. What it was I cannot imagine.

for the mountainous promontory which there extends far into the sea and landing at a village (perhaps Amalfi) where they spent the night in a chapel. Reaching the headland of the Sorrento peninsula next morning evoked inevitable memories of Ulysses and the Sirens—beings once numerous on these shores—and served as pretext for a rational explanation of what the sirens had originally been, an explanation more ingenious than convincing.[14] At Capri he speaks of the 'grots', including one with a very obscure entrance leading 'into a lightsome cave: exceeding pleasant, by reason of the water dropping from on high'. This was not the Blue Grotto, the existence of which, though known to the Romans, was not rediscovered until about a hundred and thirty years ago. There are several other caves on Capri. When approaching Naples, Sandys' companions threw all their bread into the sea in order to avoid the tax of twenty ducats a loaf by which the authorities controlled bread prices in the city.[15]

Naples naturally inspired in our traveller, as did all the places to the west which he explored, long and well-informed disquisitions on ancient history. It seems likely that on arrival here he procured two or three of the then available guide-books, possibly Pighius's *Hercules Prodicius*, a German publication of 1587, certainly Vol. III of François Schott's *Itinerarii Italiae rerumq. Romanorum* (1601) and G. C. Capaccio's *Neapolitanae Historiae . . . tomus primus* (1607). From Capaccio he translates a large number of passages, as Dr E. S. de Beer has shown in his edition of Evelyn's *Diary*.[16] This does not mean that he did not actually visit all the places described, but merely that he filled in the background (as do most travellers) from the appropriate sources. But he had learned a great deal about the present condition of the country, and this information he can only, I think, have acquired from a compatriot, one of the many English merchants established there and tolerated for fiscal reasons by the Spanish viceroy; or possibly from a Frenchman whom he met on his departure. The Spaniards, he tells us, maintain in Naples a garrison of 4,000 men, and 1,600 in the other towns of the kingdom: this 'forreine soldiery', together with the thirty-seven war-galleys, suffice to keep the whole country in subjection. Especially ingenious are the means by which the nobility have been demoralized and rendered

[14] As this was called the promontory of Minerva, he believes that here once stood an 'Athenaeum', a seat of learning and eloquence, and, one gathers, a sort of women's University: hence the fable of the Sirens on account of the sweetness of their songs 'and deepnesse of their science'. (p. 251.)

[15] P. 253.

[16] Oxford, 1955, Vol. II, pp. 578-79, and the annotations to pp. 327-54. Evelyn borrowed extensively from Sandys and others as well as from the guide-books.

impotent. The lordship they enjoy in towns and villages is merely nominal. In practice they are excluded from all important offices and commands. Their behaviour is closely scrutinized and any departure from regulations rigorously punished. They have been cunningly alienated from their vassals, and the government sedulously foments discord and envy among the nobles themselves. Small wonder if these twenty-five Dukes, thirty Marquesses, fifty-four Counts and four hundred barons, and the people as a whole, obey their oppressors with about as much love as galley-slaves feel for their task-masters.[17]

The heavy taxes on silk, and also on food, wine and even herbs, discourage trade. Sandys doubts whether, from the point of view of the King of Spain, the game is worth the candle. The annual revenue amounts to somewhat over 2,000 ducats; but as the king expends a great deal in pensions and probably more in maintaining the numerous garrisons, he cannot gain much but 'trouble and title'.

The city, however, is full of life and bustle: the tribunals 'pestered with clamorous advocates and litigious clients'; the streets thronged with citizens and foreigners whose ears are 'inured to the sound of drum and fife, as their eyes to the . . . glistering of armours[18] . . . The Gentry delight much in great Horses, whereupon they prance continually thorow the streets'. Incredible are the number of 'carosses' and also of 'segges' (sedan-chairs) which wait for fares at street corners 'as Watermen doe at our wharfes'.[19]

Sandys does not actually say that he climbed Vesuvius. 'This mountaine,' we read, 'hath a double top: that towards the North doth end in a Plaine; the other towards the South aspireth more high, which when hid in clouds prognosticates raine to the *Neapolitans*'. Now Capaccio, from whom most of this is translated, says nothing about the southern summit being the loftier;[20] but it actually was when Sandys saw it, though not on the occasion of Evelyn's visit in 1645. This we know from the Abate Braccini's account of the fearful eruption of 1631: *Del Incendio fattosi nel Vesuvio* (Naples, 1632). Braccini had explored the crater in 1612, the year following Sandys' visit, and he confirms Sandys' statement that Vesuvius (the new summit) was then higher than Monte Somma (the ancient one).[21] After 1631 it was lower. Sandys compares the crater to an amphitheatre, with a pit in the midst from which once

[17] Pp. 257-58. [18] P. 256.

[19] P. 259.

[20] *The Diary of John Evelyn*, ed. de Beer, 1955, II, 334, note 4.

[21] His work is excellently summarized in Arthur Norway's *Naples past and present* (London, 1901), pp. 182-187. After the eruption of 1631, 'the relative heights of Vesuvius and Somma were reversed' (p. 187).

had issued flames and lava but which was now choked with rocks and trees, 'the uttermost brow that declineth like the seates in a Theatre, flourishing with trees, and excellent pasturage'.[22] Braccini's description is much more circumstantial. From the rim of the crater on which nothing could grow, you descended to a level area tufted with various plants and beyond this a verdurous gulf where trees were growing and the grass was rich and thick. (Rain water evidently drained into it). This innermost crater was frequented by woodmen and domestic animals. A little smoke escaped, but only from the crater rim above.[23] Now this situation must have seemed so odd that anyone who had seen the crater would have been likely to comment on it, as Braccini did. When John Evelyn climbed Vesuvius in 1645 he saw something utterly different. In place of the deep gulf of verdure there was now an ashy hollow, from the middle of which rose a small 'hill' vomiting smoke and 'huge stones' with a noise that sounded like musketry.[24]

What had happened was this. At the beginning of December, 1631, a native of Ottajano who had climbed the mountain discovered that the chasm had filled up, the grass and trees having completely vanished. There was some alarm, though no one suspected the magnitude of the coming catastrophe. On the night of the 15th, however, a dark reddish glow was seen on the summit, and early next morning the eruption began. The upper part of the mountain was cracking, flames and stones pouring from the cracks and fearful explosions rending the air. A dark cloud like an umbrella-pine was now hanging over the peak; and Braccini who had taken down his copy of the younger Pliny, realized that what had happened in 79 A.D. was happening once again.

Repeated shocks of earthquake added to the terrors of the eruption. A huge pall of smoke was slowly covering the whole region while flashes of lightning could be seen descending from a storm-cloud above. Sulphurous fumes now poured through the streets of Naples and by the afternoon had turned day into night. Next morning (Dec. 17th) came the climax, the mountain being now in full eruption and the explosions louder than ever, while the earth suddenly heaved up, the sea receding and a little later rushing back; and then an enormous torrent of white-hot lava came pouring down from the south-eastern rim of the crater, dividing into seven different streams and destroying all the towns and villages from Boscoreale to Portici. One of them which overwhelmed Torre Annunziata ran out

[22] P. 260.
[23] Summarized by Norway, *op. cit.*, 182.
[24] *Diary*, ed. de Beer, II, 183.

into the sea where it made the water boil for several days. When at last the smoke cleared it was seen that the old peak of Vesuvius had been destroyed and was now two hundred feet lower than Monte Somma. It seemed that over 3,000 people had been killed in Torre Annunziata alone.

The eruption of 79 A.D. had been notable for the vast quantities of ash and mud which had buried Pompeii, Herculaneum and Stabiae; there had been some lava streams too. The eruption of 1631 was notable for the fiery streams of lava and for the violence of the explosions which hurled huge rocks to a great distance; the deposits of ash were less deep except quite near the mountain.[25]

After a brief description of Vesuvius, which I think he did not climb, Sandys set out on a guided tour of the ancient ruins and natural wonders of the country to the west of Naples:[26] a region once covered with populous cities, magnificent temples, palaces and villas, but in his days—save here and there—a scene of sad desolation. His account of it is livelier and more personal than Moryson's, because the tour seems to have been conducted at greater leisure, there was no attempt to push as far as Linturnum where Moryson had had such a bad time and also because Sandys was not in fear of

[25] A. H. Norway, *Naples past and present*, 183-87, summarizing the detailed account in Braccini's book.

The Vesuvius known to the Ancients was a different kind of mountain. It was in fact the Monte Somma *complete*: a flat-topped pyramid probably not more than 3,750 feet high at most. The slopes all around were covered with verdure, according to Strabo, while the top was a kind of plain of volcanic ash and calcined rocks. It was believed to be extinct, though Strabo guessed that it had once been very active. (No memory or record, however, of any activity existed). The eruption of 79 A.D. appears to have shattered the whole southern and south-western rim of the mountain (Monte Somma) and to have thrown up in its place a new and higher peak, the one now known as 'Vesuvio'; this being separated from the north and north-east rim by the deep gulf of the 'Atrio del Cavallo'. After this outbreaks occurred at longish intervals, but there had been none between 1500 and 1631, which accounts for the condition of the crater as Braccini saw it in 1612. After 1631 the crater appears to have simmered noisily, picturesquely but not dangerously for over seventy years; but the eighteenth century witnessed a number of terrifying eruptions, one of which (1794) caused great loss of life. The eruptions in the nineteenth century were still more numerous and violent, particularly that of 1872. An observatory had by this time been built on a ridge between two of the gulleys down which lava would usually flow; and in 1872 the director, Professor Palmieri, remained at his post while torrents of lava were streaming down on both sides. Loss of life in recent times has not been considerable. The people know what to expect, and a moderate eruption is economically beneficial since the lava-beds soon become extraordinarily fertile (see Norway, *op. cit.*, p. 188).

[26] Pp. 261-2. Sandys reproduces here a good picture-map of the region.

being arrested as an enemy alien. He also had more recent books to refer to. After passing through the tunnel under Posilipo, which Sandys supposed to be of remote antiquity,[27] he and his companions paid a visit to the Lago d'Agnano, where they saw the 'Stove of St German' (Le Stufe di San Germano) and the Grotta del Cane. Over the former a little house had been built from which (if we are to believe the accompanying woodcut) clouds of hot vapour were issuing. The latter was a 'mortall Cave', already known to Pliny, about seven feet high at the entrance, neither hot nor cold, but fatal to any living thing that entered it. Two prisoners who had been thrust in by order of the viceroy Don Pedro de Toledo, had 'expired in a moment', as later did three gallants 'who tempted God' by venturing in. The custom which was followed on this occasion and for the benefit of later travellers, was to place a dog in the cave. He appeared to die without a struggle.They then drew him out and threw him into the lake;[28] whereupon he recovered, swam ashore and fled yelping to the 'Osteria' near by;[29] where, if he did not receive, he deserved an appropriate stimulant.

From here one passed on to the Phlegraean Fields to inspect the 'Court of Vulcan'[30] as Solfatara was called—a rather small level area, hemmed in by cliffs, from the furthermost of which several vents were smoking. The ground was as hot as one could endure, rumblings were audible below and new vents were apt to appear anywhere.[31] Nevertheless people came from all over Italy to walk or ride over the area or be carried in sedan-chairs, as we see them in an accompanying woodcut; since the vapours were held to relieve headache and stomach-ache, and cure violent fever, itches, ulcers, etc.[32] This place lay rather over a mile from the sea. Descending now towards Pozzuoli, Sandys inspected the ruins of an amphitheatre, which gave him occasion to quote interesting passages from Martial, to descant on gladiatorial and even more revolting kinds of contest, dwelling particularly on the crimes of Nero and Domitian and breaking off to exclaim: 'But O the wicked delight of these barbarous

[27] It was probably made only in the time of Augustus. The present road-tunnel, which is further inland, was pierced between 1882 and 1885.

[28] The Lago d'Agnano occupied an extinct crater. It was drained in 1870.

[29] Pp. 265-67. This is illustrated with an amusing wood-cut of the lake, the 'Stove' and the 'Dog Grotto'. The exhalations in the latter are carbonic acid. The experiment with a dog was continued until about sixty years ago, but is now prohibited. Arthur Conway, who refused the offer of a local 'brigand' who had brought a puppy for the purpose, relates a picturesque anecdote on this subject (Naples, p. 27).

[30] 'Forum Vulcani', Strabo calls it.

[31] Sandys was right in believing the ground to be hollow.

[32] P. 268.

tyrants . . . !'[33]

It was a relief after this to find oneself on the coast at Pozzuoli: once a large and splendid city. The place, fairly populous in the later Middle Ages, had been devastated by earthquakes and the sudden appearance of a volcano; but since then Don Pedro de Toledo[34] had tempted people to return and build houses, and had himself planted a beautiful orchard and pleasaunce, bright with fountains and adorned with ancient statuary. Here 'we refreshed ourselves during the heat of the day. A place of surpassing delight'.[35] A felucca now took them across the bay to a little port from which they could visit the Lucrine Lake. It had in ancient times been separated from the sea only by a narrow causeway, while inland it had extended as far as the Lake of Avernus, dread portal to the nether world.[36] But the day of September 29, 1538, had witnessed a succession of earthquakes, after which the coast rose, the sea receding two hundred paces, a crater suddenly opened, vomiting stones and cinders and forming a 'New Mountaine'; so much so that the lake was now no more than a 'little sedgy plash'.[37]

Avernus, a circular basin girt with steep hills on all sides but one, was sombre and impressive. Hither had once come Ulysses and, after him, AEneas. The water was black, evil smelling and very deep, though not more than 253 fathoms, according to our author. The party now explored by torchlight a cave that was supposed formerly to have emerged at Baiae,[38] though it now appeared to terminate in

[33] Pp. 270-71. In the time of Diocletian, a number of Christians were thrown to the wild beasts, who, however, did not hurt them.

[34] Viceroy from 1532 to 1553: one of the few Spanish governors who appear to have conferred benefits on the region.

[35] Pp. 272-73. He does not say anything about the so-called Serapeum or Temple of Serapis, which is near the shore, because it was not excavated until 1750, in the time of Charles III, the Bourbon king.

[36] Agrippa, commissioned by Augustus, had established huge harbour-works here, building wharves and canals and turning the two lakes into sheltered 'bassins'. Were these for trading-vessels? The naval harbour was about three miles away, under Cape Misenum, in what is now called the 'Mare morto'. The whole appearance of this region in the first century must have been extraordinarily formidable, brilliant and up-to-date. Sandys relates at this point (p. 276) the story in Pliny about the Dolphin who used to carry a little boy to school, across the bay from Baiae to Puteoli and back, every day; and of the Dolphin's grief after the child's untimely death.

[37] Pp. 277-78. The Monte Nuovo is about 450 feet high. There has been no great explosion, apart from earthquakes, in these parts since 1538, the centre of activity having shifted to Vesuvius.

[38] This cave is on the south side of the Lago d'Averno; on the west side there is another tunnel about half a mile long, ventilated by shafts from the hill above, which leads to Cumae. This is called the Grotta della Pace, though it should perhaps be 'di Pace', because Pietro della Pace was the name of the man who had rediscovered it.

a rock-hewn chamber where ancient mosaics and decorations were discernible. It was here, their guide informed them, that the Sibyl used to deliver oracles; but he said this only to save himself the trouble of taking them to Cumae.[39]

They went there, however, apparently taking a path over the brow of the hill and descending into the hollow below the eminence on which the Acropolis had been built. It was not easy to approach, being beaten on one side by the surges; and of this ancient city, one of the oldest Greek colonies in Italy, nothing was now visible but the ruins of defaced temples and broken aqueducts—nothing except the entrance to the Sibyl's cave.[40] This led them into a roomy chamber, in the floor of which had been hewn three cisterns, designed perhaps for the ablutions of the prophetess;[41] and Sandys now quotes rather extensively from Virgil, including the passage from the fourth Eclogue in which is foretold the birth of the Child who should bring in a golden age. It should be noted at this point that Virgil owned a villa on Posilipo, that he wrote there the *Aeneid* and some of his other poems, and that he was buried on that headland, perhaps in the tomb popularly ascribed to him.

After inspecting the 'Arco felice', a very tall arch of brickwork which spans a hollow and once served as an aqueduct, Sandys decided to wander back by the sea-shore, so as to muse at leisure on the great men who had lived here or sought refuge from the clamour and wickedness of Rome; such as that wealthy praetor Servilius Vatia, the remains of whose mansion he at last discovered. Though unable to describe the inside, he notes its outward appearance and the little brook which there emerges from a grove of plane-trees.[42] And so he came to Baiae; a city that once extended five miles along the gulf. It had been an earthly paradise in the time of Horace, and had turned into a sink of corruption in that of Seneca. Sandys spares us the more infamous details;[43] but he naturally describes Nero's planning the murder of his mother, Agrippina.[44]

Baiae and its bay, the heights above and the headland of Misenum had been regarded by the Romans as the last word in loveliness and were converted by them into a winter-resort of exceptional luxury. Here stood many villas and mansions, including that of Lucullus. It does not appear that Sandys had time to walk round the hill, still less to climb it; but he speaks of the theatre whose ruins look out over the bay. It had contained two stages, the lower one being of

[39] Pp. 279-81.

[40] Virgil says that there were a hundred (or he may mean two hundred) openings, from which the Sibyl's voice could be heard issuing (*AEneid*, VI, v. 41). The hill is in fact honeycombed with passages.

[41] P. 285.

[42] P. 288.

[43] P. 291.

[44] Pp. 294-95.

marble, the upper, which was fronted with glass, being supported by 360 marble pillars; while 3,000 statues of brass stood between the columns. The 'semicircle' could accommodate 80,000 spectators.[45] It must have been a marvel of wealth and splendour, and probably a monument of bad taste. And now there was nothing but desolation, except for the fortress erected by Pedro de Toledo which indeed remains very impressive.

Rejoining the felucca which they had left at Porto Giulio, Sandys and his party crossed the bay to Pozzuoli and then rowed back to Naples round the headland of Posilipo. On leaving Naples he was advised not to travel overland because of the unhealthy summer, 'the dog-starre then raging'. There had been rain, and some score of travellers had recently died, presumably of fever. I therefore, says Sandys, 'agreed with a Genoese to carry me in his Feluca to Neptune [Nettuno] . . . But staying too long for my companion (an Englishman that dwelt at Ligorne) the boat put from shoare; which we were faine to follow in another'.[46] Suddenly, however, the sea grew rough, and our hero would have been in peril but for the appearance of another providential Frenchman—a fisherman this time—who rescued and conveyed him to Procida, where the felucca was waiting. On this fruitful island which abounded 'with Conies, Hares and Phesants' they were held up for a day by stormy weather and Sandys was able to survey from a distance the mountainous isle of Ischia. He would have described its history at some length if, as he explains rather engagingly, he had not been 'weary of this labour of giving so much information'.[47]

The weather now clearing, they proceeded to row up the coast, passing Cumae, the ruins of Linturnum where the younger Scipio (Africanus) was buried, and the mouth of the river Liris. The temptation to relate anecdotes was irresistible at this point, at least in retrospect. The learned will recollect that Athenaeus much commends the lobsters of Liris; and that the gourmet Apicius found them so much to his liking that he came and lived at Minturnum where he could eat them continually. He was more than a gourmet, if we are to believe Martial whose epigram Sandys renders as follows:

> Three thousand pounds upon his belly spent
> Apicius; left five hundred to prevent
> Hunger and thirst (a feare that neare thee went).
> This, after that, thou didst in poison put;
> Therein Apicius, the great greedy-gut.[48]

But it is doubtful whether Sandys was thinking of Apicius at the

[45] P. 296.
[46] P. 301.
[47] P. 302.
[48] P. 303.

time. He was more probably contemplating the hills and sea, feeling thankful that no Turkish galley was in sight, or talking with his compatriot from Livorno; while the latter would certainly be less interested in Athenaeus and Martial than in the arrangements he had probably made for the shipment of English textiles to Naples. They landed at Mola di Gaëta (the present Formia) where the Spaniards, though objecting to visitors' entering the castle, still allowed them to see the coffin of the Constable of Bourbon.[49] And here they spent the night, secure under the protection of the garrison. Better unfriendly Spaniards than no Spaniards. The coasts of the Tyrrhenian and Ligurian seas were then and remained most perilous. In 1534 Hayraddin Barbarossa had raided the town of Fondi, a little further north, with the object of kidnapping the Countess Giulia Gonzaga for Sultan Soliman II; and when she escaped him he sacked the place. The Turks had destroyed it again as recently as 1594,[50] while minor raids could be expected at any time.

After leaving Terracina, the first town in the Papal States, where they probably spent the night, they rowed round the Monte Circeo, that astonishing promontory[51] which looks like an island. This of course called to mind the misadventure of Ulysses' comrades and how the witch had turned them into swine. Sandys (writing in retrospect, I imagine, and assisted by his guide-books) proposes rational and symbolical explanations. The roaring of Circe's lions had been suggested by the roaring of waves on the beach; the Herb Moly, which Mercury gave Ulysses to guard him, represented Temperance;[52] though whether Homer had been thinking of more than a good fairy-tale is less certain.[53]

Sandys was put ashore at Nettuno, the ancient Antium, famous

[49] Charles V's general who had been killed in the storming of Rome.

[50] Sandys speaks of its having been 'recently sacked by Barbarossa' (p. 306); but he must have confused the raid of 1594 with the earlier one. The Turks sometimes established themselves on an off-shore island as a basis for operations. Towards 1630, when the Duca d'Alcala was viceroy, a party landed in the dead of night on the Chiaia, just outside Naples, with a view to seizing the Marchesa del Vasto and holding her to ransom. She, however, had gone to an inland Spa to take the waters, so they consoled themselves by seizing as many people as opened their doors; and when the viceroy, an old man afflicted with gout, appeared on horseback leading his soldiers, they made off to the isle of Nisida. From here they parleyed next day, releasing their captives in return for ransom-money (A. H. Norway, *op. cit.*, 77-79).

[51] It is nearly 2,000 feet high.

[52] P. 308.

[53] Victor Bérard, in his beautiful *Album Odysséen* thinks that the early navigators who explored this wild coast had seen the wild pigs which still haunt the tangled forest at the foot of the mountain, and that this detail, brought back to Ionia, gave rise to the story of Circe's enchantments.

in our day as one of the principal landing-beaches (Anzio) in the Allies' invasion of Italy. He seems to have snatched a few hours' rest and, to avoid as much as possible travelling during the heat of the day, set out at 1 o'clock next morning with a guide who was to take him to Rome. After traversing a great forest,[54] they rode through 'a champian[55] Country, rich in wines and graine', and took refuge from the heat at an inn about fifteen miles from Rome; reaching the city in the cool of the evening. And here he stayed only four days '(as long as I durst) secured by the faith and care of Master *Nicolas Fitz-Herbert*,[56] who accompanied me' in seeing 'all the antiquities and glories of that City'.

And here, for practical purposes, Sandys concludes his book; adding only that he travelled by way of Siena, Florence and Bologna to Ferrara, where he embarked on the Po, 'and so returned into Venice'.

Sandys' book differs from Fynes Moryson's both in what it aims at and in what it furnishes. Moryson's *Itinerary*, which took much longer to compose, is more than a record of travel. It is a systematic guide-book, full of up-to-date information, and it remains today a primary source for the historian. His obsession with finance must have been wearisome for him, but it is interesting for us. Sandys, on the other hand, was mainly interested in pagan and Christian antiquities. His instincts were more artistic than Moryson's: he was a poet, a great figure in the elaboration of the rhymed couplet and perhaps the most skilful translator of the *Metamorphoses* that we have ever had. By comparison with his contemporary, he appears indifferent to questions of finance and economics, or the material side of life in general. We do not even know how he managed in Italy for money; he must have brought back currency from the Levant, sewn up perhaps in the lining of his doublet. He was a product of Oxford, though without a degree; Moryson was a Fellow of a Cambridge College. The difference may be significant.

But if he *appears* indifferent to finance, this did not prevent his doing very well in later life, when poor Moryson had been struggling to make ends meet. It has been remarked that a study of the ancient classics furnishes the best preparation for a career in government or diplomacy. It seems to have done so for Sandys. After being appointed Colonial Treasurer of the Virginia Company in 1621, he

54 Part of the 'Macchia' which skirts the coast.

55 I.e. 'champaign'—open lowlands. Evelyn uses the form 'champion', another seventeenth century variant.

56 Presumably one of the Fitzherberts of Norbury in south Derbyshire, who had remained Catholics and were cruelly persecuted. Sir Thomas, in the time of Elizabeth I, had spent thirty years of his life in prison.

went to North America (undeterred by his horrible experience in the Mediterranean), was a member of the Council of Virginia from 1624 onwards, and returned home only in 1631. In Jamestown he employed part of his leisure in completing the translation of the *Metamorphoses*; perhaps also in regaling his colleagues on reminiscences of Malta and Naples.

CHAPTER XII

Lithgow, Mundy and Gage

The Totall Discourse of the Rare Adventures and Painfull Peregrinations of long nineteen Yeares,[1] by William Lithgow (1582-1645), scarcely possesses the literary value of the earlier travel-books, written as it is in the artificial style which good writers had discarded. But Lithgow was a tireless, almost fanatical, traveller who covered more ground than his predecessors, performed audacious deeds and suffered dire tribulations; and though much of his travel was in central Europe, Greece, Turkey, Palestine, Egypt and Algeria, he was in Italy on four separate occasions and signalized each by a notable adventure.

He spent some weeks in Rome in the spring of 1610 without apparently seeking the protection of the English College. The Inquisition got on his tracks, but he made his escape, visited Naples and Loreto, and then finding his way to Venice took ship for Corfu and the Levant. Here he lived still more dangerously; but in Jerusalem he obtained a Pilgrim's Certificate which was to stand him in good stead during a later visit to Italy. From Egypt he sailed to Malta (much like Sandys about the same time) and thence to Sicily where he was responsible for the capture of a Moorish pirate-ship. The handsome reward he received for this exploit replenished his funds, which had need of replenishment, and enabled him to take passage by sea for Naples and so to return to his native Scotland.

Setting out again in 1614, he this time ventured into the mountain-country of Calabria, famous for tarantulas and brigands. Here his peregrinations would have come to a painful end, had he not produced for the ruffians who were threatening his life, the best of all passports—the certificate of a visit to the Holy Places. On seeing this, *on lui fit fête*: the whole company made merry with him. He then passed over into Sicily (second visit). Faring across the island he discovered the bodies of two gentlemen who had killed each other in a solitary duel. As no one was about he rifled their purses, took their diamond rings, and then coolly announced his

[1] London, 1632, 807 p. See the article by Mr F. H. Groome in the *D.N.B.*, ed. 1949-50, XI, pp. 1238-40.

discovery. Following his previous route, but in the opposite direction, he sailed next to Malta and from there to Algiers. After wandering some time in the desert he visited Tunis, returned to Malta and Sicily (third visit), climbed Etna, crossed again into Italy (fourth visit) and again arrived in Naples, where he saw that most thrilling of show-places, already described by Sandys, the 'Grotta di Cane'. From here he pushed on to Rome, then to Venice and after exploring the Istrian peninsula, made his way to Sweden and finally, in 1617, back to Scotland. While one may admit with La Rochefoucauld that '*Qui vit sans folie n'est pas si sage qu'il croit*', it is true that to go on living dangerously is scarcely sensible. It was not wise to travel in Spain, as he did in 1620, and when he was caught and tortured in Granada, he was fortunate in being rescued and shipped home by the British Consul.

Adventures had sprung up in his path like mushrooms: or were they, rather, simply provoked by his character? and could one apply to such a man the verses that Corneille was to write some years later:

> *Et comme il met en nous des âmes peu communes,*
> *Hors de l'ordre commun il nous fait des fortunes?*

Peter Mundy devoted a few pages to northern Italy, which he crossed in 1640 in the course of his extensive travels;[2] and Thomas Gage, the so-called 'English American', was in Rome about the same time. Gage, who belonged to a Catholic family, had been educated as a Jesuit at St Omer. He had later, in Spain, joined the Dominican Order and then gone to Guatemala and Mexico as a missionary. After a short sojourn at home, he decided to visit Italy towards the winter of 1639. He travelled apparently by way of Innsbrück and Trent, where he suffered an attack of ague, and then proceeded to Milan, Genoa, Livorno, Florence, Civita Vecchia and Rome. Here he stayed with a Scot named Pendrick,[3] who seems to have kept a pension near S. Trinita de' Monti. He met Father Fitzherbert, Father Courtney[4] and other English Jesuits, including his half-brother George Gage; and he speaks at some length of their plans for the conversion of England. More particularly he mentions a design for creating an English Cardinal; the hopes entertained by Sir William Hamilton, Queen Henrietta Maria's agent in Rome, that he might be given this honour, and the possibility of its being accorded to some

[2] *Travels of Peter Mundy in Europe and Asia, 1608-1667*, London, the Hakluyt Society.

[3] J. W. Stoye, *English Travellers abroad (1604-1667)*, London, 1952, p. 188.

[4] For John Evelyn's visit to the English College in 1644 see below, pp. 193-4, 197.

other Englishman, whether Sir Kenelm Digby, Sir Toby Mathew or Walter Montague.[5] If Gage recalls the kindness he received from 'Don Francisco Barbarini',[6] he also emphasises the 'exorbitances and scandals' he found 'in the lives of some cardinals at Rome while I was there'.[7] His book—which was not written until 1645—conveys the impression that he had left England in search of the true religion; that he was impressed by the German Lutherans and shocked by the Roman ecclesiastics.[8] But, as Professor Newton observes, 'we have only his word for it, and it seems more probable that as late as 1640 he still thought only of opportunities to gratify his ambition within the Catholic Church'.[9]

In England, however, it soon became apparent which way the wind was blowing, and Gage bent all his efforts towards being recognized as a Protestant. In 1642 he gave evidence against Father Thomas Holland, a Jesuit who had been his schoolfellow at St Omer; and Holland was hanged, drawn and quartered. Later, in 1650, at the trial of Father Wright, pressure was brought on Gage to testify; and Wright was hanged at Tyburn. Gage's relatives were not the only persons who felt quite strongly about his conduct. But his book, which had appeared in 1648, contained valuable information regarding the West Indies and Central America; it was republished in 1655, 1677, 1699 and 1711, and there were French editions in 1680, 1691, 1721 and 1722.[10]

[5] *The English-American; his Travail by Sea and Land: or, a New Survey of the West Indies,* London, 1648. New edition (The Argonaut Series), edited by A. P. Newton, London and New York, 1929, pp. 391-94.

[6] P. 390.

[7] P. 394.

[8] Is it hazardous to surmise that, if he had been offered preferment in Rome, he would not have been shocked?

[9] Introduction, p. xxii.

[10] A. P. Newton, Introduction to *The English-American,* pp. x-xi.

CHAPTER XIII

John Evelyn

THE dangers that men like Moryson, Coryate and Sandys had faced in the Papal States or Naples diminished greatly after 1630 or 1635. Mr J. W. Stoye points out that Charles I's marriage and the milder policy that was adopted towards the English Catholics were followed by a corresponding era of tolerance in Italy.[1] In some respects this tolerance appears to have been greater. The Jesuits at the English College in Rome regularly entertained visiting Englishmen and in no perfunctory manner. Several instances could be cited;[2] but the experience of Milton in October, 1638, and of Evelyn in the winter of 1644-45 were outstanding. Cardinal Francesco Barberini, a nephew of Urban VIII, showed such kindness to visitors and was so solicitous in their behalf[3] that he came justly to be known as Protector of the English. We have records of the part he played in this matter from 1638 or earlier until 1660; and by that time other eminent churchmen were receiving English visitors and discussing scientific questions with them. In 1650 the future Marquess of Halifax, then a boy of sixteen, was received by Cardinal Savelli; while Lord Chesterfield enjoyed the hospitality of Cardinals Barberini, Spada and Copponi so much that he stayed in Rome for the better part of a year. Robert Southwell, on the eve of the Restoration, appears to have been surrounded by a whole bevy of Cardinals.[4] And it was not wholly unusual to be received by the Pope. Evelyn in 1645 was presented to Innocent X, and in 1660 or early 1661, Lord Banister Maynard, a Presbyterian, was granted an audience of Clement IX.[5]

All this had a good effect on Protestant morals. How could one hate a religion of which the churches were so beautiful and the

[1] J. W. Stoye, *English Travellers abroad* (1604-1667), London, 1952, p. 178.

[2] *Ibid.*, 181-82.

[3] Hugh Popham described Barberini as 'the gallantest gentleman in the whole world'. On the morrow of his arrival in February, 1639, the Cardinal sent one of his gentlemen to invite the visitor to call on him, after which 'he sent continually to visit me, and with all a present of the bravest wine' (Cited by Mr Stoye, 182-83).

[4] *Ibid.*, 183. I owe all these details to Mr Stoye, who has examined a vast amount of unpublished material.

[5] *Ibid.*

priests so cultured, courteous and kindly? On the other hand, converse with gentlemanly and intelligent heretics must have gradually mollified the feelings of the Roman hierarchy. The policy of Innocent XI, himself an apostle of tolerance and moderation in an era that had suddenly grown unreasonable, may not have been due simply to his own great intelligence and charitable disposition. Mutual acquaintance was of benefit to everyone.

It was especially, in the mid seventeenth century, advantageous to the English. Rome had more art treasures to offer than any other city in the world and, as a school of art, it was second to none. It was here that the greatest painters assembled and that the most fruitful innovations, like those of Salvator Rosa, were made. Nicholas Stone had studied here under Bernini, prior to 1647[6]; while two or three of our eminent portraitists were associated at one time or another with the Academy of St Luke.[7]

Finally, the attractions and facilities afforded by Rome made it easier to visit Naples and even Sicily. After about 1635 Naples became a regular stage in the tour of Italy. Milton, after visiting the Marchese di Villa in Naples, had hoped to see Sicily, but one or two, like Lithgow, had already done so, and others like Sandys and George Courthop[8] had at least touched there. John Ray, the eminent botanist, was in Sicily in the spring of 1664.[9] But it was the cordiality of the Papal Court that explains why a sometimes prolonged sojourn in Rome now figures in the diaries and travel-books.

The Diary of John Evelyn which was first published in 1818 and of which we now, thanks to Mr E. S. de Beer, have an admirable critical edition,[10] contains an interesting and detailed account of his travels in Italy. Evelyn was not a more intelligent man than Moryson, but his interests were wider, he had more scientific curiosity, above all he was wealthy and suffered under no such difficulties as had handicapped his predecessors. He was able to make prolonged sojourns in Rome where, so far from being in personal danger, he was entertained and assisted in every possible way. All this compensates for what his diary, by its very nature, lacks in consecutive literary interest.

He had kept a sort of diary at the time but did not apparently

[6] Stoye, 303.

[7] See below, p. 198.

[8] Stoye, 177.

[9] See below, pp. 225-26.

[10] Oxford, 1955, 5 vols. For a description of the manuscripts see vol. I, 44-51. Of these only two concern us here: the *De Vita Propria* which contains an account of his life up to the time in his travels when he first reached Siena; and the *Kalendarium* which covers the same ground in more detail and continues the narrative until 1697. My references for the travels in Italy (1644-46) are to the *Kalendarium* in Vol. II of Mr de Beer's edition.

begin to write it up until about 1660,[11] and he then revised and filled it out with notes taken now from John Raymond's *Itinerary: Il Mercurio Italico* of 1648, now from Pflaumern's *Mercurius Italicus*, from George Sandys' *Relation*, and other sources.[12] It would be unfair to reproach him with this or to describe his account of France and Italy as a patchwork. He wrote it for his own interest and never intended it for publication. That certain parts of it should seem tedious is natural enough.

Evelyn was a sincere but prudent Royalist, a strong Anglican, a man of great piety but without fanaticism. He had left England in November, 1643, and after passing several months in Paris and Tours, had travelled down to Marseilles and thence to Cannes, from which port on October 12, 1644, he took ship for Genoa.[13] Some bad weather was encountered and they kept close in shore, as there was risk of being seized by a Barbary pirate or a Spanish warship, Spain and France being then at war. Among the other passengers was a Frenchman, who was in particular jeopardy, and an Irish Bishop and his brother, a priest.[14] Just as they were trying to round the cape at Savona, a fearful wind began to blow from landward, raising high seas which began to swamp and threaten to sink them. The Captain thought they were lost, the priest began to confess the faithful: when lo! the tempest abated, and they were able to sail inshore again. Approaching Genoa, Evelyn marvelled at the princely villas and palaces along the coast and was enchanted by the scent of orange, citron and jasmine flowers wafted out to sea.

They landed on the 16th. It was necessary first to pass through 'the Prattique-house' and present the bills of health they had obtained at Cannes, and next to register their names in the Ducal Palace; after which they put up at an inn belonging to an Englishman named Zacharias. The account of the perils they had escaped scarcely impressed their host, whose own story of shipwreck in the West Indies 'put us quite downe', says Evelyn.[15] Two days were spent in viewing 'the rarities' under the guidance of an English merchant named Tomson who had been long established in Genoa. Evelyn was impressed with the evil repute of the place, 'this beautifull Citty' being 'more stayn'd with such horrid acts of revenge & murthers, than any one place in Europ . . . which renders it very unsafe to strangers: This makes it a gally matter to carry a knife

11 De Beer, Introduction, I, 46.

12 See De Beer's Bibliographical Notes, II, 573-79.

13 *Kalendarium*, II, 167-68.

14 *Ibid.*, 170. Evelyn's mention of the various Riviera towns which they passed is taken largely from Raymond. (Note that Raymond's visit was in 1646, and therefore subsequent to Evelyn's).

15 Pp. 171-72.

about one whose poynt is not broken off'.[16] But he was even more impressed by the magnificence of the place and the strange contrast between the bare, silent hills behind and the wealth and splendour of this narrow strip of land; especially by the Strada Nova, which 'is for statlinesse of the buildings, paving & evenesse of the Streete, certainly far superior to any in Europ for the number of houses'.[17] His description of the Palazzo Doria[18] and its gardens is of interest, since most of the latter have disappeared; though the Strada Nova, now the Via Garibaldi, remains much as it was then.[19]

On October 19th he embarked on a felucca bound for Livorno, but high seas were running and they were forced to put in at Porto Venere, 'betweene two such narrow & horrid rocks, as the waves dashing with extraordinary velocity against them, put us in no small peril'.[20] Being now, however, in quiet waters, he and his fellow-voyagers decided to land at Lerici, and from there to take post-horses to Pisa. At Pisa he met an old friend named Thomas Henshaw, who remained in his company for over a year. The wonderful group of Campanile (the Leaning Tower), Duomo and Battistero, standing in pale, coloured marble on their green lawn, struck him as beautiful (they well might!) as did the Campo Santo where the old Pisans lie buried in earth which had been brought from Jerusalem;[21] but they inspired no such raptures as were later to be felt when entering St Peter's in Rome, or even when viewing the more recent Church of the Gesù, the work of Vignola and della Porta. Passing through the forest of cork-oaks which lay between Pisa and Livorno he noticed many buffaloes[22] feeding, and he describes them and the way in which the herdsmen handled them in one of the few passages of this part of his Diary in which he is not indebted to Raymond or Pflaumern. At Livorno he probably drew money, proceeding next day to Empoli and thence on the 23rd to Florence.

Here he was 'exceedingly wel treated' at his lodging with 'Signor Baritiere' in the Piazza dello Spirito Santo. And Florence filled him with enthusiasm. He speaks in particular of the Boboli gardens beside the Palazzo Pitti where 'the Duke ordinarily resides, living

[16] P. 173.

[17] II, 176.

[18] As distinct from 'Don Carlo d'Orias' house in the Strada Nova, which is now the Municipio (II, 176, note 3).

[19] See Mr de Beer's annotations. Evelyn certainly visited a number of palaces and churches, though many of the details he gives are taken from Raymond's observations, which are more original, or from Pflaumern's guide which Evelyn afterwards obtained in Rome.

[20] II, 178.

[21] II, 180-81.

[22] II, 182-83. Smaller than most domestic cattle, they may be indigenous to Italy. One saw several before the war in the fields round Paestum, and they may still be there.

with his Swisse Guards after the frugal Italian way, and even Selling what he can spare of his Wines . . .'[23] The Palazzo Vecchio with the statuary in the Piazza della Signoria and under the Loggia dei Lanzi —all of which remain much as they were in Evelyn's time—and also the galleries of the Uffizi, are described rather confusedly. Evelyn was probably more sensitive to works of art than Moryson had been, but his knowledge was deficient and his taste undiscriminating.[24] It is odd to read that 'st. *Crosse* is the chiefe Cathedrall . . .' —or would be if Dr de Beer had not discovered that this passage is partly taken from Pflaumern—since Santa Croce would be more properly described as the Westminster Abbey of Florence; and equally odd when in the next paragraph he refers to the Duomo as 'St Mary Florida'. His description of the menagerie[25] is better: 'I tooke greate pleasure to see what an incredible height one of the Lyons would leape, for which I caused to be hung downe a joynt of mutton: They are loose in a deepe, Walld-Court, & therefore to be seene with much more delight than at the Tower of Lond, in their grates.'[26]

Proceeding now on horseback to Siena (October 29th) he slept at San Casciano and dined next day at Poggibonsi, famous for the manufacture of snuff 'which the *Italians* of both sexes take excessively'.[27] At Siena the air was 'incomparable', and the city as one approached presented 'an incomparable Prospect, occasion'd by the many playne brick Towers . . . the tallest where off is call'd the Mangio . . .'[28] This, for an appreciation of the Torre del Mangia, seems rather tepid. Evelyn adds, however, that the brick used here is of such rare quality as to look almost as well as porphyry; while as to the Duomo, it is 'both without and within of large square stones of black & white marble polish'd, of inexpressable beauty'.[29]

Two or three days later, as he climbed to the famous inn at Radicofani, he witnessed 'one of the most pleasant, new & altogether surprizing' things he had ever beheld; and he describes it well. The inn stands on a considerable height; the road led up through a belt of dark clouds for upwards of a mile, when suddenly he emerged

[23] II, 187.

[24] And the numerous and confused borrowings from Pflaumern (1628), Raymond (1648) and Balthasar de Monconys' *Journal des voyages* (1665-66)—writers who did not all see the Uffizi (where the collection did not remain static) at the same time—make his account worse.

[25] 'The serraglio delle fiere' which Mr de Beer says was probably the best zoo in Europe (II, 195, note 6).

[26] II, 195.

[27] But they do not appear to have been given to excessive pipe-smoking, as our countrymen had been since the time of James I.

[28] II, 201. Most of the towers had been or were being demolished.

[29] II, 204.

'into a most serene heaven'. Up here the mountain seemed like an island, with a sea of clouds rolling beneath, and here and there, through a gap in the mists, a vision of 'Landskips and Villages'.[30] Though it would have been pleasant to linger, Evelyn had been anxious to reach Rome in time to see 'the Cavalcad of the new Pope', Cardinal Pamphilij, who had assumed the name of Innocent X. When at last he came in sight of 'that prowd Mistriss of the World', his 'thoughts were strangely elevated, but as soone allayed' by a heavy rainstorm, so that when he rode into the city (about 5 p.m. on November 4th) he was 'wett to the skin'.

After wandering in search of shelter for some time he was directed to a French pension kept by a Monsieur Petit on the left side of the slope leading up to Santa Trinità de' Monti from the Piazza di Spagna.[31] Here he delivered up his horse to the vetturino who had brought him from Florence, agreed with his host for twenty crowns a month,[32] 'causd a good fire to be made in my Chamber, and so went to bed . . .'

He immediately next day began a round of visits among his compatriots: Father John Selby, a Benedictine who was Superior of the English College at Douai; Father Patrick Cary, a brother of Lord Falkland, 'a pretty witty young priest' who afterwards returned to the Anglican Communion; the Jesuit Father Thomas Courtney, Principal of the English College; Dr Bacon and Dr Gibbs, who was head-physician at the hospital in the Via Triumphalis; Lord Somerset and others. These gentlemen instructed him as to behaviour in Rome, the purchase of books and the best means of visiting palaces, churches and museums; and so, having resolved 'to spend no moment idly here' he 'began to be very pragmatical'.[33]

Apart from a short visit to Naples in early February, Evelyn spent the winter and spring of 1645 in Rome. His description is detailed and conscientious. The modern reader would welcome more of personal impressions—some sign of the wonderful sensations of which Rome is so prodigal. But Evelyn had no feeling for the ancient world and was deficient in historical imagination. When he speaks of visiting the Campo Vacino he does not even mention that this pasture-ground for cattle concealed the remains of the Roman

30 II, 208.

31 II, 212. It was therefore opposite, but higher up than the corner house (still standing) where Keats and Severn were to take up their lodging. The great stairway had not been built in 1644.

32 About £5 10s. od. in the English currency of the time.

33 II, 214. He hired one of the many guides available. Hans Gross of Lucerne, a member of the Swiss Guard, was the most famous of these men, says de Beer (note 2).

Forum.[34] He thought that Sallust had been a poet.[35] On the other hand he had a great sense of beauty, a keen interest in Christian antiquities and a genuine appreciation of recent and contemporary architecture.[36] If the word 'incomparable' recurs rather often under his pen, if his enthusiasm for Bernini may appear a shade uncritical, his taste was that of his age. Bernini was a man of immense talent, versatility and virtuosity. And as to the buildings in general, it was better to enjoy the spectacle of so much splendour than to argue about the comparative merits of the classical style in architecture and the 'mannered', or discuss *when* the 'baroque' began and just what it was—and was not.

But science and natural history held as great an appeal for him. On November 8th the Jesuit Professor of Mathematics, Athanasius Kircher, showed him round his laboratory and demonstrated the use of the apparatus he had invented for research in optics and magnetism.[37] On the 15th he was charmed by a visit to the gardens of the Villa Borghese, by the trees and fountains that made it an 'Elysium of delight' and by the vivaria for exotic and other birds and animals.[38] On the 23rd he witnessed the splendid and long-awaited procession in which the new Pope was conducted to the Basilica of St John Lateran; and the great display of fireworks that followed in the evening.[39] He entertained and was entertained by distinguished Romans. On Christmas Eve he did not go to bed at all, but spent the whole night in moving from church to church, hearing midnight mass and sermons, and admiring the ingenious pageantry; and on December 29th the Jesuits invited him to a sort of gala dinner at the English College, followed by the performance of an Italian comedy.[40]

Towards the end of January[41] (1645) he and Henshaw set out on a visit to Naples, availing themselves of the *procaccio*[42] who provided the mules they were to ride and arranged for board and lodging en route. The company included Sir John Manwood, an English soldier; a Dutchman whose perfect command of English concealed his nationality from the Spaniards travelling with them; 'two Cortizans

[34] Nov. 7th, 1644. II, 217-220. [35] P. 234.

[36] For a description of the general appearance of Rome at this time, see de Beer's note on II, 212 and his many annotations pp. 212-313. Evelyn, he points out, obtained his copy of Pflaumern's guide on Nov. 14th; and for his description of Rome Evelyn also used P. Totti's *Ritratto di Roma antica* and his *Ritratto di Roma moderna*, both of them recent works (1627 and 1638).

[37] P. 230. [38] P. 251.

[39] Pp. 279-82. [40] Pp. 290-91.

[41] Probably on Saturday, the 28th (see de Beer, II, 315-16, note).

[42] The *procaccio* ran a public service, leaving Rome on Wednesdays and Saturdays (see de Beer's note on p. 315).

in Mans Apparell, who ridd astride, booted, Sworded and Spurd, & whereof one was marvelous pretty, and the Milaneze Squire Signor Jo. Baptist their Gallant, our servants & some others'.[43] Travelling by way of Velletri and Tres Tabernae, they reached their goal on February 1st, 'allighting at the 3 Kings,[44] a place of treatement to excesse, as we found by our very plentifull fare all the time we were in Naples, where provisions are miraculously cheape, & we seldome sat downe to fewer than 18 or 20 dishes of the most exquisite meate and fruites, enjoying the Creature'.[45] The size and magnificence of Naples, with its large, well-paved streets, greatly impressed him, as did the 'gallants' on horseback, the sedan-chairs which, as he remarks, Sir Sanders Duncombe had introduced from here into England,[46] and the gaiety of the country-folk with their love of music and singing.[47]

Nothing remarkable in the way of classical antiquities existed in Naples itself at that time. The museum of Ferrante Imperato was indeed 'full of incomparable rarities'; but so far from being the exquisite statues and wall-paintings which are now the glory of the Naples museum, they consisted of unusual marine and other plants, such as mandrake-roots; reptiles including cameleons; and various kinds of tarantula.[48] Certain excursions were already *de rigueur*. Evelyn and his companions went up Vesuvius on mule-back and spent 'some whole houres there':

I layd my selfe on my belly to look over & into that most frightfull . . . vorago, a stupendious pit . . . of neere three miles in Circuit, and halfe a mile in depth . . . The area at the bottom is plaine . . .: in the middle & center, is a rising, or hill shaped like a greate browne loaf . . . continually vomiting a foggy exhalation, & ejecting huge stones with an impetuous noise & roaring, like the reports of many musquets discharging . . .[49]

Evelyn actually made an etching of the crater; but it is curious to reflect that, as Dr de Beer points out,[50] a part of his description including the probably exaggerated estimate of the size of the crater,[51]

[43] Pp. 315-16.

[44] One of the best hotels. The charges, a few years later, were a crown a day for *pension complète*, including wine.

[45] P. 325.

[46] P. 14, note 4.

[47] Pp. 353-54.

[48] Pp. 330-31.

[49] P. 335.

[50] See the notes to pp. 334-35.

[51] It may, however, I think, have been much larger than it is now. The eruption of 1631 (of which Evelyn gives an account a little further on) blew off the summit of Vesuvius and greatly reduced its height. As the mountain gradually built itself up in later years, the size of the actual crater may well have diminished.

is taken from John Raymond's description and that Evelyn's subsequent references to the elder Pliny and to the 'rebell Spartacus' seem to have been inspired by Raymond (whose book he constantly used) and by George Sandys respectively. Evelyn himself knew little about ancient history.

The visit to Cumae, by way of the Lago d'Agnano, Solfatara (the Phlegraean Fields), Pozzuoli, Baiae and the Lago d'Averno, was the standard excursion, the same as the one described by Sandys, and Evelyn's description of it owes a good deal to Sandys, Raymond and others.[52] Naples and the region, he admits, offer a feast of 'fine sights & good cheere', but when invited to record his name and impressions in the Hotel Album, this being 'the Non ultra of my Travells', the best he could think of was an Ode in honour of Home.[53]

Evelyn and Henshaw appear to have been back in Rome on the 11th, when they immediately resumed sight-seeing. On the 17th he 'was invited . . . to the Academie of the *Humorists*, kept in a spacious Hall, belonging to Signor Mancini, where the Witts of the Towne meete on certaine daies, to recite poems, & prevaricate on severall Subjects &c . . .: by these ingenious Exercises . . . is the purity of the Italian Tongue daily improv'd'.[54] On February 25th a Dominican whom he had heard preaching to the Jews, actually invited him to be godfather to a Turk and a Jew who were being baptized in the Church of Santa Maria sopra Minerva, near the Forum.[55] Evelyn took his duties very seriously. During one week in March he went every day to hear the sermons in St Peter's, 'that most stupendious & incomparable Basilicam' (sic).[56] He also attended service in St Peter's on Good Friday and Easter Sunday.[57] It is pleasant to notice that Evelyn, though a confirmed Anglican, was on friendly and courteous terms with the Roman clergy. He could not but be impressed by the paternal care which the Pope took of his subjects, and the institution of the *zitelle* is mentioned more than once in his *Kalendarium*. These young girls were selected annually, to the number of two or three hundred, from poor working-class homes, and they received dowries to enable them either to marry or to become nuns.[58]

[52] Pp. 336-352.
[53] Pp. 354-55.
[54] P. 364. M.-L. Mancini, the owner of this mansion, was Cardinal Mazarin's brother-in-law and father of those attractive girls, one of whom Louis XIV wanted to marry. Another, the Duchess, later became an ornament of Charles II's court and was a great friend of Saint-Evremond's. Evelyn must have seen her at court in the 1670's.
[55] Pp. 376-77.
[56] As he had previously (p. 255) described it.
[57] P. 386.
[58] P. 378 and 384 and note.

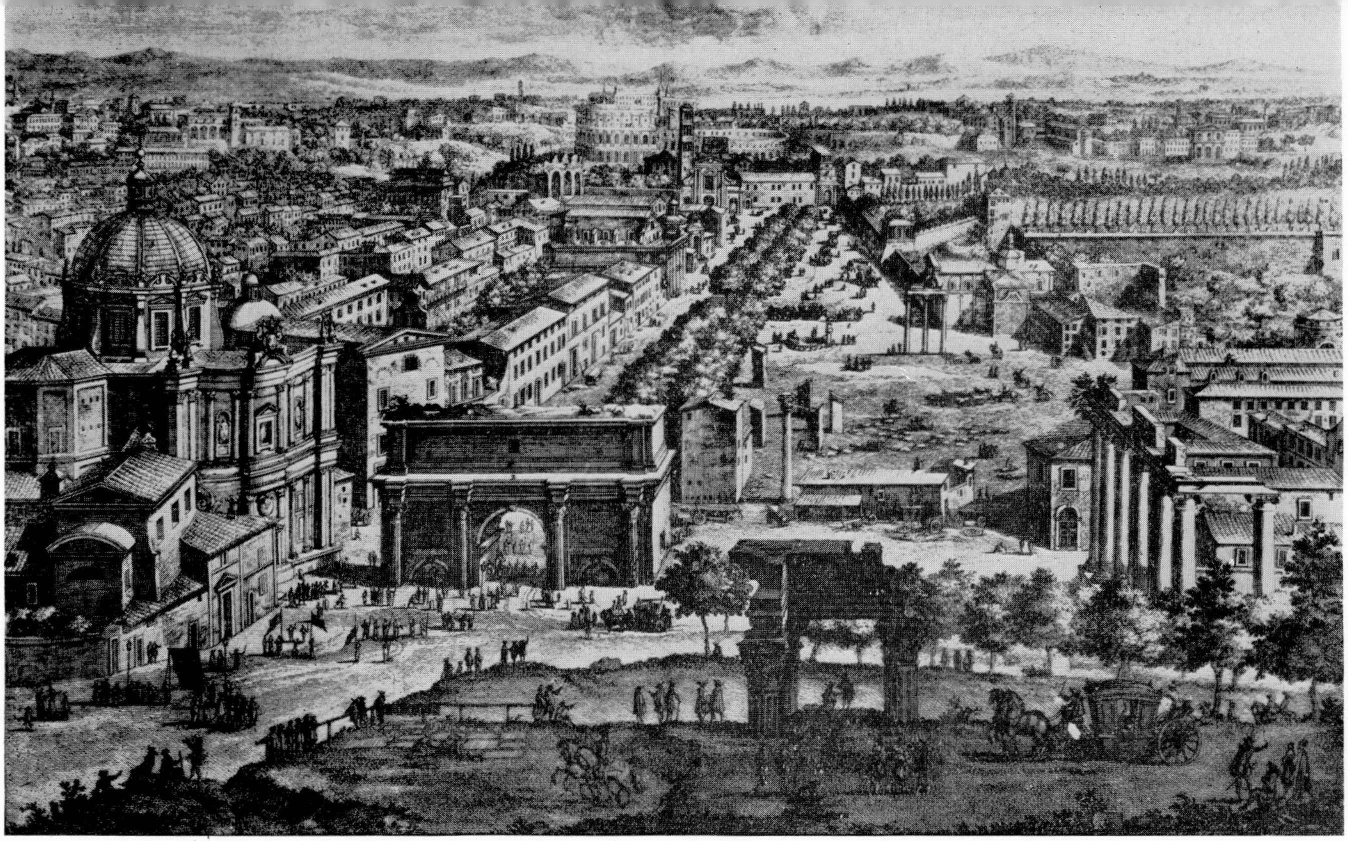

10. *The Roman Forum in 1650, by Livinus Cruyl*

11. *Bird's Eye View of Venice*

On May 2nd Evelyn and his companions 'were entertain'd at Night with an English play, at the *Jesuites* where we before had dined, & the next [day?] at the *Prince Galicanos*,[59] who himself compos'd the Musique to a magnificent Opera . . .: after a Just & Turnament of severall young Gentlemen upon a formal Defy . . . The Launces & swords running at tilt at the Barrieres with a greate deele of clatter, but without any bloud shed, which . . . was very new to us Travellers'.[60]

He had called on Lord John Somerset immediately after his first arrival. In February he again called on him in his 'Appartment in *Palazzo della Cancellaria*, belonging to Card: Francesco Barberini, as Vice-Chancellor of the Church of Rome, & Protector of the English'.[61] And on May 14th, 'by favour of our Cardinal Protector . . . I was admitted into the Consistorie, heard the Ambassador [of Lucca] make his oration in Latine to the Pope . . . After which I was presented to kisse his Toe, that is his embrodr'd Slipper . . . so as sufficiently bless'd with his thumb & two fingers for that day I returned home to dinner'.[62]

So there was some similarity between Evelyn's experiences in Rome in 1644-45, and Milton's some six years earlier: the reception by Cardinal Barberini, the musical entertainment, the dinner with the English Jesuits. Only whereas Milton in the *Defensio Secunda* was silent about the English College, but conveyed the impression that Italy was decadent and that intellectual life was being stifled by Papal obscurantism,[63] Evelyn conveys no such impression. The fact is that Italy was still in the van of scientific research and was to remain so until the 1660's.[64] The Accademia Secretorum Naturae, founded in Naples in 1560, was the first scientific society in Europe; although the Florentine Accademia del Cimento which was organized towards 1655 was, prior to the formation of the Royal Society, the most outstanding. Now it is true that Milton had some

[59] Pompeo Colonna. The opera was apparently the *Proserpina rapita* (De Beer, 389, note 1).

[60] Pp. 388-89.

[61] P. 367.

[62] P. 391.

[63] The Roman curia had been understandably alarmed by Galileo's discoveries, but after a few years it receded from the position it had taken up and tacitly admitted them. Besides, what man of sense today has not speculated on the ultimate benefit to mankind of more than one recent discovery? In any case, the obscurantism in question has been greatly exaggerated.

[64] For example, by using a compound microscope, Malpighi, who was professor at Pisa, discovered the capillaries and thus completed Harvey's demonstration of the circulation of the blood. And he was only one of many Italians engaged in various branches of research. The great centres were of course in Padua and Pisa; but important work in Mathematics and optics was being done at the University of Bologna which was under Papal control.

knowledge of the science of his time and was interested in medicine and mathematics; but he did not possess the varied curiosity of Evelyn who attended lectures on chemistry, made a serious study of medicine and was a great authority on horticulture and arboriculture.

He was also, without being a specialist, something of a connoisseur of painting, and a notable collector. He could not but be impressed by Michelangelo's frescoes in the Sistine Chapel, by the Vatican galleries in general[65] and by many other paintings he saw and described. He makes a brief mention of the Roman school of art,[66] though he did not perhaps realize that it was the best in Europe and the one that attracted the great painters. Most of our English portraitists of the seventeenth century either drew inspiration from Italian technique as did William Dobson in his portraits of Royalist soldiers and gentlemen, and Robert Walker whose picture of Evelyn himself is very Italianate; or studied in Rome like William Sheppard and especially Michael Wright, the interpreter of society in Restoration England, who in 1648 had been a member of the Accademia di S. Luca at the same time as Poussin and Velasquez.[67] Evelyn had the insight to employ a young artist with a great future, Carlo Maratti, to make a number of drawings for him; and before leaving Rome he had also 'purchas'd many books, Pictures & several Curiosities',[68] as a result of which he had spent 616 *ducati di banco*' since his arrival in Italy.[69] As the remittance he was expecting had not arrived, he cancelled a proposed visit to Loreto and decided to return to Livorno for further funds.

He first, however, made an excursion to Frascati and two days later to Tivoli to see the gardens of the Villa d'Este and the falls of the Anio; and then on May 18th, he and, apparently, his friend Thicknesse,[70] joined 'two courteous *Italian* Gentlemen' in hiring a coach to Siena and Pisa[71] At Livorno he drew ninety crowns, complained with some heat of his failure to get funds in Rome, secured a

[65] On Jan. 18, 1645. Pp. 298-99.

[66] P. 399.

[67] Ellis Waterhouse, *Painting in Britain: 1530-1790*. London, 1953, pp. 53-71. I hope in a companion volume to study the influence of Italian architecture and painting in England.

[68] P. 401.

[69] The ducat, a Venetian coin, was worth about 4/5, according to Mr de Beer's calculation. This means that Evelyn had spent about £136—a great deal of money at that time.

[70] See II, 470 (sojourn at Padua) where he speaks of Thicknesse as 'my deare friend & 'til now Constant Fellow traveller'.

[71] Pp. 405-6.

letter of credit for Venice[72] and then set out for Padua, seeing as much as he could on the way. He went round by Lucca and Pistoia, lingered a few days in Florence to see the Uffizi again, visit S. Lorenzo and Prince Leopold's collection and also to inspect the famous Accademia della Crusca. He then took leave of his 'two jolly Companions, Signor Giovanni and his Fellow', and hired horses for Bologna.[73] This place retained him a short time. He remarked, following earlier writers, that it appears like a ship of which the Torre Asinelli is the main-mast, while the lower Torre Garisenda looks always as if ready to fall.[74] He also commented on the famous sausages and cheeses, and on the breeding of a race of lap-dogs then very popular. It will be recalled that Sir John Finch obtained one for his sister.[75] They were very small and extremely expensive.[76] From Bologna he embarked on a canal boat towed by horses and, after passing through several lock-gates, an invention which was new to him, stopped for dinner at an inn called 'Mal Albergo'. It lived up to its reputation, and he was not sorry to be back in the boat, gliding on through a night so illumined with fireflies that by capturing a number of them he was able to read in the dark.[77] Ferrara, aside from its fortifications, did not much attract him, and in the afternoon he proceeded still by canal-boat until they reached the Po and finally, after changing into a larger vessel, the Adige. On this part of the journey he made friends with a Polish bishop who 'afterwards did me many kindnesses at *Venice*', he says.[78]

It was on the evening of the second day after leaving Ferrara that Evelyn landed in the great city, and after passing through the Customs—probably on the site of the present *Dogana*—put up 'at honest *Signor Paulo Rhodomants* at the *Aquila Nera* neere the Rialto'.[79] Next morning, feeling very weary and travel-stained, he went to an oriental bathing-place where they washed him in hot and

[72] He had been using bills of exchange and these had evidently not been honoured owing (apparently) to the confirmatory notes not having reached the Roman banker.

[73] Pp. 411-18.

[74] Pp. 420-21. Dante alludes to it in the passage in the *Inferno* about Antaeus. It looks just the same today when a cloud is passing over it.

[75] See above, p. 120.

[76] Mr de Beer (p. 425, note 1) says that the smallest would go inside a lady's muff, and that they might cost up to £40.

[77] P. 427.

[78] P. 428.

[79] Evelyn appears to have made his headquarters at first in Venice. He went to Padua for a day towards the middle of June, and had settled there by the latter part of July. He lived in Padua from the late summer of 1645 until April, 1646, but paid several visits to Venice—too numerous to deserve mention, the more so as he did not always record the exact dates. He was in Venice for Ascension week (June, 1645) and for the Carnival (January, 1646). For his description of Venice (partly derivative) see ed. de Beer, II, 430-452.

cold water, rubbed him with oil, brought 'a world of dirt' off his limbs, then applied a depilatory to remove the hairs; after which he caught one of the worst colds he had ever had.[80] The silence of the city, due to the absence of horses and carriages, impressed him; as did the remarkable attire of the Patrician dames and the still more remarkable 'high heeld shoos', *calcaznetti* (or 'Choppines' as foreigners called them), which they alone were allowed to wear.[81] They looked very ridiculous, he thought, when crawling in and out of their gondolas, '& what dwarfes they appeare when taken down from their Wooden Scafolds!' To Evelyn's eyes, no doubt, but not to Venetian. How very gratifying it must have been for the said ladies, in the Piazza San Marco or on the Rialto, to queen it high above the heads of mere citizens' wives and especially of the most famous courtesans; the more so, as these *nobildonne* had their fair hair set thickly with precious stones and silken flowerets, wore magnificent dresses, were extremely *décolletées* as was apparent from the fine, transparent lawn that covered their shoulders; and as the dress of the inferior orders was strictly regulated.[82] Evelyn was not old enough at this time to understand the joys and refinements of female vanity.

But he was well able to appreciate the enchantments of Italian opera, with its 'most excellent' singers, its variety of painted scenes, and 'Machines, for flying in the aire, & other wonderfull motions'. He and Lord Robert Bruce booked places for a performance of the *Hercules in Lydia*[83] at the Teatro Novissimo.[84] Anna Renzi, soprano, was the prima donna, and Hercules was apparently represented by a Genoese who 'sung an incomparable Base: This held us by the Eyes and Eares til two in the Morning'.[85] Evelyn was much taken with these people, as will appear later. At the moment, however, his thoughts were set on a visit to the Holy Land, Egypt and Turkey; and having planned to sail in an English vessel, of which the Master was a certain Captain Powell, he laid in a stock of 'some Sheepe, Poultry, Bisqit, Spirits' and drugs for the purpose. Unfortunately the Turks had just launched an attack on Crete, Powell's ship was

[80] Pp. 430-31.

[81] Evelyn says they were about 10 feet high. Mr de Beer suggests not more than 1 foot 8 ins. The original purpose had been to protect the feet and skirts from street refuse (p. 446, note 11).

[82] Pp. 447-48.

[83] Words by Bisaccioni, music by Rovetta (De Beer, p. 450, note 2).

[84] Opera properly so-called had been invented by Monteverdi, whose *Orfeo* had been produced in 1607 at Mantua; but the first opera-house was opened in Venice in 1637, with Monteverdi as the principal composer. The theatre which Evelyn saw was destroyed by fire in 1647. The *Fenice* dates only from the eighteenth century.

[85] Pp. 449-50.

requisitioned by the Republic to carry provisions for the relief of Candia, and Evelyn's arrangements were drastically altered.[86]

He went to Padua to see the Fair of St Anthony, the journey by canal-boat enabling him to admire the beautiful villas and gardens standing on both sides of the Brenta canal.[87] On the following day, which was excessively hot, he witnessed the great procession of Venetian nobles and other dignitaries to the Basilica of Sant'Antonio—which he took, mistakenly, for the Cathedral—and visited the interior. He then crossed the Prato della Valle to see the Church of Santa Giustina, which, in common with other travellers, he greatly admired, supposing it to be the work of Palladio.[88] It was perhaps at this moment that he conceived the notion of settling in Padua for a course of study. However that may be, he returned to that city late in July, met Dr George Rogers who was then Consul for the English nation, and inspected the University. Notable in particular was

the Theater for Anatomies, which is excellently contriv'd both for the discector & spectators: [89] I was this day invited to dinner, & in the afternoone being July 30th, received my *Matricula*, being resolved to spend some moneths here at study, especially Physic & Anatomie, of both which here were now the most famous Professors then in Europe.[90]

Next morning [he continues] I went to see the Garden of Simples, rarely furnished with plants, and gave order to the Gardner to make me a Collection of them for an *hortus hyemalis*, by permission of the Cavalier Dr Vestlingius[91] their Prefect, & Botanie Professor, as well as Anatomie.

Evelyn had created a great impression in Padua, for he immediately moved into the best circles. On August 2nd the Earl of Arundel invited him 'to go with him to see the Garden of Mantua' and in the afternoon to the zoo 'at the palace of Foscari all'Arena'. The garden in question was near the Eremitani, probably on the site of the present public park; the Palazzo Foscari stood in the Roman Amphitheatre a few yards away, and in front of the Madonna dell'Arena

[86] Pp. 451-52.

[87] The canal is now half-empty and out of use; and some of the villas, particularly at Mira, where Byron lived for a time, dilapidated or put to other uses. Many, however, are beautifully kept up, for example at Strà. An easy way of going to Venice today is by the motor-bus which follows the line of the canal. (Note 1963. The canal has now been refilled and a tourist vessel plies on it.)

[88] Pp. 453-55.

[89] It is still preserved in the Palazzo centrale of the University.

[90] Pp. 464-65. He had signed the Visitors' Book the previous day.

[91] Johann Vesling.

or Scrovegni chapel. This palace was demolished in 1820 leaving the arena as an open garden.

Three days later Evelyn returned to Venice, explored the glass-works on the island of Murano in the Lagoon, and was rowed out into the Adriatic to see the English vessel on which he had intended to sail for Palestine.[92]

In the meantime the election of University or rather Student officers had taken place. George Rogers was elected as Counsellor of the English Nation and Evelyn as Syndic. This news[93] embarrassed him, since he felt that the duties involved would seriously interfere with his work. He declined the honour, whereupon a German[94] was appointed, a fact 'which did not well please my Countrymen'. One could at any rate devote one's whole attention to work in the Medical School. Evelyn found a suitable apartment in the Piazza del Santo, facing the great church and near Donatello's equestrian statue of 'Gattamelata',[95] in a house where a plaque now records his sojourn. He studied hard, he tells us, ''till the arivall of Mr *Henshaw*, *Bramstone* & and some other English Gent: whom I had left at Rome';[96] and also no doubt after their arrival. Thomas Henshaw, it will be recalled, was an old acquaintance. An excellent French scholar, he afterwards handled Charles II's French correspondence, and became Secretary of the Royal Society in 1668.

On September 26th Evelyn's fellow traveller, Thicknesse, had to return to England. Evelyn himself paid another visit to Venice; but what was his dismay and alarm on returning home, to find Padua 'infested with Souldiers'—probably foreign troops hired for the war in Crete—who had broken into many houses and ill-treated the inhabitants. Far more serious was the danger he incurred by taking his wine cooled with snow and ice. This brought on an attack of quinsy, he could scarcely breathe and 'was in uttmost danger'. Johann Vesling, who was called in, failed to cure him, but the elderly Italian professor of medicine, Benedetto Selvatico, applied remedies that gave relief and enabled him, after a fortnight, to go out again. He moved to another part of the city, taking a house in the Via Pozzo Dipinto—now the Via Cesare Battisti—where he and Bramston 'lived very nobly'. The Convent of Santa Caterina stood in the same

92 Pp. 466-69.

93 Which he received on August 8th.

94 'A Dutch Gentleman.' Actually two, who were Counsellors. The Germans were then usually referred to as Dutch.

95 Erasmo da Narni, a condottiere who had been in Venetian service: known as the 'honeyed cat'.

96 P. 470. They appear to have arrived some time in November. Bramston matriculated on the 22nd (Horatio Brown, *op. cit.*, 73; Andrich, Records for 1645-46; see above, ch. VI).

street, and on October 31st, which was Evelyn's birthday, the nuns sent him a present of 'flowers of silk-work'. He bought three hundred pounds of grapes, pressed his own wine, 'which proved incomparable Liquor', avoided ice and was very studious until Christmas.[97]

In January, 1646 (N.S.), Edmund Waller the poet, whose wit at an awkward moment was later so much to amuse Charles II, arrived in Padua. A less prudent person than Evelyn, Waller had attempted in May, 1643, in concert with the Royalists at Oxford, to put into force the 'commission of array'. He and his fellow 'conspirators' were arrested by Parliament, two of the unfortunates were hanged outside their own doors in the City, and Waller lay in prison for over a year. His life was spared, apparently because he was a member of the House (representing St Ives in Cornwall) and because he paid a fine of £10,000 and agreed to go into exile.[98] At Padua he matriculated on January 25th,[99] and he appears to have attended, or at least looked in at, Vestlingius' lectures on anatomy which occupied a month, from mid February to mid March, and were illustrated with dissections of which Evelyn gives a brief account.[100] He afterwards wrote a poem in the professor's honour, as we know from the testimony of Edmund Warcup, a nephew of the Speaker of the House of Commons, who was in Padua at the same time.[101]

There had been a heavy snowfall and great cold in January, and Evelyn and his friends did not go to Venice to see the Carnival until Shrovetide, about February 12th. The Carnival had been in full swing since the turn of the year, but the last few days were the climax, and the staid young Englishman was astounded at the license that prevailed, the flinging about of eggs and the hunting of bulls through the narrow thoroughfares. More to his liking were 'three noble Operas'[102] in which Anna Renzi sang, along with a

[97] Pp. 471-73.

[98] P. 478. See C. V. Wedgwood, *The King's War*, London, 1958, pp. 218-19. Miss Wedgwood is very severe on Waller's action in buying 'his dishonoured life' by naming his accomplices. It is very hard today to understand the atmosphere of that troubled time when families were divided by loyalties sometimes hesitant and uncertain, when legality had gone by the board, when life or death might hang on a mere word or flash of temper and when no one could foretell the consequences of his behaviour.

[99] See above, ch. VI.

[100] P. 475.

[101] J. W. Stoye, *English Travellers Abroad (1604-1667)*. London, 1952, p. 199. In 1660 Warcup published an English translation of François Schott's *Itinerarii Italiae* . . . (1600), a version probably based on one of the many editions in Italian of this popular guide-book. He entitled his English translation: *Italy, in its original Glory, Ruine and Revival* (Stoye, 199).

[102] Evelyn does not give the titles or subjects. De Beer says that the only operas recorded for that year were Monteverdi's *Incoronazine di Poppea* and F. Cavalli's opera about Julius Caesar as dictator; the libretti being by G. F. Businello (474, note 6).

eunuch whose voice Evelyn greatly admired, and the Genoese bass. Early in Lent he invited her to a fish-dinner, after which she entertained him and his friends by singing to the harpsichord. A Venetian gentleman then came for her, to show her the war-galleys that were sailing to Crete; and when viewing these, they were invited to the house of the English Consul—probably John Hobson—who was entertaining the Genoese. This kept them late. On escorting a lady, who had had supper with them, to her gondola, 'we were shot at by two *Carbines* from out another *Gundala*, in which was a *Noble Venetian* & his *Curtezana*, unwilling it seemes to be disturb'd, which made us run in . . .'[103]

Back in Padua Evelyn attended the demonstrations in dissection and anatomy, and from Vesling's assistant 'I purchased those rare Tables of *Veines* & *Nerves*, & caused him to prepare a third of the *Lungs, liver,* & *Nervi sexti par:* with the *Gastric* vaines, which I transported into England . . .' and which he afterwards gave to the Royal Society.[104] He also visited the hospitals, marvelling at the care that was bestowed on the sick and the charity with which these humane Italians treated even diseases arising from vice. Late in March he went again to Venice, where he took leave of the patriarch G. F. Morosini and of Hugo Grotius's son who was accompanying the expeditionary force to Crete, with the rank of Commander[105]—probably of a Dutch contingent.[106] He also called on his banker, or 'Merchant', Vandervort (another Dutchman) and drew three hundred ducats for his journey to Paris; and, intending to pass through the Milanese, paid his respects to the Spanish ambassador, 'Don Gaspar de Teves, y Guzman, Marques de la Fuente', who presented him with a passport of extraordinary length and magnificence to ensure his safe passage.[107]

April, with the trees bursting into leaf, was a pleasant month in Padua. On the 30th, George Rogers received his M.D. and was congratulated in a number of Latin poems, including one by Evelyn. The latter had already (on the 25th) begun to take leave of his friends, especially the Earl of Arundel who was then in great dis-

[103] P. 475.

[104] P. 475. These were similar to the ones which John Finch was to obtain towards 1659 (see above, ch. VI). Evelyn's specimens, however, became known soon after his return home in 1651. In 1652 Sir Charles Scarborough, who had succeeded to Harvey's lectureship, borrowed them for his own lectures on anatomy, as Evelyn intimates in his Diary for Nov. 5, 1652. He appears to have paid 150 scudi for them (de Beer, 476 note), i.e. about £41.

[105] Pp. 476-77.

[106] The *Serenissima* recruited a great many troops, and even sailors, from Protestant countries: England, the United Provinces and Switzerland.

[107] Pp. 477-78.

tress, owing to his grandson's having taken orders[108] and to his belief that the Countess, who was in the Netherlands, was unkind. At Arundel's house he met another grandson, Henry Howard, later to become Duke of Norfolk; and also John Digby, a son of Sir Kenelm. The whole of the English peerage was not at this time in Padua or Venice, but one feels that those members of it who were not, ought to have been—unless they were fighting for the King (or the Parliament).

Finally, having received from Lord Arundel carefully written-out instructions as to all the interesting objects (not female) which he was to look out for on his journey, and being armed also with Dr Selvatico's advice as to the care of his health, he set out. His companions in the coach were Edmund Waller and John Abdy, a Fellow of Trinity College, Cambridge, 'a modest & learned man'; the fly in the ointment was a certain Captain Wray, whose father had been in arms against His Majesty and who was 'therefore by no means wellcome to us'.[109] He was neither modest nor learned, and he had a large and enterprising hound, as we shall see.

It was early May, and Evelyn was charmed with the sight of the Euganean hills and the well-watered plain. In Vicenza he visited Palladio's theatre and Count Valmarano's gardens, and very much wished to see the Rotonda, which stands on the hill to the south, but was prevented by one of his companions (no doubt the objectionable Wray) who minded little 'save drinking and folly' and who forced them to proceed by coach earlier than they wished.[110] The late afternoon and all the next day were spent in Verona. Evelyn considered the amphitheatre 'one of the noblest Antiquities in Europ'; but the crowning pleasure came in the evening, in the Giardino dei Giusti, with its huge and magnificent cypress and the terrace from which the eye ranges, from the roof-tops of Verona beneath, far over the plain to distant Mantua.[111] Verona, Evelyn concludes, is 'situated in one of the most delightfullst places that ever I came in, so sweetly mixed with risings, & Vallies . . . & here of all places I have travelld in *Italy*, would I fix preferable to any other . . .'[112]

Reaching the Lake of Garda next day, they visited Sirmione. This enchanted spot evoked no mention of Catullus and Lesbia (save perhaps in the minds of Abdy and Waller), perhaps because the unspeakable Wray 'bought a pretty Nag of the Master of our Inn', in spite of the tearful reluctance of the hostess to part with it.[113] From

[108] Philip Howard became a cardinal in 1675.

[109] P. 480.

[110] P. 484.

[111] P. 487. See also the articles on ' "Rose-Red" City of Verona' in *The Times*, February 1, 1958.

[112] P. 488.

[113] P. 489.

Brescia they would have liked to turn south to see Mantua and Parma; but the presence of bandits decided them to push on by way of Lodi to Milan. They were now in Spanish territory; some 'Cavalieres' they met looked suspicious; and 'dread of the Inquisition' began to exercise some of their minds. They were admitted by the officers, however, without losing more than the necessary tip and reached the inn of the Three Kings in safety.[114]

The Italian population was kind. Francesco Ferrari, prefect of the Ambrosiana,[115] to whom Evelyn had a letter of introduction, showed them round the marble Duomo and various churches. Evelyn himself ventured imprudently into the governor's palace and even peeped into a room 'where the greate Man' (no less a person than Don Bernardino de Velasco y Tovar, Constable of Castile and Duke of Frias[116]) was in the hands of his barber; whereupon the Duke sent a negro to investigate. Evelyn made what excuse he could, but on hearing the Duke exclaim that 'It was some Spie', retired with all speed and rejoined his companions. The day concluded with a visit to the Madonna delle Grazie and Leonardo's great fresco of the Last Supper. François Ier, he mentions, was so enamoured of this picture that he wished to have the whole wall bound with ribs of iron and wood, and removed intact to France. 'But this incomparable piece,' he concludes, 'is now exceedingly impaired:'[117] It escaped by a miracle in the last German war when the remainder of the room was destroyed by a bomb.

Ferrari[118] called for them next morning and conducted them round the Ambrosian Library and the Church of S. Ambrogio. On returning to their inn they passed a cavalier who overheard them speaking English and sent his servant to invite them to dinner on the following day. This struck them as rather odd and they were uncertain whether to accept; but on learning that he was a Scottish Colonel who had a command in the city, they decided to go. He lived in a noble palace and provided a sumptuous repast, with tempting wine; after which he showed them his arms and trophies, bestowed a pair of pistols on Wray (whom Evelyn describes at this point as 'a good drinking Gent:') and on Evelyn himself a Turkish bridle with silk trappings from which a half-moon was suspended—a 'glorious spoil' which he had taken in war and which his guest conveyed safely back to England. But the day was to end in tragedy. Their host, who appears to have been Alexander Burnet, next took them to see

[114] P. 491.
[115] P. 492.
[116] P. 493, note 8.
[117] P. 497.
[118] The Directors of the Ambrosiana remain distinguished for their courtesy. The present writer recalls with gratitude the manner in which he was received in 1947 by the successor of Monsignore Achille Ratti, who was at that time Pope Pius VI.

his stables and 'manège'. Here, being an excellent horseman, he put various animals through their paces, and then, contrary to the advice of his groom, mounted a beautiful creature that had not yet been broken in. It immediately plunged off in full career and rising on its hind legs crushed the Colonel against the wall of the riding school. It failed to throw him, but he asked to be taken down and helped into the house and to bed. He was unable to speak. His guests took leave of him in consternation.[119]

When they called next morning, they found an Irish friar confessing him, or pretending to do so, for the Colonel was secretly a Protestant and the friar was his confidant. He was still unable to speak, and he vomited blood. But he took them all by the hand, and made signs that they should see him no more.[120] This dreadful experience filled them with grief for their kind host, and with a renewed fear of the Inquisition, so much so that they left Milan the very next day.

After crossing in a boat the lower reaches of Lago Maggiore, they landed at Arona, where 'the horrid prospect of the *Alps*, coverd with Pine trees, & Firrs & above them Snow' and starting up 'as it were suddainly' from the plain,[121] was to some extent offset by a view of the Borromean islands with their gardens and formal buildings.[122] At Mergozzo Evelyn could obtain no better mount than a donkey, with looped ropes for stirrups, to carry him to Domodossola. Here he had to show his Spanish passport to the governor who made him pay a crown for another one; but here also they hired a guide and secured mules which were surer-footed than the 'gallant steedes' they had just been riding. The next two days were a time of fear and of tribulation. The Simplon was not then in frequent use and the 'road', now cut out of the rock-faces, now carried over the torrent flowing below at a 'stupendous depth' on a narrow bridge consisting of huge fir-trees, was of the most primitive. The huge precipices towering overhead as they mounted through the Gorge of Gondo, the deafening roar of the cataracts, were the same as those which Wordsworth was to see many years later; but very different was the impression they produced on Evelyn.[123] The natives were a gigantic folk, 'ex-

[119] Pp. 503-4.

[120] He can scarcely have outlived the day. Mr de Beer cites an epitaph in the Church of S Angelo which apparently refers to him, as it gives his name and the year but not the day of his death (505, note 1). He belonged to the same family as Bishop Gilbert Burnet.

[121] Pp. 503-4.

[122] Isola Bella and Isola Madre. The gardens and palace on the former, which Evelyn correctly calls 'Isabella' (its original name) were being constructed at this time (De Beer, 506, note 8).

[123] P. 509.

tremely fierce & rude', yet honest; many of them, especially the women, suffered from goitre. It was altogether very unpleasant, and there was worse to come. As they were approaching the hospice, Wray's spaniel, 'a huge filthy Curr, that had follow'd him out of England', chased a herd of goats down the rocks into the torrent.[124] Nothing more was heard of this at the moment. In the hospice, still half-covered with snow, they were given a rough meal and slept in 'Cupboards' between those loose feather-beds still strangely popular in parts of the Alps. But next morning there appeared a 'huge young fellow' demanding compensation for a goat that the dog had killed. Our travellers, who were by now feeling thoroughly miserable, set spurs to their mules and attempted to ride away; whereupon the crowd which had assembled to hear Mass pulled them off their mounts, seized their carbines and set a watch on them until Mass was over. A summary court was then set up by these 'grim Swisse' who condemned them to pay a pistol for the goat and ten for trying to escape. Rather than face imprisonment and a regular magistrate, with the additional charge that they were preparing to use their carbines, 'as indeede the Captain was about to do', they deemed it better to follow the advice the Gospel gives us for such contingencies and pay. Which they did;[125] all of them apparently contributing. It may be assumed that Wray's popularity went down by several points at this time.

The pass was deep in snow, and as they were beginning the descent Wray's horse, which was carrying the baggage, appears to have stepped on to a snow-cornice. This gave way and he slid a long way down the declivity; which so incensed his choleric master that he was about to send two bullets into the poor beast. His companions, who seem to have been rather afraid of Wray (his father was a powerful figure in the Eastern Association) contrived, by a Machiavellian manoeuvre, to prevent this folly. But the horse, plunging about in the snow, was by no means out of danger. He again lost his footing and was precipitated down a further slope, coming to rest in a deep gully near which the winding track descended. He had fallen about two miles, Evelyn calculated. When they at last reached the spot, they removed the pack-baggage, hauled the animal out of the snow (which alone had saved his life), rubbed and chafed his legs until the circulation began to return, and so were able to proceed.[126] And it must have been a rather subdued and miserable party that rode late that night into the streets of Brigue.

The following day, as they moved down the Rhone valley, was brighter and indeed 'excessively hot'. At Sion they were entertained

[124] P. 511.

[125] Pp. 512-13.

[126] Pp. 513-14.

with the utmost kindness by one of the principal citizens, a former Colonel in the French army—'a true old blade'—who was much displeased at the treatment they had received on the Simplon. A man of culture, a collector of pictures and antiquities, he invited them to stay for a time, to see his country house and go hunting with him, as wolves and bears then abounded in the region. This, however, they declined, as they did a further pressing invitation from the governor of the canton at Saint-Maurice,[127] being now 'so neere France, which we reckon'd as good as home'. Evelyn was nevertheless charmed with Switzerland which he rightly regarded as 'the safest spot of all *Europ*'.[128]

Evelyn marks an advance on his predecessors by virtue of his curiosity regarding all matters artistic and scientific. The future Fellow of the Royal Society was a genuine connoisseur, sensitive to beauty of various kinds, even to the beauty of landscape and conceiving the notion—still very original—of attempting on occasion to render it. He had not, it is true, thought of describing the Campagna and the Alban hills, nor could he have done so. The art of landscape-*painting* was only then being explored by the French and the Italians and invented—and with what brilliance!—by the Dutch. The art of *describing* landscape was still to come. But the Dutch paintings had perhaps given Evelyn an idea of its possibilities. He notes the contrast between the calm serenity of Lac Léman and the snow-capped Alps, 'shewing their aspiring tops' in the distance.[129] His long description of the Gorge of Gondo above Domodossola suggests comparison with Wordsworth's impressions of the same scenery, as recorded in the *Prelude*. Evelyn writes:

Next morning we mount againe through strange, horrid & firefull Craggs & tracts abounding in Pine trees . . . nor could we any where see above a pistole shoote before us, the horizon being terminated with rocks, & mountaines, whose tops cover'd with Snow, seem'd to touch the Skies, & in many places piered the Clowdes. Some of these mountaines were but one intire stone, 'twixt whose clefts now & then precipitated greate Cataracts of Mealted Snow . . . which made a tirrible roaring, Echoing from the rocks and cavities, & these

[127] Still in Canton Valais.

[128] P. 518. Readers of the *Diary* will be familiar with his subsequent experiences; how on leaving Le Bouveret (in Savoy) he developed small-pox, owing, as he believed mistakenly, to an act of selfishness on his part (see De Beer, 519, note 4); how he lay very ill in Geneva but, after five weeks, had some most interesting experiences there; and how he spent over a year in Paris, where he married Sir Richard Browne's daughter.

[129] Pp. 519-20.

Waters in some places, breaking in the fall, wett us as if we had pass'd through a mist, so as we could neither see, nor heare one another, but trusting to our honest Mules, jog on our way.[130]

This is an original passage, not, like so many of his apparently personal observations, borrowed from Raymond, Monconys[131] or one of the guide-books. And indeed it is not hard to disengage from Evelyn's *Diary* (which, one cannot too often remind oneself, he compiled entirely for his personal interest) the elements of an excellent book of travel in the company of a charming and good-tempered companion, a perfect gentleman, and already something of a 'man of feeling' in an age not conspicuous for tenderness.

130 P. 509.

131 Balthasar de Monconys, *Journal des Voyages*, Paris, 1665-66, 3 vols.

CHAPTER XIV

John Raymond

BY far the best of the seventeenth-century travel-books that concern us is *Il Mercurio Italico* or, in its alternative title, *An Itinerary contayning a Voyage made through Italy In the yeare* 1646 & 1647. *By Jo: Raymond. Gent.* It was 'printed for Humphrey Mosely . . . at the Princes Armes in St Pauls Churchyard 1648' and boldly dedicated 'To the most Illustrious Prince Charles'.

To give a fair description of the country, a writer was obliged to take some information from the standard guide-books, and Raymond from time to time uses François Schott's *Itinerarii Italiae* and, in a lesser degree, J. H. von Pflaumern's *Mercurius Italicus* (1628),[1] the title of which he borrows. With this reservation, his book is original and by far the liveliest and most entertaining that I have read. By copying from almost every part of it a vast number of passages and observations, John Evelyn has unwittingly acquired in our own time much credit that rightly belongs to his gifted contemporary.

Raymond's itinerary was the one increasingly followed at this time, that is, by entering Italy from Cannes or Antibes and leaving by the Simplon. Naturally therefore he saw the standard marvels. With a shrewd and humorous mind, an eye for the essential detail and the art of expressing himself quickly and well, he must have been a delightful companion for Bargrave[2] and Chapman who, like him, hailed from Kent and were with him most of the time. After explaining in his Introduction *why* one should go to Italy, *what* one should be on one's guard against, and *how* one should proceed, and after enumerating some of the wonders of the peninsula, he asks us to 'behold' Rome the Holy, Venice the Rich, Naples the Gentle, 'Florence the faire, Genua the superbe', Milan the Great, Bolonia the Fat, Padua the Learned, and Verona the Ancient; and he shows us them, though not in that order.

It was in early December, 1646, that, having reached Antibes, 'the utmost city of France', the young Kentishmen procured a 'bill

[1] De Beer, *Evelyn's Diary*, ed. 1955, II, 573. De Beer has studied and compared all the travel-books of the period.

[2] John Bargrave; to be distinguished from Robert B. who was in Rome in 1654 (Stoye, p. 193).

of health' from the governor and hired a felucca to take them to Genoa.[3] The splendour of this place, with the houses rising in tiers up the hillside like the seats in a theatre, provoked the usual and merited admiration. '. . . the Genuesians live in a Kingly luxury, and I believe it is the best built and compacted City, not only of Italy, but also of *Europe*.'[4] The fact that no coaches were allowed in the narrow streets under the towering palaces 'preserves the wayes more cleane and neater'. He may not have been aware that much of this magnificence was based on an extensive business in banking and marine insurance. The party next proceeded by sea to Lerici where the boatmen contrived delays so as to force the travellers to pay the whole fare to Livorno but actually to take horse from Lerici. This was Raymond's fate. At Pisa he was greatly impressed by 'that worthy peece of arte the Falling Tower';[5] which he apparently supposed had been intended to lean. In describing the marble Duomo, he noted that the roof is supported by three-score pillars[6] of great beauty. The semi-domesticated 'Buffolos'—creatures very strange to northern eyes—that haunted the forest, drew his attention[7] when he and his friends took a boat like a gondola down the canal to 'Ligorne' to draw money. Returning thence to Pisa 'we tooke Coach (a very unpleasant journey over hilly way)' to Empoli and Florence.[8] Twenty pages of the book are devoted to Florence and the government of Tuscany. He describes in succession the Piazza della Signoria; 'the Great Duke's Gallery', that is, the Uffizi; the covered way leading across the river to the Pitti Palace; the Boboli gardens; the Duomo which was 'the fairest Cathedrall without, that ever man laid eyes on';[9] and then 'that mirrour of Art, and wonder of this present age, Saint Laurents Chappell', where one feels oneself 'in some place above terrestriall';[10] and of course the Library with its manuscript treasures.[11] One notes as regards the Uffizi that Raymond describes the statues and jewels but says very little about the pictures. 'The Florentins,' he observes, 'have commonly notable headpieces, so that from hence spring notable Polititians, and States-men,'

[3] *Il Mercurio Italico*, 1648, p. 2. His description of the voyage from Antibes to Genoa was of great help to Evelyn when compiling his Diary.

[4] *Ibid.*, 10-13.

[5] P. 19.

[6] Evelyn, glancing at this, wrote 'six'! These columns had been taken by the Pisans from ancient Greek or Roman buildings in Sicily and southern Italy, in the course of their forays back in the Middle Ages.

[7] Pp. 26-27. Evelyn had also seen them, but from the public coach.

[8] Pp. 27-28.

[9] Pp. 31-39.

[10] The Medici chapel in San Lorenzo. Evelyn, who used this passage, calls the chapel 'the third heaven if any be on Earth' (II, 198). It was in particular the facing of the walls with marble of varied colours and with precious stones that inspired these ecstasies in visitors.

[11] Pp. 40-41.

and he tells how three ambassadors from three several kings met once by accident and found they were all Florentines.[12]

Siena, however, was the place best suited for a long sojourn. The quality of the air, the courtesy of the people, the purity of the language—'these and the like conveniences . . . mov'd us to settle ourselves there for Some moneths'. The streets were well paved with brick, so that even 'in the fowlest weather one may walke as cleane as within dores'. The Torre del Mangia, or Lily-Tower as it is now more pleasantly called, seemed to Raymond a 'hidious Structure', but the façade of the Duomo was 'admirable'.[13] In April at last, 'After two moneths stay, the time of Easter . . . urging, together with good company, and the holy week, we set on for Rome'.[14] They saw the great hostelry that Ferdinand I had built at Radicofani[15] and then, crossing the frontier, proceeded to Montefiascone, famous as the name implies for its wines, famous also for the German bishop who sampled too many of them and too much. This ecclesiastic, a member of the Fugger family, had on arriving at Montefiascone sent his servant round all the taverns to see where the wine was best and to mark the appropriate doors with the words 'Est, Est'. He marked a good many; and the bishop who heartily approved the choice, 'so filld his body with wine, that hee left no roome for his Soule'. He was buried there, and the following epitaph was written by the servant: *Propter Est Est, Dominus meus mortuus Est.*[16]

Raymond had prepared himself not to expect too much of Rome, but 'I found that it flourisheth beyond all expectation, this new even emulous to exceed the old, the remnants of the old adding to the splendour of the new'. It deserved the name of 'Mistriss of the World'.[17] Although he felt 'confounded' in knowing how to describe Rome, his description in some forty pages is a masterpiece of judgment and selection. 'A man may spend many Moneths at *Rome*, and yet have something of Note to see every day.' The Arches of Constantine and Titus 'speak *Roman* History more palpably than any Author', says Raymond, noting very shrewdly the wonderful eloquence of bas-relief or sculpture.[18] As to St Peter's, ''tis the most perfect modell of decent Magnificence in the world'. In the Vatican Library he was shown copies of Virgil, Terence and others, 'written with their own hands' (as he supposed); and 'there are likewise . . . King Harry the eights Letters to *Anne of Bulloyne*, some in *French*, some in English, those beginning commonly with *My Darling*, or a

[12] P. 47.
[13] Pp. 51-5.
[14] P. 57.
[15] It belonged to the state.
[16] P. 62.
[17] Pp. 67-8. Evelyn borrowed this phrase, as he borrowed so much else from Raymond's book.
[18] Pp. 77-8.

lascivious expression; together with his Book against Luther, which procurd him the Title of *Defender of the Faith*'.[19] To turn to less humorous topics, the Villa Borghese was 'to bee preferred before any other . . . in Italy'. The park and gardens 'want nothing which should make a man conceive himselfe in Paradise'.[20] This is no exaggeration. Papal Rome was then, and remained until 1870, a far more enchanting city than it is today.

It was becoming usual, as we have seen, for travellers so to plan their tour that they could spend Holy Week in Rome. Raymond and his friends visited the Sistine Chapel on Good Friday (1647) and attended a service in St Peter's on Easter Sunday. They then left for Naples. Along the post-road[21] through Velletri and the hill-country they noted the frequent watch-towers that were manned by Papal guards to protect travellers against the banditti.[22] The ruins supposed to mark the site of the Three Taverns, where the brethren from Rome came to meet Paul on his arrival, spoke strongly to Raymond's imagination. Approaching Terracina, the road emerged into the ancient Via Appia, which Raymond describes as 'smooth and shining . . . like a Silver Highway'.[23] But, in common with other tourists, he was less sensitive to such beauties of the landscape as the towering promontory of Monte Circeo or the flowers and foliage of springtime than to the vestiges of antiquity. Thus, just outside Formia, the ancient Mola, he was thrilled at the sight of the tomb of Cicero,[24] who had been murdered near his villa there in 48 B.C.

Naples[25] furnishes 'great delights', he tells us, and 'is still frequented by men of high condition'. At the approach to the Mole 'all the Gentry at the evening retire to take the Fresco',[26] that is, they parade on horseback and in carriages. The city, however, 'is extremely populous, and consequently vitious'. The English party went the usual round of classical sites, marvelled at the road-tunnel under Posilipo[27] and inspected the places already described by Moryson and Sandys. After taking horse to some height on Vesuvius,

[19] P. 89. [20] P. 95.

[21] Most travellers seem to have taken this for the Appian Way. The real Via Appia ran further west, through the Pontine marshes, and was impassible for a long distance (see De Beer, *Evelyn*, II, 317, note 7).

[22] P. 120.

[23] Much of the detail in Evelyn's description of the journey was taken from Raymond's book.

[24] P. 131. On the route as a whole, the halts for meals (as at Formia) and for sleeping (as at S. Agata and elsewhere) seem to have been arranged and standardized by the Vetturini or other carriers.

[25] See pp. 114-156.

[26] P. 139. The daily ceremony known as the Corso, in vogue also at Messina (see Sandys), Milan and elsewhere.

[27] P. 149.

Raymond crawled up the steeper slope to the top 'where the *Vorago* is so terrifying a spectacle, that if I would paint Hell, this would be the best Patterne; it is a hole about three mile in compasse[28] . . . in the midst is a new hill that still vomits thick smoke . . . it daily increaseth, and when tis growne to a fuller Bulke caveat Neapolis'.[29]

Returning now to Rome, our travellers visited the catacombs of San Sebastiano, made an excursion to Tivoli, saw the gardens of the Villa d'Este and the rainbow in the falls of the Anio.[30] Raymond understood, in conclusion, that there is no place like Rome:

Roma Capo e Compendio del Mondo
A cui non è cosa simile ne seconda.[31]

But the practical advantages of Siena had not been forgotten and Raymond again settled down there, this time for the better part of three months. One night in the Sala del Consiglio he saw a production of the *Statira*, an opera presented by the Accademia dei Filomati;[32] otherwise he did little else than study Italian. Early in September he and his friends left for Florence where they arranged with a *Procaccio* to take them to Venice. The 'Pietra mala', a kind of volcanic vent in the Apennines, naturally provoked their astonishment. At 'Bolonia the Fat', they tasted the 'famous Saltsages' and contemplated the towers Asinelli and Garisenda,[33] before embarking in the usual way for Ferrara. The canal took them 'through about nine *Sustegne*, Machines not much unlike our Sluses, to keep up and let down the water for the turning of all sorts of Milles, and the passage of Boates'.[34] At Ferrara they stayed, like most gentlemen, at the 'Angel'. The mighty waters of the Po—or Padanus, or Eridanus, to mention its more distinguished names—made him think of Io[35] when he should have been thinking of Phaethon; but he had not yet seen the opera which showed that imprudent charioteer being precipitated into the said waters. And so at last they came to Venice.

The three weeks Raymond spent here afforded sensations and amusement. He noted the quarter of San Giovanni e Paolo as 'much frequented by the Venetian walking *May Poles*, I meane the women'. They wear 'their haire (their own or counterfeit)' flowing

[28] Evelyn repeated this exaggerated estimate.
[29] P. 162.
[30] Pp. 171-2. Evelyn's description is taken from this passage (*Diary*, ed. de Beer, II, 397, note 1).
[31] P. 173.
[32] P. 174.
[33] See pp. 179-182. Evelyn repeats what Raymond says about the city's being like a ship with two masts; but this comparison, suggested perhaps by Alberti's guide-book, had become a commonplace (De Beer, *Evelyn*, 420, note 7).
[34] P. 183.
[35] P. 185.

over their shoulders and 'trim'd with gemmes'. In their long coats and

> mounted on their Chippeens (which are as high as a mans leg) they walke between two handmaids, majestickly deliberating of every step they take.
>
> This fashion was invented, & appropriated to the noble *Venetians* wives, to bee constant to distinguish them from the Courtesans, who goe coverd in a vaile of white Taffety.[36]

'Padua the Learned' inspired some rather surprising reservations. It is true that foreign students enjoy great privileges there, 'yet the ill government of the schollars . . . much dissuades others from likeing the place'. The students, he explains, are commonly armed with a brace of pistols and a stiletto, a habit ascribed to some old feud between the Vicentines and the Brescians, 'which two parties so fill the towne with slaughter, that no man can walke the streets late at night for fear of their *Chi va là?*'—and, what was equally alarming, the bullet-holes in pillars and archways.[37] Notwithstanding all this, Padua is 'a very worthy University', with its 'Anatomick Theatre' and its 'Physick Garden, fild with simples'.[38]

Raymond now 'joynd company' with 'a Northern Baronet' and his son for the journey across the Alps. It was almost Vintage time, he says, and the country they traversed, the great plain where the trees were ranged in order, 'the Vines embracing the Elmes' and an 'incredible quantity of grapes', seemed to him a paradise.[39] 'Wee lodgd every night in some memorable City, where we found good accommodation . . .' Vicenza inspired him to appropriate eulogies. It was full of rich gentry, 'the common title to a gentleman here being Signor Conte'; men, too, who 'delight to goe abroad . . . to see foreigne customes'; a city full also of noble buildings and beautified by the art of Palladio. The great piazza, the theatre which holds 5,000 people, the Villa Valmarana, the Madonna del Monte—all are described,[40] and especially the Rotonda, Palladio's 'masterpiece . . . it containes Geometrically a Round, a Crosse & a Square'. As they were descending from the Rotonda where they had probably been served by the steward with wine, they met the master of the house who invited them to come back the next day. He 'uses all strangers very civilly. His Sellars are the best, & the best furnished

[36] Pp. 202-3.

[37] Pp. 209-10. Evelyn repeats this (*Diary*, II, 472) but with fewer picturesque and circumstantial details.

[38] Pp. 210-18.

[39] P. 220.

[40] Pp. 221-25.

I met with'.[41] Captain Wray had made a serious blunder the year before, in preventing Evelyn from visiting the Rotonda.

Nothing of special note occurred in Verona. Raymond describes the city in adequate detail. A little further on he remarks that the Lago di Garda abounds with 'Troutes . . . which wee tasted of that night at supper at Lunato'[42]—another experience which shows how much has remained unchanged in the past three hundred years.

After spending four days in Milan where the churches were 'divine',[43] they agreed with a guide 'that hee should beare all our charges [by way of the Simplon] for horse, Diet, & lodging, till wee came to *Geneva*, wee paying him eight pistolls a man'.[44] It was not long now before the Alps came into sight. Near Sesto Calende 'wee had in full view the Mount *San Bernardo Il grande*, the highest Terrasse in *Europe*. And wee could perfectly discerne it about four *English* miles to out top the Cloudes'.[45] What they must have been looking at was the cluster of peaks beyond and above the Val d'Ossola. The Grand Saint Bernard lay far away to the west, hidden from the shores of Maggiore by the great spurs that radiate southward from Monte Rosa. They crossed Lago Maggiore by boat and after dining at Domodossola, changed horses. 'Presently wee met with extreame hazardous way' and

> entered into the Paese de'Valesi; a most barbarous disconsolate place, a Habitation for Wolves & Beares.
>
> Our *terminus Visus* was most hideous Mountaines, coverd with snow, on all sides terrible Precipices, monstruous Rockes, passages over narrow Bridges, cataracts of water . . . wee could not heare one another speake.[46]
>
> This strange . . . Landskip continued not above five houres, but presently wee met with a new People, a new Phisiognomy, a new genius, a new Dresse, a new Language . . .[47]

After dining at 'Sampion' on the top,[48] they started down, but

[41] Pp. 224-25. [42] P. 235.

[43] I do not quote his observations (pp. 238-45).

[44] P. 246.

[45] P. 247. Evelyn (II, 506) repeats this curious observation, and De Beer discusses the point (p. 506, note 3). I think the error may have arisen from the fact that one can also from this point look north-eastward to the Lepontine Alps, which can be crossed, beyond Bellinzona, by the *San Bernardino*. It was probably the guide who flattered travellers with the notion that they were beholding the highest mountains in the Alps.

[46] Observations more or less repeated by Evelyn.—The gorge is still subject to rock falls and landslides which may, as a few years ago, block both road and railway for some days.

[47] Pp. 248-49. [48] P. 251.

below the snow-line had 'to alight, to crawle down the steeper part'. When they remounted one jade broke loose and ran away.

Twas my ill Fortune to be set upon a Mule, a . . . headstrong beast, which seeing the other Horse, a great way before, ranne headlong up and downe, and carried the Rider over such terrible places that all the company gave me for lost.

However, both mule and horse came to a timely halt and the party reached 'Briga' safely that evening. And they were in Geneva on October 16th, eight days after leaving Milan.

The minor risks of travel in Italy can easily be obviated, Raymond explains. As Protestants are connived at, 'so tis rashnesse to proclaime ones opinion, weaknesse to disclose it'. In general one is let alone. A 'Tramontano is held contemptible by the multitude' and this reserves privacy for the foreigner. He adds, however, that 'One of my Cotemporaries discoursing with a Fryar, in a Complement protested he did reverence Clergy men *for that he was the Sonne of a Priest in England*: which the Monke could not conster but either an *Irony* to his Order, or Infamous to the gentlemans own descent'—an episode that has been paralleled and even bettered in an experience of Edmund Gosse's related by Sir Edward Marsh.[49]

Some annoyance may arise when bargaining with Vetturini and innkeepers, these latter being 'very peremptory and crosse'. One should never threaten them, as the inns are usually remote from villages: 'the safest way is dissimulation'—and commendation. 'The *Cimici* [that is, 'zanzari' or mosquitoes] are most Troublesome bedfellowes; but Fleas in *Folio*, yet so dainty, as they will chuse their flesh . . .' Other insects are more agreeable. 'The *Cantherides* are greene flies by day, and in the night passe about the fields (a pleasing spectacle) like flying Glowwormes with fire in their Tayles'—possibly the first mention of fireflies in our literature.

Raymond believes that '*Southern climates* (Philosophically) *refine the braine*; those that have adorn'd *Italy* with their singular endowments, owe perhaps as much to their Country, as She to them'. The air naturally favours inventiveness. 'What Braine but *Italian* could contrive Engines to raise . . . the *Vatican Obelisque*? And he goes

[49] On this occasion Bishop Stubbs 'in company with four strapping sons on a walking-tour slept the night at an inn where Gosse was staying in some remote part of France. Next morning the landlady came to Gosse with an air of concern. 'Pardon, monsieur—that gentleman who was here last night—those four young men—is it true that they are his sons?' Gosse told her they were. 'Oh, monsieur!' cried the devout old thing, 'un évêque! quel cynisme!' " (A *Number of People*. London, 1939, p. 111).

on to mention some of the 'machivillian unheard of weapons they devise to surprize an enemy unawares', such as the 'Pockit stone-Bow, which held under a Cloake shoots needles with violence to pierce a mans body, yet leaves a wound scarce discernable'; the walking-stick containing a spring that shoots out a rapier; and the air-gun which makes 'small or no report'.

Raymond, as we have seen, was more interested in statuary than painting; but of all the arts in which Italy excelled, he especially praised those of landscape gardening and opera. In Florence he appears to have seen a '*Balletta*, or dance of Horses; whilst an Ape playde the ayre on a Gittarre'; he saw an opera in Siena; and in Venice he saw Phaethon in a chariot drawn by four real horses 'all hurld over the Theater in an Artificiall cloud'.[50] It is difficult to exaggerate the merits of Italy. 'To her we owe our Civility', he says, that is, our Civilization (the word was not invented until the eighteenth century).

Raymond's book is illustrated with several drawings, apparently his own: pictures of the Tres Tabernae, of Cicero's tomb, and Virgil's, and a very funny picture of Vesuvius with men sliding down the lava-screes on their backs.

[50] Such marvels were, a few years later, to be imitated in Paris.

CHAPTER XV

Reresby, Mortoft and Ray

RAYMOND'S tour was now, as we have seen, the favourite *giro d'Italia*, and other books or manuscripts of travel repeated or amplified what he tells us. Not that everyone entered Italy by the Genoese Riviera and left by the Simplon. Sir John Reresby, after spending two and a half years in France, travelled by way of Geneva and Zürich. From hur he and his party crossed the Albula, put up with 'a very mean' lodging at 'Pontrazin', and then crossed the Bernina to Tirano. He noted here that the wine was good and that the mountain-forests abounded with wild beasts, including bears and wolves. His tour was via Verona, Vicenza, Padua, Venice, Bologna, Florence, Pisa and then back to Venice and over the Brenner to Innsbruck; the whole journey lasting about nine months, from October, 1656, to early August, 1657.[1]

A feature one notices in the travel records of the mid-Seicento is the growing and absorbing interest of Englishmen in Rome. It is already well marked in Evelyn's *Diary*. Francis Mortoft devotes to Rome 106 pages of a book which numbers only 189. Richard Lassels, in a formal and documented guide to Italian travel, which also contains general advice regarding the educational purpose of travel on the Continent, devotes to Rome 153 out of 434 pages; that is, more than a third of his book concerns Rome. This was not primarily due to the facilities for Protestants afforded by the Papal Court. The explanation lies in the unique attractions that Papal Rome offered and was to offer until the later nineteenth century. It possessed the greatest art-treasures in the world. Rome spoke to the imagination, as it still speaks, with great memories of the past; it kindled sentiments which nothing short of the destruction of our planet can efface. But it also had other and quite different merits. The organization of social services and charities was far in advance of that of any other city or state in Europe. And the city of Rome had been modernized at a time when London and Paris were still in large measure, as to their buildings, medieval. This is a point on which

[1] *Memoirs and Travels of Sir John Reresby*, ed. A. Ivatt. London, 1904, pp. 44-95.

Malcolm Letts has rightly insisted. 'Rome at this time,' he writes,[2] 'was no longer a city of the Renaissance, but a modern city, the product of Sixtus V,—Paul V,—Bernini and his friends and rivals'. It was 'one of the most brilliant intellectual resorts in Europe—a world wonderfully complete within itself . . .'

Another feature of the travel-books is that, covering much the same ground, they inevitably repeat much that was said before. For this reason Francis Mortoft's book, which was not published until 1925, can be described more rapidly than Raymond's. Mortoft with his companions Hare and Stanley, travelled on mule-back along the Corniche-track from Nice to Mentone—the most dangerous and terrifying 'road' in western Europe. On reaching Genoa (December 1st, 1658) they had to surrender their pistols to the guard. Few of the Genoese travel, he tells us, as they think no other city comparable to theirs—and with some reason, when one contemplates 'such rare and superb buildings'. Exile for a Genoese is counted as death.[3] Passing through Massa Carrara and Lucca—'one of the Prettyest contrivedst Cittyes in Italy'—they reached Livorno on December 12th. Here 'the Marchants . . . have a very convenient place to meete in, where one shal hardly meete with any but English men'.[4] At Pisa they were invited with their friends from Livorno to hunt in the Grand Duke's park and to share in the bountiful collation he provided. In Florence, Mortoft was impressed by the suits of armour in the Uffizi and the cabinets and tables inlaid with rubies, diamonds, pearls and other precious stones. 'One would esteeme the great Duke for the Richest Prince in Christendome.' Mortoft speaks of the paintings in the Palazzo Pitti, but without specifying any of them. It was disappointing that the 'water worke' in the Boboli Gardens was not playing on account of the frost.[5]

Reaching Rome on December 27th, they went on January 1st 'to the Pallace of the Queene of Sweth land', that is, the daughter of Gustavus Adolphus who had been received into the Catholic Church in 1656 and had taken up her residence in the Palazzo Rospigliosi. She was on good terms with the Jesuits but frequently at odds with Alexander VII, as Mortoft indicates. She was also one of the sights, if not the wonders, of Rome. Mortoft and his friends went for another glimpse of her on January 7th. She is, he tells us, 'one of the greatest witts . . . in this Age, her whole delight . . . being to converse with Men of Witt and Spirit . . . Here she was very merry'. This is no understatement. David Ogg says that 'her fêtes, mas-

[2] *Francis Mortoft: his book. Being his travels through France and Italy 1658-1659.* Edited by Malcolm Letts. London, 1925, pp. xiii-xiv.
[3] Ed. Letts, pp. 41-42.
[4] P. 48. [5] Pp. 51-57.

querades, theatricals, library and funeral were on a scale of unprecedented splendour, while the most austere cardinals were charmed by her vivacity'.[6]

The Campidoglio had, even before Mortoft's time, assumed its present appearance. The great stairway had been built by 1536 and the statues of Marcus Aurelius and Castor and Pollux stood where they stand today. The Capitoline Museum had just been opened.[7] Mortoft comments on the statues, including one of Nero as a little boy with 'a kind of a fierce looke with him'.[8] The Forum, which the Englishmen next visited, had not yet been excavated. Its level, owing to the masses of rubbish which had been deposited there, was of course much higher than it is now and a handsome avenue of elms ran down it as far as the Arch of Titus.[9]

On January 6th Mortoft and his friends went to the Vatican to see Pope Alexander VII, 'a very handsome old man', 'in all his greatnesse'.

We saw some thirty-five Cardinals . . . Every Cardinal having a Gentleman before him to carry a great silver Mace, and many Gentlemen and attendants following, where followed two English Lords (My Lord Candish and my Lord Rosse Commons); Cardinal Barbarin, in regard he is esteemed to be the Protector of the English here in Rome.[10]

At the present moment Roscommon appears to have been accompanying the Duke of Newcastle (William Cavendish) who had been Commander-in-chief of the Royalist Army. They were to leave Rome for Naples on March 25th,[11] and, as we have already seen, Roscommon was to be visiting Padua in June.[12]

Mortoft next describes the seven most famous churches in Rome[13] and then passes on to a survey of the seven hills. Although he speaks of 'the Viminal, where is the church of St Pudentiana', he does not mention that on the site of this church, which has since been destroyed, had once stood the house of that Pudens whom St Paul mentions in *II Timothy*, IV, 21. He and his daughters Praxedis and Pudentiana are believed to have been the hosts of St Peter during the latter's sojourn in Rome, and to have been converted by him. The Church of Santa Pudenziana was subsequently built on the site of

[6] *Europe in the Seventeenth Century*. London, 1925, p. 406.
[7] Malcolm Letts, p. 63, note 1, of *Mortoft: his book*.
[8] P. 68.
[9] Letts, p. 69, note 1.
[10] P. 76.
[11] *Calendar of State Papers, Domestic*, 1658-59.
[12] See above, p. 117.
[13] Pp. 78-94.

this house, and it appears to have been the Christian Cathedral of ancient Rome.[14] Between January 20th and March 21st Mortoft and his friends visited a number of the more famous Villas and Palaces, and he described the works of art they contained: the Villa Montalto on January 20th, the Villa Medici on February 7th, then the Villa Ludovisi, the Palazzo Mattei on February 13th, the Palazzo Farnese on March 12th, the Villa Borghese on March 16th, and the Palazzo Giustiniani on March 21st. He particularly admired and commented on the paintings in the Villa Montalto, and the beautiful gardens with their 'waterworks'. These were set going; the visitors got wet and thoroughly amused themselves.[15] At the Villa Medici Mortoft considered that the lifelike appearance of the marble group of Niobe and her children would 'bring grief and sorrow into any person's heart';[16] and when contemplating the statues in the

[14] Rodolfo Lanciani, *Pagan and Christian Rome*. Boston, 1896, p. 112. Lanciani did not commit himself to the belief that St Peter was ever in Rome; but subsequent study and research on the part of Protestant scholars and impartial archaeologists strongly supports a tradition which 'seems to have been accepted without question in Antiquity' (J. Toynbee and J. W. Perkins, *The Shrine of St Peter and the Vatican Excavations*. London, New York & Toronto, 1956, p. 128). The first inference in support of Peter's presence in Rome is in *I Peter*, V, 13: 'She that is in Babylon, elect together with you, saluteth you; and so does Mark, my son.'

The majority of Protestant scholars now agree that 'Babylon' is here a code-name for Rome—probably adopted for reasons of security (*Ibid.*, p. 132). The mention of Mark, who was associated also with Paul, fits in with this view. (Mark may have written his gospel about this time?) The first *documentary evidence* following the Apostolic age is in a letter to the Church in Rome from Dionysius of Corinth (quoted by Eusebius), dating from c. 170 A.D. Here he expressly describes Paul *and* Peter as having 'planted' [Christianity] in Rome and as having suffered martyrdom 'on the same occasion'. But now the excavations of 1939 have laid bare on the Vatican hillside a shrine of St Peter which dates from not later than 170 A.D.—a shrine on the spot on which Constantine was later to erect the first Church of St. Peter (*Ibid.*, pp. 127-8). This suggests, if it does not prove, that the Christian community in Rome believed that Peter had been in Rome and had died there (by crucifixion: *John XXI*, 18, 19—the last words having probably been added after the Apostle's death). Now it is certain that Paul had lived and died in Rome; and it would be extraordinary if, as early as a century later—and probably less than a century—records had been so completely lost, and memories were so utterly at fault, that St Peter, and not St Paul, was not recognized as the first head of the Christian Church in Rome (cf. Toynbee and Perkins, p. 128). One may reasonably suppose that he was. It is true that Paul never mentions Peter in the messages of salutation in his epistles; but a Cambridge scholar (Miss E. M. Chrystal of Newnham College) has suggested very cogently that this may have been for security reasons (*Ibid.*, p. 134).

[15] The Villa Montalto and its gardens were destroyed after 1870 to make a building site for the Railway Station.

[16] P. 121.

Villa Ludovisi, especially Bernini's Proserpine, he lost himself in superlatives.[17]

There were other kinds of diversion. One day in January they had seen a play about Elizabeth and Essex which was performed behind the Palazzo Farnese. The girl who acted the Queen 'did so . . . with much grace'. On February 16th they managed to get into the Roman College to see a play about an English king in pagan times, whose sons had been converted to Christianity. He had had them put to death, but had afterwards repented and been baptized. This was 'such a rare Comody, that I never looke to hear the like again'. As to the acting, 'it was impossible to doe better'.[18] The Carnival in the Corso, which began on February 15th, offered diversions of a less refined character, and he was shocked by the orgies of eating on the last day (February 25th), when all who could afford it 'stuffed there (sic) paunches full of flesh'. Nothing, however, in Italy seems to have fascinated Mortoft as much as the music. At Sant'Ambrogio in Genoa, 'wee heard the most ravishingst musicke that wee ever heard in our lives'. These pleasures were renewed at the Jesuit Church ('Il Gesù') in Rome (February 23rd) where there was 'very sweete and heavenly Musicke'. In the afternoon of the same Sunday, they 'heard very Sweet and ravishing Musicke' at S. Apollinare, and in the evening, music and a sermon at the Chiesa Nova. And on the following Sunday (March 2nd) they went twice to S. Apollinare where the music-master was said to have a salary of 3,000 crowns a year.[19] Finally, after paying another visit to the English College and making an excursion to Frascati and Tivoli, Mortoft and his friends rode (March 27th) across the Apennines to Loreto and then up the coast to Rimini and so to Bologna.

The remainder of the tour, during part of which Mortoft joined forces with a Frenchman named Pillat, calls for no special mention. On Easter Sunday in Venice, they witnessed a magnificent assembly in St Mark's, when the Doge and Senators attended High Mass. From Padua Mortoft followed the usual route to Brescia: here he noted the 'fiercenesse' of the people, 'both by the cruelty of their lookes, and guns and swords which they continually cary about them'[20]—a trait which survived until recent times. The young Stendhal in 1800 says there were something like eight hundred and forty assassinations every year in Brescia—a magnificent example of the Italian energy he admired. The Fascisti called Brescia 'leonessa d'Italia'. From Brescia onwards their way, over the Bergamasque Alps to Chiavenna and thence by the Septimer or the Splügen, was

[17] P. 126.
[18] Pp. 136-37.
[19] P. 143.
[20] P. 187.

rough—and the cold on the pass intense. Mortoft's manuscript ends with his arrival in Zürich on May 9th, 1659.

We have seen that it remained in manuscript until 1925; it could not therefore serve, like Raymond's account, as a guide. Edmund Warcup's *Italy, in its original Glory, Ruine and Revivial* (London, 1660) is, however, a real guide-book and in fact a translation of François Schott's *Itinerarii Italiae*, of which several editions had appeared in Italy.[21] But Warcup had travelled in Italy and knew the language. Several other translations, mostly from the Italian, were appearing about this time. James Howell's *History of Venice* (1650) is partly adapted, partly original. Henry Cogan's *Directions for such as shall travel to Rome* (1654) is translated from Martinelli's *Roma Ricercata*, while Nani's History of Venice from 1613 to 1660 was put into English by Sir Robert Honywood and published in 1673.[22]

The last of the notable travel-books prior to the time of Addison was John Ray's *Travels through the Low-Countries, Germany, Italy and France . . . with curious observations, . . . also a Catalogue of Plants found in those Parts*. It appeared in 1673 and was reprinted in 1738. Ray was a clergyman, a Fellow of the Royal Society and the first of our great botanists.[23] Descending into Italy in October, 1663, by way of Linz and Treviso, he visited Venice and settled in Padua for the winter. He gives us a list of all the professors in the University. He himself attended Pietro Marchetti's lectures on Anatomy, inspected 'the physick-garden, well stored with simples', and described the hot springs at Abano. Padua was less tranquil than Cambridge. 'The citizens and strangers . . . dare not stir abroad in the dark', on account of the unruly students who roam the streets; when two parties meet, each man stands behind a pillar and shoots.[24] Ray's interests, however, were almost exclusively scientific. He travelled over most of northern Italy in the early part of 1664, botanizing and compiling catalogues of plants.[25] Taking ship from Livorno to Naples, he climbed Vesuvius; then sailed to Messina, where he arrived at the end of April. The dazzling splendour of the Sicilian spring, the mountain-sides ablaze with marigolds, must have impressed him, though he was mainly occupied with the identifica-

[21] 1600, 1601, 1610 (first Italian edition) and several others (De Beer, *Evelyn's Diary*, II, 574). Warcup may have translated from one of the editions in Italian.

[22] See Stoye, p. 200.

[23] See C. E. Raven, *John Ray Naturalist. His Life and Works*. Cambridge, 1942.

[24] *Travels*, ed. 1738, p. 182.

[25] One such list is printed after the account of his visit to Livorno.

tion of genera and species. His list of the plants found in Sicily alone occupies nearly four pages.[26] After a visit to Malta, Ray returned to Sicily, and from Catania climbed the slopes of Etna as far as the snow-line (May 20, 1664). He then returned to Italy, visited Salerno and Naples, and spent the summer in Florence. During this time he was collecting a mass of specimens, geological and zoological as well as botanical. Edward Browne, who met him in Rome early in 1665, describes this huge collection.[27] Ray's expedition may in fact be regarded as the most thorough-going scientific exploration of Italy which had yet been made by an Englishman. Even his return north was original. He reached the Grisons, not from Brescia or Milan, but by way of Trento and Bolzano: he made his way up the little known Münstertal, then apparently over the Ofen Pass to Zernetz, up the valley to Zuoz and Ponte, and thence over the Albula to Chur.[28]

[26] *Travels*, pp. 241-44. [27] C. E. Raven, *op. cit.*, p. 136.

[28] Ray being one of the great naturalists, a detailed study of his Italian experiences is reserved for a later volume; as also is an account of Bishop Burnet's

CHAPTER XVI

Richard Lassels

THE best and most up-to-date of the English guide-books, as distinct from travel-records, was Richard Lassels' *An Italian Voyage, or a Compleat Journey through Italy. In two parts.* This appeared posthumously in Paris and London in 1670. There was a French translation in two volumes (Paris 1671), a second English edition (London 1698) and apparently later English editions. It was probably, with Misson's *Voyage d'Italie*,[1] the most popular book on the subject.

Lassels (c. 1603-1668) was a Lincolnshire man. He had been educated at Oxford and Douai, where he was appointed Professor of Classics in 1629. He subsequently acted as 'governor' to various young nobles during their tour of the Continent, and, as he tells us in his Preface, had spent half his lifetime abroad, having made 'three long Voyages into *Flanders*, six into *France*, five into *Italy*, one into *Germany* and *Holland* . . .' This had certainly fitted him to give advice on travel and education. Travel lowers our self-conceit and, since all the world's akin, enables us to visit our relations. In travel we study 'the great Book' of the world, and fit ourselves for the service of our country. The common course is first to make a sojourn in France and then to go to Italy. Lassels, however, recommends that the 'Governour' should take his young man at the age of fifteen or sixteen straight to Italy 'and there season his mind with the gravity and wise maxims of that Nation, which hath civilized the whole world, and taught Mankind what it is to be a Man'. After two or three years spent in learning the language and studying music, painting and mathematics, 'he will at his return know what true use to make of *France*. And having spent three more years there . . . he will be ready to come home . . . a Man most compleat both in Body and Mind'.

After this preamble the book opens with a general eulogy of Italy, 'Nature's Darling'. It is the warm sun that 'has helpt to make so many brave soldiers and scholars . . . While (according to the observation of Charles V) the *French* appear not wise, but are wise;

[1] Travellers could also consult Monconys' *Journal des voyages* (1665-66) and Grangier de Liverdis' *Journal d'un voyage de France et d'Italie* (1661). See De Beer, *Evelyn's Diary*, 570, 572.

the *Spaniards* appear wise, but are not wise; the *Dutch*[2] neither appear wise, nor are wise . . . the *Italians* anciently afforded us those prodigies of Wit and Learning . . . which all men would follow . . .'[3] The Italian humour is midway between Spanish gravity and French levity. The Italians are generally men of sound judgment, although apt to be melancholy and, on occasion, jealous. Their principal vice is that 'they are most extravagant in their Revenge'. But their virtues are outstanding. 'They neither eat nor drink to excess.' They are ambitious of honours. Their manners 'are most commendable'; not only are they courteous to strangers, but gentle and considerate to each other. 'They call Men much by their Christian Names, Signor Pietro . . . &c.' Their cooking is 'more lean and dry than ours'; and they use snow and ice 'which they keep all summer' to cool their wines.[4]

Lassels next outlines the various routes by which he had entered Italy and one notices here that he had crossed both the Bernina and the Splügen, as well as the Mont Cenis, the Simplon and the St Gothard. He begins his description of Italy by supposing that we cross the Mont Cenis to Turin, and then visit Genoa, Milan, Bologna, Florence, Pisa, Livorno, Siena, Rome, Naples, back to Rome, Loreto, Ferrara, Padua, Venice, Padua again, Vicenza, Verona, Milan and back north by the St Gothard, 'and so home to my dear Country, *England*, by way of *Dover*'. Lassels' descriptions are more systematic and generally more detailed than those of his predecessors. In connexion with each great city he gives a list of the standard books relating to it. He tells us a good deal about the great paintings in Milan, Florence and Rome—a topic which travellers had sometimes come near to ignoring. And the information about social customs and institutions is unique in its way. He has, finally, an eye for the curious and picturesque, and his observations are often charming.

Genoa, though less wealthy and less strong than Venice, is thoroughly modern in outlook. 'The rich *Banquier* is more esteemed here than the learned Divine.'[5] The Strada Nova with its superb palaces, 'would be the true Queen-Street of Europe', if it were only a little longer. *Milan* has 'great store of Artizans' as well as of gentry, but is, though Lassels does not use the word, bled by the Spaniards who draw from it 2,400,000 crowns a year 'as well as the Thirds'.[6] The Biblioteca Ambrosiana 'opens its Doors publickly to all

[2] The Germans were frequently referred to as 'Dutch' in the seventeenth century, though the country was called Germany: 'I like not their endless drinking in feasts, which is able to make them freemen of all vices,' Lassels observes.

[3] P. 5.

[4] Pp. 9-19.

[5] P. 69.

[6] P. 89.

comers . . . and suffers them to read what book they please'.[7] *Bologna* is convenient for the arcades that line the streets and notable for the two towers Asinelli and 'Carissenda'. Lassels does not believe that the latter was built crooked on purpose.[8] 'Their *Traffick* consisteth much in Silks, Velvets, Olives, Leather-bottles,' etc. The Academy is known as that of 'Gli Otiosi, *per antiphrasin*' because they are not idle. *Florence* enjoys peace and other benefits owing to the 'goodness & wisdom' of its prince. 'The Gentry are Ingenious and Rich . . . their good Husbandry, and underhand Traffick [.e. private commerce] have put them notably into Purse.' The Grand Duke himself willingly receives men of condition: '. . . having entertain'd you in his Chamber with wise discourse, he will entertain you in your own Chamber too with a *Regalo* of dainty Meats and Wines, which he will be sure to send you.'[9]

Lassels, unlike his predecessors, devotes some space to the paintings in the Uffizi, the Pitti Palace, and the Annunziata. He especially admires the work of Andrea del Sarto.[10] The Duke's famous diamond weighs 138 carats, is nearly an inch thick and is valued at from 100,000 to 150,000 crowns.[11] While Florence has its Accademia della Crusca, there is no academy at *Ligorne*. 'All the *Latin* here is only *Meum and Tuum* . . .

Yet I must confess they study here *belle Lettere*: for, if the true *belle Lettere* be Letters of Exchange, your Merchant here, if you present him with a Letter of Exchange from his Correspondent, will read it over and over again, and study upon it, before he gives you the contents of it in Money.[12]

'Many strangers draw Bridle [in] *Siena*, the *Orleans* of Italy,' and pass the summer there on account of the good air and the good language.

Part II of Lassels' book opens with his arrival in *Rome* where 'we lodg'd in an Inn for three or four days, till we had found out, and furnished a House to our Satisfaction'. Of the many titles bestowed upon Rome, he thinks that 'Roma la Santa' is the most honourable. It is the most deserved, and not only for religious reasons. Rome is full of hospitals for the sick or the insane; hostels for foundlings, and also for young girls whose parents are 'poor' and 'suspected'; here the girls are brought up 'under careful matrons' until they are ready to marry or take the veil. Many of the clergy and especially the Oratorians devote themselves to the task of recon-

[7] P. 83.
[8] P. 100.
[9] P. 141.
[10] P. 129.
[11] P. 120.
[12] P. 151.

ciling 'disagreeing Families'. There is even a house 'per le donne mal maritate'. There is a committee whose members 'go into every corner of Rome to seek out poor Men who are asham'd to beg'; and there are 'hospitals for poor gentlemen'. A 'Congregation of Advocates and Attornies' acts, in effect, as poor men's lawyers. In the 'Convent of Penitent Whores', many of these 'poor Magdalens' have led very penitential lives. In Rome also 'you shall find an *Apothecaries-Shop*, founded by Cardinal *Francis Barberin*, with a yearly revenue of 12,000 crowns . . . to furnish the Poor with Physick *gratis*'; and a number of Church Schools where poor boys receive a free education. Not only then are the public services, in what was a genuine welfare-state, intelligently organized, but the Pope and a number of the Cardinals dispense private charity in a munificent fashion.[13]

Rome possesses several libraries where the books are catalogued and there is 'a courteous gentleman to reach you any book'. The paintings by Raphael and Michelangelo, in the Vatican galleries and the Sistine Chapel are themselves a book, for 'it belongs only to *Rome* to have the Bible set out thus in its own colours'.[14] For the rest, there are few churches or sites of interest in Rome and its environs which were not visited and described by Lassels. He descended several times into the Catacombs; and he saw some operas, which seem to have been brilliantly mounted, with 'machines' to take men flying through the air. Rome, in conclusion, is a city 'where every Stone almost is a Book; every Statue a Master; every inscription a Lesson; every Antichamber an Academy'.[15]

In the pages devoted to *Naples*,[16] Lassels describes the crater of Vesuvius, which he climbed, and especially the classical sites and natural wonders along the north-west shore. His account of the excursions to Albano, Castel Gandolfo, Frascati and Tivoli is placed after the return to Rome, and this, as we have seen, was the usual order in the itineraries. So too was the journey, by way of Terni and Spoleto, to Loreto. From Padua he took a horse-drawn barge down the canal, admiring the 'world of stately Pallaces and Gardens' on its banks, some of which—especially at Strà—still retain much of their beauty. He had been three times in Venice, he tells us, once at Ascensiontide when he witnessed the ceremony of the wedding of the Adriatic. The 'horrible *Cioppini*, or high shooes' worn by the ladies he did not approve; but the men seemed to him the most grave and handsome he had seen anywhere. The forbidding of periwigs also pleased him. Tintoretto's 'Paradise' is described. No place in Italy, Lassels thinks, 'has so many, and so rare pieces of painting'.[17]

13 For the above, see Part II, pp. 4-12.

14 Pp. 31-35.

15 P. 156.

16 Pp. 165-195.

17 P. 241.

Padua is briefly and systematically described, but Lassels dwells in some detail on St Anthony's Church, and also on the tomb of Lady Katherine Whitehall in the Church of St Thomas of Canterbury. He had escorted this lady from Brussels to Italy in 1650 and there still exists in the British Museum a manuscript account of this journey. Finally he notes that Padua possesses two Academies, that of the Ricoverati and that of the Infiammati. The descriptions of Vicenza, Verona, Mantua and Mirandola are, however, of the briefest.

Lassels' 'Voyage' is a very readable guide-book, as witness the passage about the thrifty gentlewomen of Piacenza,

> who make no scruple to be carried to their Country Houses . . . in Coaches drawn by two Cows . . . .these will carry the *Signora* a pretty round trot unto her Villa; they afford her also a dish of their Milk, and after collation, bring her home again at night, without spending a penny.[18]

His description of the fireflies, which 'the Country People call . . . *Lucciole*', is not without its poetry. One night after sunset he 'saw Millions of little Flies in the Air, carrying a bright Light about them like Glow-worms . . . especially upon the Corn Fields and high Grass. It was huge pretty me thought, to see Heaven upon Earth almost, and flying Stars conduct us to our Lodging'.[19]

A charming book, which honours its author as much as the country he describes.

[18] P. 90. [19] P. 221.

Conclusion

THE foregoing enquiry has given rise to some strange conclusions. The interest which today people take—and are compelled to take—in the language and literature of a foreign country is determined not by the intrinsic merits of that language and literature but by the military and economic importance of the country in question. This explains the emphasis on Russian and German Studies, and, negatively, the comparative neglect of Italian.

But do such reasons fit the situation we find in the Seicento?

England had for long past been a considerable power, especially at sea, and a nation always to be taken into account. By 1640 she had produced a poetic literature as varied and brilliant as any in modern times. And yet, prior to the 1660's few people on the Continent seem to have realized its existence and hardly anyone, apart from a number of Frenchmen, knew English or even thought of learning it. It was the Restoration—which drew French people in numbers to London—and the establishment of the Royal Society—which announced the achievements of British science—that first led foreigners seriously to study the language. The publication in France of English grammars and conversation-books is one of the notable phenomena of the time. The discovery of English literature followed rather slowly, and it was partly due to the 'rayonnement' of English science. The French were the first to become aware of it and few things are more interesting in this period than to read La Fontaine's impressions of a people whom he had never visited but who had aroused his curiosity.

At the same time and in face of this ignorance of English literature on the Continent, we note that French and Italian writings had been familiar to Englishmen for centuries. Why were the English so much interested in Italy? Hardly on account of the military importance of the country as a whole, because Italy was not a nation and only the Venetian Republic remained a notable power. It was of course very necessary to prevent the Spaniards from extending their empire, and trade with Italy was important, although that would have gone on even if Spain had dominated the whole peninsula. From the thirteenth century onward there had been opportunities of raising loans in Milan, Genoa, and Florence, but these sources of capital were pretty well exhausted in the early Seicento, except for Genoa which, however, was now in the Spanish orbit. Such reasons, in short, do not explain the prestige which Italy continued to enjoy.

That prestige had been built up in the course of centuries. It was a matter of tradition and experience. Italy was a land of superior culture and the home of the most refined and civilized of peoples. In that land stood the monuments of ancient Rome which evoked in the traveller's mind the heroic days of the Republic and the sensational days of the Empire, the poems of Virgil, Horace and Ovid—everything which had been the background of his reading at school or university. The world these studies conjured up was full of glamour and to some travellers seemed more real than the contemporary world. As they stood in Rome or Naples or by the lake of Garda, it came vividly to life for them. Add to this the fact that medicine, anatomy and other branches of science were (prior to the Restoration) best studied in Italian Universities, and that the Academy of St Luke in Rome was the best Art-School in the world, and we can understand why Italy enjoyed a fame hardly affected by the misfortunes of foreign domination and economic recession.

The diaries and travel records do not always take us into the heart of the seventeenth century as we see it now in the perspective of time. But the Italian experiences of Hobbes, Finch, Boyle and Ray make it clear what was happening: an intellectual revolution was taking place under the stimulus of France and Italy. Of these great figures, only Ray published a formal account of his journey. Most of the other travel-books are documents for what we know as the 'daily-life' genre. But there are marked differences between the Italian attitude to England and the English to Italy. The English, aware that they are among a people more advanced in manners and the refinements of living, are not unnaturally disinclined to stress the fact. If they rarely say much about food (Fynes Moryson is an exception), this is because the Italian cuisine does not seem to have differed materially from ours. It was more refined and less copious. But veal, mutton, venison, poultry and fish were not novelties to Englishmen; the latter would merely notice the absence of beef (except very tough beef) and the presence of salads. The truth is that the Italian cuisine was markedly different from what it is now. Some of the *paste alimentari*, associated with tomatoes, which are now the basis of Italian cooking, seem to have existed but not in any quantity. They had been introduced, probably from China, in the Middle Ages;[1] but these *paste* had to be made by hand, and it was not until the early nineteenth century that machinery was invented and machines

[1] Boccaccio, in a fantastic passage in the *Decameron*, describes people who are doing nothing but make '*maccheroni e raviuoli e euocerli in brodo di capponi*', that is, cook them in chicken broth. The process must have been slow and even expensive.

multiplied for the mass-production of spaghetti, macaroni, ravioli and so on. The tomato, a South American plant, was brought to Europe at the end of the fifteenth century, and maize or Indian corn[2] in the sixteenth. Both were grown in Italy, but it seems doubtful whether they figured very much in the daily fare before the eighteenth century.

When, in the next volume, we turn to the picture of life in England, we shall find that the Italians are surprised, sometimes offended, by indelicacies of behaviour on the part of the upper classes, not to speak of the brutishness of the lower; but that, with a few exceptions, their comments are relatively mild.

[2] Widely cultivated by the North American Indians. Polenta is made from maize.

INDEX